SOFT SKILLS

FOR

HARD

BUSINESS

DAVID L. LOSEBY

ISBN 1903-499-93-3
978-1903-499-93-1

Printed and bound in the United Kingdom by 4edge Ltd, 7a Eldon Way Industrial Estate, Hockley, Essex, SS5 4AD.

FSC
www.fsc.org
FSC® C102342

The mark of
responsible forestry

Contents

Preface 1

Acknowledgements 1

Foreword 2

Introduction 4

Structure of the Book 7

Part A: Setting the Scene 9

Chapter 1 | Foundations of Behavioural Economics 11

History and commentary 11

Key concepts and principles 17

The Birth of behavioural procurement 20

Definition of Behavioural Procurement 24

Chapter 2 | An Overview of Non-technical Skills (the things we already know and use) 27

2.1 Am I hearing you right? 27

2.2 Are we in touch? (Emotional Intelligence) 30

2.3 Stakeholder management 32

2.5 Active listening skills 40

2.6 Development and Chronology of Contributors to the Theory of Emotional Intelligence 43

Chapter 3 | Soft Skills (Behavioural Competences) 45

3.1 The As and Bs of professionalism in Procurement and Supply Chain Management (Attitudes and Behaviours) 45

3.2 Working together (Positive indicators of Collaboration) 49

3.3 What goes around comes around (Relationship Lifecycle Management) 51

3.4 Have you got my back covered? (Developing Trust and Reciprocity) 54

Chapter 4 | Overview of Psychology 59

4.1 Human Nature and Society 59

4.2 The unthinkable can happen! (Black Swan Events) 61

4.3 Did I get the right deal in the end? (Fairness) 63

4.4 Functions and Systems of the Human Brain 67

4.5 Are we wired the right way? (Neuroscience and how it supports the understanding of behaviours) 69

Part B | The Application of Behavioural Science in Purchasing and Supply Chain Management   71

Chapter 5 | The Application of Behavioural Science in Purchasing and Supply Chain Management   73
5.1 Overview of the Behavioural Landscape   73
5.2 Heuristics   78
5.3 System 1 and System 2 Judgements   82

Chapter 6 | Self Biases   87
6.1 Overview   87
6.2 Predictions and Forecasts   95
6.3 Dealing with Self Biases and Overconfidence   98
6.4 Cognitive Framing   100
6.5 Reciprocity   105

Chapter 7 | Group Biases   107
7.1 Overview   107
7.2 Planning Fallacy and GroupThink   112
7.3 Peltzman Effect (Risk Compensation)   116
7.4 Bringing it all together   117

Chapter 8 | Societal Biases   119
8.1 Overview and the Significance of Trust   119
8.2 Framing Effect   124
8.3 Loss Aversion   126
8.4 Negativity Effect (Bias)   130
8.5 Group Serving Biases   130

Chapter 9 | Institutional Biases   133
9.1 Overview   133
9.2 Anchoring or Focalism, and Zero Risk Bias   136
9.3 Sunk Cost Fallacy   140
9.4 Status Quo Bias   142

Part C | Game Theory and Nudging   **147**

**Chapter 10 | Game Theory Applied to Negotiation in Procurement
and Supply Chain Management**   **149**

10.1 What is Game Theory? Key principles and terminology   149
10.2 Strategies for Negotiation   154
10.3 Negotiation models and practice   155
10.4 Summarising Game Theory   161

Chapter 11 | Prospect Theory   **165**
11.1 Prospect Theory: an Analysis of Decision under Risk   165
11.2 The use of Libertarian Paternalism in Procurement   170
11.3 What does this have to do with Political, Economic, Social,
Technology, Legal and Environmental (PESTLE)?   172

Chapter 12 | Nudging (including Ethics and Governance)   **177**
12.1 What is Nudging?   177
12.2 Nudging applied to Decision-making   180
12.3 Ethics and Governance of Good Nudges   181
12.4 Nudge applied to Policy-making and Case Studies   186
12.5 Nudge: Beware of the Marketers and Sellers (an inside story!)   188

Part D | Change Management and Allied Subjects   **191**

Chapter 13 | Frictionless   **193**
13.1 Concept and Approaches to easier Decision-making
in Purchasing and Supply Chain Management   193
13.2 How can Frictionless help?   199
13.3 Frictionless by design   201

Chapter 14 | Cultural Practices and the Social Sciences   **205**
14.1 An overview of Cultural Dynamics and Differences   205
14.2 The Social Sciences as Applied to Purchasing and Supply
Chain Management   211
14.3 Cultural Layers and Models, and Practical Steps for Purchasing
and Supply Chain Management   214
14.4 Managing Diverse Teams – Globally   217

Chapter 15 | Change Management Essentials   **225**
15.1 The Change Process and Phases   225
15.2 Behavioural Interventions and Prerequisites   230
15.3 Cognitive Hurdles   236
15.4 Anchoring, Framing, Status Quo Bias and Optimism Bias
in Change Programmes   239
15.5 Change Leadership from a Behavioural Perspective   241

Chapter 16 | The Silent Pillar: Supplier Relationship Management   **243**
16.1 The Traditional Pillars of Supplier Relationship Management   243
16.2 The Behavioural Pillars (People behaviours, Trust,
Power Distance Index (PDI) and Cognitive Diversity)   246
16.3 Attitudes and Behaviours Matter   251

Chapter 17 | Leadership, Innovation and More   **257**
17.1 Leadership Styles and Impacts   257
17.2 Surveys and Interviews   258
17.2 Innovation through Behavioural Practice in Purchasing and
Supply Chain Management   262
17.3 A summary and some concluding thoughts   266

Glossary and Definitions   269
Recommended reading list   282
Case Study 1: Behavioural Assessments   287
Case Study 2: Potential Behavioural Biases in a Project or Programme   299
Case Study 3: Taking Parallels from Other Behavioural Interventions   305
Index   311

Preface

In an attempt to understand and recognise the influence of behaviour and what sometimes seems to be the irrational elements that prevent us from delivering outcomes, this book will explore the relevance of the Behavioural Sciences as it relates the broad spectrum of Procurement, Supplier Relationship Management, Contract Management and other related disciplines.

The current view and indeed the training and teaching so far has generally been focused on how procurement and the associated disciplines of Supply Chain Management, Supplier Relationship Management, Contract Management and all other related activities has been focused on the logical and rational approaches, such as Category Management.

This has further been reinforced by the use of many electronic platforms and systems and more recently digitalisation, AI, robotics and many other variants in this domain. However, despite the thoroughness and robustness of many of these processes, the profession has failed to consistently deliver competitive advantage that can be sustained from one enterprise to another.

Moving forwards, we need to recognise the significance and relevance of all that the Behavioural Sciences has to offer to deliver significantly more complex and robust outcomes. In seeking competitive advantage, we need to recognise more consciously and prominently the impact of and collective individual behaviours that have been shaped and moulded by our ancestry as well as modern experiences. This contrasts sharply with the advances and more prevalent use of data, AI, robotics, etc.

Interestingly this is not a new concept, as the interplay of behaviours, passions, biases, prejudices and so forth have been recognised for many centuries particularly in the fields of economics, sociology, psychology, politics, to name but a few.

Acknowledgements

I wish to thank all those who have freely and willingly shared their thinking and their insights allow this book to be written and as such represents a concentrate of associated beliefs and thoughts that bring to life all things behavioural.

I would particularly like to thank Gerard Chick, who freely and voluntarily entertained my thoughts and encouraged me to write this book. I also want to thank my family – Amelia, Jared, Eugene and my wife Rebecca – who encouraged and supported me to produce this book.

Foreword

The Procurement and Supply Management profession could either be on the precipice of a terminal decline or at the point of evolving to be one of the most valued and admired professions in the corporate world. Its ability to adapt and learn new skills and behaviours will determine which outcome is achieved but one thing is for certain: 'What got us here as a profession will not keep us here!'. David's book *Soft Skills for Hard Business* provides us with a rich understanding of why business outcomes rely on more than just facts, data and sound processes to deliver sustainable value, and sets out in clear and practical language why the profession needs to evolve with the support of Behavioural Sciences, Decision Sciences and Social Sciences to assure its long-term success.

I have been fortunate to have been part of the Procurement and Supply Management profession for over 25 years, working mainly for large multinational companies such as Motorola, Microsoft and Ericsson in both regional and global roles. For the past 8 years I have been working as a Director for the Chartered Institute of Procurement and Supply (CIPS) which is the largest professional association dedicated to the Procurement and Supply Management profession, with over 60,000 members around the world and operations in 7 countries.

During my time at CIPS I have engaged with hundreds of procurement professionals around the world from those in entry level roles to Chief Procurement Officers, and have often been astonished by how little the definition of what 'successful procurement' looks like has changed over the years.

Of course, we have progressed and without doubt technology has enabled better use of data and more efficient processes, but in many cases the essence of how procurement performance is measured has made little progress beyond right cost, right time and right quality since I first started as a Buyer in the early 1980s.

The correlation between good procurement performance, in its broadest sense, and good business performance is generally misunderstood. How often does a Procurement team pat itself on the back for achieving its cost savings objectives, only to find turmoil ensuing within the stakeholder community because the chosen supplier is underperforming and difficult to deal with? The 'reality gap' is often caused by a lack of understanding, complexity, ineffective stakeholder engagement and changing priorities. Under these circumstances no arsenal of good data and procurement processes is going to deliver the value that is increasingly being demanded of Procurement.

It was in my role as Director of Business Solutions at CIPS that I first met David when he was the Chief Procurement Officer for Westminster City Council in London. In that role and those that followed I was always struck by David's ability to transform the team he was leading and to drive improved outcomes though better engagement with internal and external stakeholders. On reflection David's success as a leading practitioner has not been so much about working harder (although I am sure that was part of the mix!), but working smarter and putting in to practice the key 'people skills' that are discussed in the book. Not that I am suggesting that people skills alone are the answer, but it is the skilful blending of technical skills and self-awareness and an understanding of how other people's values, behaviours, biases and culture that can all have a bearing on how business is conducted and what outcomes can be expected.

This book sets out to explain why long-term value and competitive advantage cannot be secured by simply following traditional well-rehearsed approaches to Procurement and Supply Management. Whilst many of the tools and techniques we learn though our professional and academic qualifications continue to be relevant it will be the non-technical skills that differentiate the professional of the future. How these skills are flexibly applied in a rapidly changing and often complex business environment will be the principal drivers of value.

Whilst many of the concepts in the book at first glance seem unrelated and almost alien to our profession they are explained clearly and with the practitioner in mind at all times. When I have listened to David speak about these concepts at conferences I have found his style very easy to relate to and can readily see how concepts such as Biases and Emotional Intelligence have had a profound bearing on my professional life and perhaps, more importantly, what we can do to be more self-aware and how we can make often simple changes to improve our interactions with people and secure improved business value.

As a profession we will increasingly recruit based on competency not process capability, and on behaviours not seniority, so understanding how to nurture and develop these aspects of our 'DNA' are an essential part of our personal and professional development. I firmly believe that to be successful in the Procurement and Supply Management profession you need to have a firm understanding of the underpinning knowledge required across a broad range of technical subject matter, but as *Soft Skills for Hard Business* suggests, the professional of the future will require a complementary range of skills that help navigate the uncertainties and vagaries of the modern business world.

Andrew Coulcher FCIPS

Introduction

How a CPO (Chief Procurement Officer) conference that I really didn't want to go to ended up with years of research and interest!

I have had a very diverse career, which has included living and working in many different countries and many different sectors (public, private and venture capital) and as a consequence this has given me a unique view of the way enterprises and the supply chain interact. Over the last four or five years I have researched both formally and informally many aspects of the Behavioural Sciences, to explore and understand why rational and logical approaches do not necessarily deliver a linear line of decision-making.

In my early career as a surveyor and project manager in the field of construction and property development I was grounded in the very precise disciplines of architecture, structural engineering, civil engineering and material sciences, all of which demanded attention to detail and delivery to a precise specification. The sector and the industry itself was very much governed and regulated by a traditional and well-established hierarchy. On the surface, it suggested a culture and working practice that had little or no room for interpretation or tolerances. However, as many people know this industry and sector suffers from many disputes, claims and counter claims, much of which is seen as par for the course and nothing out of the ordinary.

Considering this and the many times we have or will face decisions that either purport to be or are seen as completely irrational and simply not logical, have you ever wondered or stopped to consider something as simple as what defines the best person you have ever worked for or with, and why your working practices resonated so well?

By the end of this book, you will know the answers to questions like, "It's not rational or logical, why did they choose the option that didn't deliver the maximum amount of savings or benefit?", and many similar questions that on the face of it do not conform to the way we expect outcomes to be.

Having read through countless journals, research papers, white papers and many other forms of academic literature, I have chosen to write this book in a way that makes it accessible to all the practitioners. Many of the practices, competences and approaches are intended to be set out in a way that allows the practitioner to see how these may be implemented in real-world situations, whilst at the same time gaining a primary understanding of some of the key concepts, arguments, theories and experimental outcomes from parallel work from those anchored in the Behavioural Sciences such as Behavioural Economics, Cognitive Behaviour, Psychology, Decision Sciences, Social Sciences and many other related fields.

I have used many of my own personal experiences over the last 30 years and more to set into context many of the principles and parallel studies to show dissonance within the field of procurement and commercial management. Equally, it is my belief that many of the principles, concepts and competences are valid across many functions and management practices in general, and in particular the specific vocation of leadership.

Many of the things that I have discovered through my research allow me to understand more clearly why certain events both in my life and in my career turned out the way they did! I have also spent nearly 10 years of my working career working in countries where English is not the first language – this has allowed me to witness first-hand a diversity of cultures, practices and social norms that have augmented my knowledge and understanding. This has enabled me to make reasonable adjustment for such factors when examining human and corporate behaviour. Further, the many global roles I have had the fortune to discharge over the many years, outside of my native country England, have taken me extensively and comprehensively across Australasia, China, Asia, Europe, Russia, the Baltics, North and South America as well as the UK.

As my research began I quickly realised that certain fundamental understandings of practices or ways of working had already been researched, defined and more formally categorised through Behavioural Science. Accordingly, I cannot go much further without making reference to heuristics and cognitive biases[1], which you'll come to recognise and familiarise yourself with as you tune into the comprehensive world of Behavioural Science.

The "light bulb" moment for me came when I attended a CPO event a few years ago, where one particular session was the spark that set things in motion. Therefore, I attribute my interest and passion in this area of Behavioural Science to Professor John Henke, who has spent many years studying the supplier relationships between the major US motor manufacturers and their supply chains in detail. Further, Professor John Henke has also worked in 18 other industries since 1990 – experience that has led to the development of a *working relations index*, a system that is owned and proprietary to Prof. Henke (and his company PPI Inc.). What struck me about this particular presentation was the need to recognise how human behaviours played a pivotal role in determining critical

---

1. Heuristics and Cognitive biases: Heuristics are strategies derived from previous experiences with similar problems. These strategies rely on using readily accessible, though loosely applicable, information to control problem-solving in human beings, machines, and abstract issues. The most fundamental heuristic is trial and error, which can be used in everything from matching nuts and bolts to finding the values of variables in algebra problems. Cognitive Biases are tendencies to think in certain ways that can lead to systematic deviations from a standard of rationality or good judgment, and are often studied in psychology and Behavioural Economics. Cognitive biases can be organized into four categories: biases that arise from too much information, not enough meaning, the need to act quickly, and the limits of memory.

factors such as Earnings Before Income and Taxes (EBIT) value being directly correlated to the way the major motor manufacturers in the US interacted and behaved towards the many tiers within their supply chains. For the first time, I saw referenced, in a quantitative way how the changes in behaviour towards the supply chain directly correlated with the fortunes of the buying organisations.

This led me to some very early and simplistic thinking that was subsequently borne out by real-life exchanges with sales and business development directors regarding contractual negotiations I had carried out in previous years, wherein large organisations behaving in a non-collaborative and at times abusive way towards the supply chain did not yield the best results.

Whilst I cannot reveal the names and identities of companies and people involved in prior commercial negotiations, there are very clear examples I can offer. For example, a sales director of a major drinks manufacturer and distributor had offered the company (I represented at the time) – a mid-tier pubs, clubs and restaurants chain – more favourable pricing, by some considerable margin, than several top tier companies in the same sector. This was simply attributed to the way the team and I behaved towards them as a company, not our size or buying power!

Clearly the expectation of the top tier company was that it would receive the most preferential pricing in the marketplace (a 'logical expectation' due to size). However, their hostile behaviour towards a branded supplier of alcoholic beverages had failed to recognise that their size and non-collaborative approach towards their supply chain had acted against them, rather than in their favour.

In essence, the rationality and logic of outcomes can and will continue to be altered as a consequence of key factors that sit outside of the traditional domain of systems, processes, contract terms – all as a consequence of human behaviour.

Finally, the conventional assumption is that all parties to any form of decision-making, evaluation and the general performance of procurement, contract and commercial duties are achieved solely through rational and logical decision-making. In other words, that approaches that deliver the optimum commercial outcome in terms of value and resource allocation consider and mitigate all known reasonable risks in an objective and structured manner is simply not true.

My hope is that – as a result of what you are about to read – you will be able to reflect and consider the behaviours and intentions of the other party (and all parties) as well as your own, to give you a better understanding of human nature.

Structure of the Book

The book is structured to take the reader through a journey that begins with an understanding of the "catalyst" for this book – and also my PhD in Behavioural Science. This then transitions into an overview of the areas we already know and relate to in the field of procurement and allied disciplines such as Supply Chain Management, Contract Management, Supplier Relationship Management, etc. So, if you are familiar with these areas, feel free to use it as a refresher. However, I will refer back to these from time to time. Perhaps as you begin the journey into Behavioural Procurement the linkage to soft (people) skills) will allow you to begin to realise the broader set of competences that I will signpost in the first section.

From there we launch into areas of Behavioural Science that set out not only definitions, but how this is anchored back into everyday life for many professionals. These will lead us to a better understanding of how people are at the centre of change when it comes to strategic and complex issues in Procurement, Supply Chain or Supplier Relationship Management.

As a profession, we have for long recognised the need for robust processes, systems and good data, and that isn't about to change. However, we have been missing the fourth leg of the stool – the softer people skills. That then is the focus of this book, plain and simple. The parts build to give a wider comprehension of the aspects that connect to allow change to be more effective and leadership to be more cognitive and inclusive of diversity. This then leads to deliver better and more sustainable outcomes.

Ultimately it is not just about others but about your behaviours too, and the impact that they may have on outcomes. The book reminds us all that trust, fairness, integrity, collaboration and similar characteristics are core competences for everyone, even the leader, if not more so. Hopefully, you will come to see it as reference book too, that in time that you can dip in and out of as needed, as there isn't a one-size-fits-all way for every situation, environment and set of people.

PART A
//
SETTING THE SCENE

CHAPTER 1 | FOUNDATIONS OF BEHAVIOURAL ECONOMICS

1.1 History and Commentary

History plays a great part in the story and development Behavioural Economics and as you will begin to realise this subject has been the focus of attention and research for many centuries. In setting out my case, I fundamentally believe that to accept that all matters and exchanges between human beings is rational and logical is unrealistic. Further, our interactions and negotiations are governed by *the situation, the circumstances and the people involved in it*!

The fact that we do not act rationally is not a new concept – in fact it can be traced back to the very early philosophers such as Plato, René Descartes, Aristotle, and Friedrich Nietzsche. But perhaps more importantly, in the context of economics and all things commercial, is Adam Smith's book the *Theory of Moral Sentiments*[1], which he wrote in 1759. In my book, I will focus on aspects relating to economics and commercial matters and how they have been influenced by the introduction of Behavioural Science into this paradigm from the late 1970s onwards.

It is pivotal in gaining an understanding of how and where Behavioural Procurement (BP) has been developed over a relatively short period of time, and why it should come as no great surprise that behaviours are frequently the missing consideration in what all commercial agents do, every day. For me there are three primary attributes:

- Data – The use of it and the ability to be able to factually record and project what has happened, what can happen or what the impact of different approaches and scenarios will be through numbers.
- Processes – The methodology and approach we need to take in order to understand the sequence of events, duration, risks we may encounter, who we need to engage with, and so on.
- People – Who we need to work with, communicate with, persuade, influence, engage, and what their contribution and/or impact upon our work (both positive and negative) will be.

Before we go any further I will let you ponder on the definition of Behavioural Procurement, so that elements of the concept and approach are in your conscious mind as we move from Behavioural Economics to Behavioural Procurement.

---

1. Smith, A. (1759). *The Theory of Moral Sentiments*. Printed for Andrew Millar, in the Strand; and Alexander Kincaid and J. Bell, in Edinburgh.

The definition is as follows:

> *BP and the related field of BE study the effects of psychological, social, cognitive and emotional factors on the commercial decisions of individuals and institutions, and the consequences for competitive advantage, innovation and resource allocation. BP is primarily concerned with bounds of rationality of commercial agents and factors. BP models typically integrate insights from BE, psychology, Decision Sciences, Social Sciences, market theory, as well as Nudging; in so doing these behavioural models cover a range of concepts methods and fields.*

Adam Smith's seminal book *The Wealth of Nations*, published in 1776, is arguably his best known work. However, it was his first book *The Theory of Moral Sentiments* which provided the ethical, philosophical, psychological and methodological underpinning to Smith's later works. In it he records and documents the significance of our experiences and behaviour and how this materially affects every aspect of our life.

In the initial chapter Smith states, "*We have of course no immediate experience of what other men feel; so the only way we can get an idea of what someone else is feeling is by thinking about what we would feel if we were in his situation. Our imagination comes into this, but only by representing to us the feelings we would have if etc. We see or think about a man being tortured on the rack; we think of ourselves enduring all the same torments, entering into his body (so to speak) and becoming in a way the same person as he is. In this manner we form some idea of his sensations, and even feel something that somewhat resembles them, though it is less intense. When his agonies are brought home to us in this way, when we have adopted them and made them our own, they start to affect us and we then tremble and shudder at the thought of what he feels.*"[2]

Smith is clearly setting out his observations and perceptions of how our feelings are unique, and that others may feel completely different things to us in a given circumstance. Moreover, different circumstances can alter our perception and understanding of how others may feel in the same or a similar situation. Therefore, we must learn to understand that in conducting our business we cannot possibly know all there is to know about how the other party may or may not understand, respond to or value what we ourselves choose to acknowledge.

Understanding needs to lead to us being cognizant of the fact that our assumption that how we act, behave, engage and indeed view what we believe to be something described as objective, can in fact, appear subjective to others. This understanding is critical to our development as managers and leaders; and in so

2. Smith, A. (1759). *The Theory of Moral Sentiments.* Printed for Andrew Millar, in the Strand; and Alexander Kincaid and J. Bell, in Edinburgh. P1.

doing to create certainty we have to imagine that we exist in a set, predetermined, unchanging reality.

However, the things that always change are the situation, the circumstances and the people involved. So, the promotion of rational, logical models and outcomes is impossible, as this only reflects theory and not reality – particularly since we are all born with a fully self-serving, self-justifying nature and the resulting introverted, subjective perception is by default subjective.

Smith believed that we are driven by an internal struggle between our impulses, passions and perhaps a sense of conscience (which he describes as the impartial spectator)[3]. Therefore, we generally place a greater focus on more trivial matters (which he describes as out-of-pocket expenses) versus perhaps some of the more fundamental aspects of an agreement. This kind of behaviour, which is often seen as being erratic but consistently concerned with fairness and justice, is evident. Further, he references people's motivation by ego and pure self-interest rather than multidimensional and realistic rational-thinking people.

Smith's also uses the term "commercial society" – a phrase that emphasises his belief that the economic attribute is only one component of the human condition. David Hume, a professor who worked with Smith, argued that whilst you may be able to teach what it means to be moral, "only their passions not their rational capacities can actually inspire them to be ethical".[4] This position has roots in Aristotle's distinction between moral and intellectual virtue. Essentially, the foundations of virtues, morals, ethics, fairness and justice, etc. are always present in any rational or logical exchange, and become key factors in governing their outcomes.

There are a number of people who have been attributed with the establishment of Behavioural Economics. One in particular is Herbert A. Simon, who became best-known for his Theory of Corporate Decision-making, in his book *Administrative Behaviour* (first published in 1947). Simon highlights the multiple factors that contribute to decision-making. His Theory of Administration is largely based upon human decision-making and focuses on both economics and psychology. Simon defines rational decision-making as being "a process that selects the alternative that results in the more preferred or optimal set of all possible consequences". He argued that the two factors needed to achieve administrative decisions was measured by:

- The adequacy of achieving the desired objective
- The efficiency of which the result was obtained

3. Smith, A. (1759). *The Theory of Moral Sentiments*. "They are led by an **invisible hand** to share out life's necessities in just about the same way that they would have been shared out if the earth been divided into equal portions among all its inhabitants."
4. Hume, D. (1738). A Treatise of Human Nature, Book III. Publisher unknown.

The rational decision-making task was therefore divided into three required steps:

- Identifying and listing all alternatives
- Contemplating the consequences resulting from each of the alternatives
- Establishing the accuracy and efficiency of each of these sets of consequences.

In his work, Simon recognised that the knowledge of all alternative options and of all consequences that follow from each step is truly impossible to calculate. He concluded that his theory provided a framework, conditioned by our human cognitive limitations. He asserted that administrative behaviour addresses a wide range of human behaviours, cognitive abilities, management techniques, personal policies, training goals and procedures, specialised roles, criteria for evaluation of accuracy and efficiency and all the ramifications of communication processes.

He was particularly interested in how these factors influence decision-making both directly and indirectly. He also recognised that we must pay particular attention to the efficiency with which the desired result was achieved, and that organisational decisions are distinctly different from personal decisions. However, we cannot ignore the fact that individuals make decisions for and on behalf of organisations and therefore impart decision-making both in the personal and in the organisational context insofar as intent, purpose and effect are concerned.

Simon recognised that certain organisations are well-studied and as such offer a primary benchmark of organisational behaviour, which can be defined in the organisational context as the ability and right of an individual of higher rank to guide the decisions of an 'individual of a lower rank'. The actions, attitudes and relationships of executives to junior members of staff constitute the components of role behaviour that may vary wildly in form, style and content, but do not vary in the expectation of the obedience by the one of superior status and consequently the willingness to obey, from the junior status.

Further, it was defined by Simon as the "process whereby the individual substitutes organisational objectives (service objectives or conservation objectives) or his own aims as the value indices, which determine his organisational decisions". This entailed evaluating alternative choices in terms of their consequences for the group, rather than the individual or immediate family.

Clearly decisions can be a complex mixture of facts and values. This again serves to establish that pure logic and rationality as we know it are not the only determining factors of an outcome or a decision. In any given decision-making process, Simon believed that agents face uncertainty about the future and costs in acquiring information in the present. These factors alone limit the extent to which we can make fully rational decisions, and thus we possess only "bounded rationality"[5] and must make decisions to "satisfice" [sic] them, using that which might not be optimal, but which will make them happy enough.

Another key figure in the development of Behavioural Economics was George Katona, who saw Behavioural Economics as a discipline within Economics, and which was primarily concerned with the human element in economic affairs. The use of the word *Behavioural* was intentional, to signal that this was central to the research around human decision-making as opposed to traditional economic theory, which was concerned solely with the behaviour of markets.

Katona viewed the scope of Behavioural Economics to include all human economic behaviour (consumer spending, saving behaviour, entrepreneurship, work-related behaviour, job choice, investment in human capital, business behaviour in terms of prices, output, investments, financing, policies and the like). His research focused on the rationality of the process of decision-making, and in doing so fused the disciplines of psychology and economics into one.

Katona was influenced by John Maynard Keynes and his seminal Keynesian Theory[6] of 1936, which lead a revolution in economic thinking, challenging the ideas of neoclassical economics. Keynes' theory was a compelling explanation of how uncertainty and ambiguity influence the expectations and decisions of economic agents (or more specifically a decision-maker in a model of some aspect of the economy by solving a well or ill-defined optimisation or choice problem).

Keynes placed special emphasis on the decisions of business, as well as those of government policymakers in the management of the national economy. However, Simon disagreed with Keynes' "fundamental psychological law" that proposed that consumers were passive responders to current income and their importance in consumer investment expenditures in the course of shaping macroeconomics as a whole.

Simon essentially believed that economic behaviour is a learned behaviour and that it is dependent on how people perceive and utilise information. Therefore,

---

5. Bounded Rationality relates to the concept that when individuals make decisions, their rationality is limited by the tractability of the decision problem, the cognitive limitations of their minds, and the time available to make the decision. Decision-makers in this view act as satisficers, seeking a satisfactory solution rather than an optimal one. Herbert A. Simon proposed bounded rationality as an alternative basis for the mathematical modelling of decision-making, as used in economics, political science and related disciplines.

6. *The General Theory of Employment, Interest and Money* was written by the English economist John Maynard Keynes. The book, generally considered to be his magnum opus, is largely credited with creating the terminology and shape of modern macroeconomics. Published in February 1936, it sought to bring about a revolution, commonly referred to as the "Keynesian Revolution", in the way some economists believe – especially in relation to the proposition that a market economy tends naturally to restore itself to full employment after temporary shocks. Regarded widely as the cornerstone of Keynesian thought, the book challenged the established classical economics theories of the time, and introduced important concepts such as the consumption function, the multiplier, the marginal efficiency of capital, the principle of effective demand and liquidity preference.

the development of Katona's theories about how people learn was influenced by the Gestalt Theories[7] of Max Wertheimer, Kurt Lewin and others. Accordingly, we only recognise the aspects that show the way information is framed to determine its meaning. Further, Katona believed that there was no other concept that played a larger or more important role in shaping economic behaviour than expectations. However, the bounds of expectations as a determinant of behaviour was largely missing in psychology.

Katona believed the expectations had both cognitive as well as effective components, meaning expectations contained information about future states of economic variables as well as how people evaluated those expected outcomes. Finally, scientific advancement requires not just models that can accurately predict behaviour, but theories that represent a comprehensive understanding of the underlying causal pathways, and the such this cannot be the end of the journey.

Another key piece of work came from the collaboration of mathematician John von Neumann and economist Oskar Morgenstern, who wrote *The Theory of Games and Economic Behaviour* (1944) – considered the ground-breaking text that created the interdisciplinary research field of Game Theory[8]. Von Neumann

---

7. Gestalt Theories or Principles: The school of gestalt practiced a series of theoretical and methodological principles that attempted to redefine the approach to psychological research. This is in contrast to investigations developed at the beginning of the 20th century, based on traditional scientific methodology, which divided the object of study into a set of elements that could be analysed separately with the objective of reducing the complexity of this object.

The theoretical principles of Gestalt are the following:

Principle of Totality – The conscious experience must be considered globally (by taking into account all the physical and mental aspects of the individual simultaneously) because the nature of the mind demands that each component be considered as part of a system of dynamic relationships.

Principle of psychophysical isomorphism – A correlation exists between conscious experience and cerebral activity.

Based on the principles above the following methodological principles are defined:

Phenomenon experimental analysis – In relation to the Totality Principle any psychological research should take phenomena as a starting point and not be solely focused on sensory qualities.

Biotic experiment – The school of Gestalt established a need to conduct real experiments that sharply contrasted with and opposed classic laboratory experiments. This signified experimenting in natural situations, developed in real conditions, in which it would be possible to reproduce, with higher fidelity, what would be habitual for a subject.

8. Game Theory is "the study of mathematical models of conflict and cooperation between intelligent rational decision-makers". Game Theory is mainly used in economics, political science, and psychology, as well as logic, computer science and biology. Originally, it addressed zero-sum games, in which one person's gains result in losses for the other participants. Today, Game Theory applies to a wide range of behavioural relations, and is now an umbrella term for the science of logical decision-making in humans, animals, and computers. Modern Game Theory began with the idea regarding the existence of mixed-strategy equilibria in two-person zero-sum games and its proof by John von Neumann. Von Neumann's original proof used the Brouwer fixed-point theorem on continuous mappings into compact convex sets, which became a standard method in Game Theory and mathematical economics. His paper was followed by the 1944 book *Theory of Games and Economic Behaviour*, co-written with Oskar Morgenstern, which considered cooperative games of several players. The second edition of this book provided an axiomatic theory of expected

and Morgenstern used objective probabilities, supposing that all the agents had the same probability distribution, as a convenient, yet simplistic way of modelling. Moreover, Neumann and Morgenstern mentioned that a theory of *subjective probability*, as part of the theory, could be provided, which was instrumental in moving away from simple linear models. The subjective probability was provided by Jimmie Savage (1954) and expanded later by Johann Pfanzagl (1967) based on von Neumann and Morgenstern's axioms of rational preferences to transform the traditional probability models and make it subjective and hence more realistic in the real world.

Only by developing selfless, altruistic and objective point of view and leaving a limited and subjective state behind can we begin to reach a point of view where the subjective and objective fuse into one. Even Adam Smith recognises that "we the self" will need an impartial spectator, to allow us to act in an impartial and objective way. This recognises and balances the short-term gratification we naturally seek versus the long-term benefits or costs (or value). Maybe this was again a signpost to not simply rely upon the things as we know them (our heuristics) and/or be led by our biases, of which there are nearly 200, all of which affect our judgement.

The "Utopian Principle", which Adam Smith described as a world where there was equal division among all men of the wealth and goods, etc.), in which both buyer and seller benefit or profit from an exchange or contract/ agreement, is a noble one, but hardly reflects the true reality in every situation, as we cannot possibly foretell the future and how events will allow this new state of affairs to play out.

1.2 Key Concepts and Principles

There has been considerable work carried out more recently which augments the foundations of Behavioural Economics. Luminaries such as Daniel Kahneman, Amos Tversky, Richard H. Thaler, Cass R. Sunstein, Dan Ariely, Nassim Nicholas Taleb, who are broadly recognised as the modern thought leaders of Behavioural Economics (science), have added considerable detail and salience to everyday life.

The more recent research and findings from the 1950s onwards are key and most relevant to the concepts and principles that apply to the modern commercial world of procurement and Purchasing and Supply Chain Management. There are many more that I could add to the list of contributors who have developed the concepts and principles, but for me the above group is the most relevant and proximate to the profession as a whole.

utility, which allowed mathematical statisticians and economists to treat decision-making under uncertainty.

A critical aspect of the development of these theories is a concept Adam Smith introduced, called "the invisible hand"[9]. This theory suggests that there is a certain degree of individualism in any decision-making process which produces an inherent lack of certainty in outcomes and decisions that is not always evident or visible to the other party. So even Smith recognises that we "the self" will need an impartial spectator to allow us to act in an impartial and objective way, to allow us to balance short-term gratification (our natural instinct) with long-term costs (or value). In simple terms the key principle here as I see it is as follows:

We simply cannot rely upon facts and data, logic and rationality as being the sole determinants of outcomes, decisions and the way in which we will deliver value and competitive advantage either in the public or private sector.

The key concepts behind this have been established by empiricism through scientific experimentation and a greater understanding of Social Sciences, Psychology, Neuroscience, Decision Sciences, etc. Therefore, the way in which we operate in buyer-seller situations and life in general is more greatly dominated by Behavioural Science as a whole – quite often much more so than we currently recognise.

Research has continued to reaffirm that our decision-making, negotiating, processing of information and so forth is not linear, and very much influenced by factors such as inbuilt or acquired knowledge on the part of the decision-maker (holistic), biases and prejudices of both past and current events and circumstances, as well as a vast array of assumptions by all the parties who are involved in the decision to be made.

We, as professionals, must look to progress to a new form of procurement theory and practice that is balanced by and with the assistance of the Behavioural Sciences, Decision Sciences and Social Sciences in order to create sustainable competitive advantage for the organisations we serve. In establishing the key concepts, I will draw upon research carried out in many allied and parallel disciplines in order to set them out in a way which can be readily understood by practitioners. This is an intentional approach to "make sense and translate" the volumes and richness of academic research that has allowed us to reach a

9. "Every individual necessarily labours to render the annual revenue of the society as great as you can. He generally, indeed, neither intends to promote the public interest, nor knows how much he is promoting it. By preferring the support of domestic to that of foreign industry, he intends only his own security; and by directing that industry in such a manner as its produce may be of the greatest value, he intends only his own game, and he is in this, as in many other cases, led by an **invisible hand** to promote an end which has no part of his intention nor is it always the worst for the society that it was no part of it. In pursuing his own interest, he frequently promotes that of the society more effectually than when he really intends to promote it. I have never known much good done by those who affected to trade for the public good."

greater understanding of how behaviours fundamentally impact outcomes and decisions, particularly – but not specifically or solely – in the area procurement and allied subjects.

The Chartered Institute of Purchasing and Supply (CIPS) have defined the practice of procurement as follows:

Procurement is the business management function that ensures identification, sourcing, access and management of the external resources that an organisation needs or may need to fulfil its strategic objectives.

Procurement exists to explore supply market opportunities and to implement resourcing strategies that deliver the best possible supply outcome to the organisation, its stakeholders and customers.

Procurement applies the science and art of external resource and supply management through a body of knowledge interpreted by competent practitioners and professionals.[10]

I would suggest that the key concepts of **Behavioural Procurement** can be identified as follows:

1. Behavioural Procurement is a sub-field of Behavioural Economics.
2. We understand and recognise the effects of behaviour as related to ourselves and other parties, insofar as they may impact or affect the outcomes of otherwise pure and unbiased and impartial activities and interactions.
3. The impact of social, cognitive and emotional factors in terms of outcomes, decisions and commercial factors is fundamental.
4. Current environmental and unrelated events have a determining effect on the delivery and relativity of decision-making.
5. Salience: as relative to our mental state relative to distinctiveness, prominence, obviousness and our/other parties' perception and/or cognition of a stimulus that, for any of many reasons, stands out from the rest. (Salience may be the result of emotional, motivational or cognitive factors and is not necessarily associated with physical factors).
6. Outcomes are and will be impacted by our own and other parties' "bounded rationality".
7. Risk is a dynamic consideration, not a static one. Over time it will change outcomes and consequences as related to the initial decisions.
8. Pure maximisation of gain is not the only determinant of value or competitive advantage.

10. CIPS official Definition of Procurement, accessed at https://www.cips.org/Documents/CIP-SAWhitePapers/2006/Definition_of_Procurement.pdf

Implicit within these key concepts is the recognition of factors such as governance, ethics and sustainability (of outcomes).

1.3 The Birth of Behavioural Procurement

In the same way that financial management became a sub-field of Behavioural Economics, we can argue that Procurement and Supply Chain Management is also a sub-field. From my experience, it was the realisation that behaviours not only matter, but have a significant impact on outcomes and decisions, that enabled me to focus on the professional possibilities. This was a "light bulb" moment for me in terms of the potential for the organisations I represented – a prospect that was endorsed by my peer group of Chief Procurement Officers working in similar roles.

My ability to recognise that there are explanations for what appeared in the past as a series of either irrational or illogical outcomes, as a professional who began work as a Surveyor and Project Manager, was suddenly reassuring. My ability to *"make sense and translate"* processes and events as a consequence of my newly-found understanding of things such things as bounded rationality, heuristics, biases and many other factors besides was akin to the lifting of a mental fog in the world in which I operated.

I will return to this term "make sense and translate" in future chapters as I believe this simple principle of understanding and playing back in different ways for different audiences has a profound effect on our decision-making ability.

Most humans are born with five senses (sight, sound, touch, taste and smell). I feel too that in our professional lives there must be a combination of multiple attributes to work in a holistic manner. If we were simply to operate with processes and data alone we would be performing in a suboptimal manner in delivering the best possible outcome. Adding additional dimensions by way of competences such as behavioural competences provides a more holistic approach which in turn produces better outcomes.

When we consider that most interactions related to the field of Purchasing and Supply Chain Management, i.e. Contract Management, Supplier Relationship Management (SRM),[11] Supply Chain Management (SCM)[12] etc. centre around

11. Supplier Relationship Management (Supplier Relationship Management) is the systematic, enterprise-wide assessment of suppliers' assets and capabilities with respect to overall business strategy, determination of what activities to engage in with different suppliers, and planning and execution of all interactions with suppliers, in a coordinated fashion across the relationship life cycle, to maximise the value realised through those interactions. The focus of Supplier Relationship Management is to develop two-way, mutually beneficial relationships with strategic supply partners to deliver greater levels of innovation and competitive advantage than could be achieved by operating independently or through a traditional, transactional purchasing arrangements.
12. Supply Chain Management (SCM) is concerned with the management of the flow of goods and services, of an enterprise. This involves the movement and storage of raw materials, of

people either in the singular or in groups/whole companies, it should not come as a big surprise that simply following a category management process or similar is in itself only a means to an end. By acknowledging the very existence of behaviours not just in our everyday lives but in our commercial lives too starts to add colour to an otherwise monochrome picture. If we begin to ask ourselves, "Why do I favour the relationships of some above others, and what are the characteristics and factors that endear us towards them in our social lives?", this should then enable us to think about how this might be relevant in a commercial setting. In fact, Trust relies on the occurrence of three fundamental attributes: Ability, Integrity and Benevolence.[13]

When we stop for a moment to think about the many related issues that are shared through the various forms of social media, they often gravitate around the subject of how we need to recognise, respond, collaborate, communicate, empathise and reciprocate, but they are rarely assembled as a collective.

Some have begun to recognise and indeed utilise aspects of Game Theory in negotiation and other areas of procurement. Furthermore, the use and practice of behavioural assessments in major projects is now becoming far more mainstream in many Western areas of the world, and will continue to gain momentum as its importance as a key differentiator to project/programme success gains wider recognition. I will be as bold as to say that Behavioural Procurement is here to stay and there is still much to do to augment and increase our knowledge in this critical area, not just for procurement as a profession but for other fields too. A number of British university professors (Bath, East Anglia, Sussex, etc.) in operations management, value chain management and psychology already recognise and have begun exploring the area of Behavioural Procurement.

The introduction of Behavioural Procurement will embrace and recognise many of the things that we already know and use in Procurement and Supply Chain Management such as:

---

work-in-process inventory, and of finished goods from point of origin to point of consumption. Interconnected or interlinked networks, channels and node businesses combine in the provision of products and services required by end customers in a supply chain. Supply-chain management has been defined as the "design, planning, execution, control, and monitoring of supply chain activities with the objective of creating net value, building a competitive infrastructure, leveraging worldwide logistics, synchronising supply with demand and measuring performance globally."

13. Ability refers to an assessment of the other's knowledge, skill, or competency. This dimension recognizes that trust requires some sense that the other is able to perform in a manner that meets our expectations. Integrity is the degree to which the trustee adheres to principles that are acceptable to the trustor. This dimension leads to trust based on consistency of past actions, credibility of communication, commitment to standards of fairness, and the congruence of the other's word and deed. Benevolence is our assessment that the trusted individual is concerned enough about our welfare to either advance our interests, or at least not impede them. The other's perceived intentions or motives of the trustee are most central. Honest and open communication, delegating decisions, and sharing control indicate evidence of one's benevolence.

- Communication
- Emotional Intelligence (EI)
- Stakeholder management
- Active listening skills

These subjects will be covered in Chapter 2. In the birth of Behavioural Procurement, and its scientific base, I must give due recognition to the opportunity to both meet and understand the work of Professor John W. Henke Jr, PhD (President/CEO, Planning Perspectives Inc.; Professor of Marketing, Oakland University; Research Fellow Centre for Supply Chain Management at Rutgers University), who spent many years, amongst other things, developing the Working Relations Index® study in the North American automotive sector.

For me, this highlighted three key principles of fairness, payment on time and trust. Equally it recognised the characteristics of the purchasing agent to build the foundational activities required to create collaborative relations. The working relations activities, as defined by Planning Perspectives Inc., were as follows:

- Buyer-supplier relationship
- Buyer communication
- Buyer help
- Buyer hindrance
- Supplier profit opportunity

Work is principally aimed, although not exclusively, to maximisation of supplier contribution to company profits and the improvement of supplier relations.

This is summarised by the following:

- Basic business practices – have in place the basic practices on which collaborative supplier relations can be built and maintained.
- Purchasing agent characteristics – have in place appropriate purchasing agent behaviours and practices needed to build and maintain the desired level of collaborative supplier relations.
- Relational activities – i.e. know how suppliers perceive working with you; know your organisation's supplier relations.

In 2016 I chaired a CPO round table[14], which included thought leaders and academics. This session reaffirmed the importance of behaviours in procurement.

14. Langley Search and Interim: The Importance of Behaviours in Procurement Senior Procurement Executives on How Behaviours and Soft Skills will Shape the Future of Procurement: February 2016

The following is an extract of some of the quotations from that session, in no particular order:

- "Procurement needs to wake up from the sleep habit."
- "My most effective teams have been successful because they have connected, communicated and worked collaboratively together. It's all about the environment – connecting with people in understanding what they value and what drives them, and will give you your best performers."
- "Sometimes it can seem that procurement speaks an entirely different language to the rest of the business. We need to remedy this to ensure that we are speaking the language of our business to help them understand why we add value and how we can work together."
- "Procurement currently operates under a shield of profitability: if we are making a profit, why should we change?"
- "We need a range of skills and abilities – we need every type of procurement person, from analytical thinkers and problem-solvers to good people's people. We should examine the issue in an organisational context."
- "Procurement can often drive its own behaviours!"
- "There is still much bounded rationality, even amongst such a senior group of professionals."

At the time, I advocated a move away from more rigid toolkits to competency kits that will enable the growth and development required to help teams discover and take full advantage of all the potential opportunities for improvement. In discussion during the round table, it was felt that the top skills that procurement executives will be seeking in the new team members might include things such as:

- Determination and perseverance
- Curiosity
- Resilience
- Proficiency in establishing and maintaining relationships
- Communication skills
- Being highly personable

In conclusion, many of the forum attendees that I have had the privilege of being involved with, as well as the many peers and thought leaders I have engaged with over the years and months preceding this book, have all recognised the need to develop additional competences that recognise and harness all that Behavioural Science has to offer.

The three most influential books I have read over which offer an explanation of the concepts relating to Behavioural Economics and their application are:

- *Predictably Irrational* (Dan Ariely, 2008. HarperCollins)
- *Thinking, Fast and Slow* (Daniel Kahneman, 2011. Farrar, Straus and Giroux)
- *Nudge* (Cass Sunstein, Richard Thaler, 2008. Yale University Press)

All of these books (shown in the recommended reading section) reinforce to the reader that the process of decision-making is not logical, rational or linear. They also explain in detail the impact of well-documented psychological traps that befall most of us in our commercial exploits.

Ultimately, we face endless possibilities, especially because of the complexity of the decisions we make in our professional lives. These decision-making scenarios are likely to continue to become ever more complex. I am confident that like me, you too will experience many situations where metaphorically the simple sum of 2+2 does not equal 4! As I am realising, it is the non-tangible aspects of many of the situations I face that matter – it is more apparent that we must all dig deeper to develop a better understanding of just how many factors have an impact on the outcomes we might expect.

1.4 Definition of Behavioural Procurement

Some time ago I wrote a definition for Behavioural Procurement, and for me this still stands as strongly today as it did then. As I have set out before, I consider Behavioural Procurement to be a subfield of Behavioural Economics and therefore it relies upon much of the research and findings in that discipline.

However, if it is to have relevance to Procurement and Supply Chain Management, then we must be able to see and understand the parallels between Behavioural Economics and the definition I have set out below:

Behavioural Procurement and the related field of Behavioural Economics study the effects of psychological, social, cognitive, and emotional factors on the commercial decisions of individuals and institutions and the consequences for competitive advantage, innovation and resource allocation. BP is primarily concerned with bounds of rationality of commercial agents and factors. BP models typically integrate insights from BE, psychology, Decision Sciences, Social Sciences, market theory, as well as implicitly nudging; in so doing these behavioural models cover a range of concepts methods and fields.

It sounds complicated, so let's keep it simple! I have often used the tag line "I'm good or bad depending on the circumstances, the situation and the people involved!"

Setting out the principal contributors to Behavioural Procurement can be visually expressed as shown in Figure 1, below:

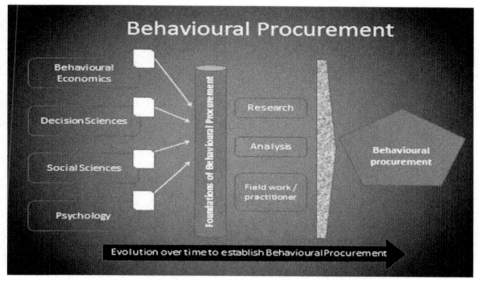

Figure 1.1. Principal contributors to Behavioural Procurement

I do not intend to comment much further beyond the definition itself, as I believe the evolution of Behavioural Economics now as a subfield of Behavioural Procurement is established, including the key concepts.

Rather than exploring the areas of competences we have traditionally known and used in Purchasing and Supply Chain Management, I suggest we begin to embrace a new ways of working that subscribe to Behavioural Procurement. So, in summary I will leave you with these final thoughts as considerations about those competences outside of the technical toolbox of procurement and Contract Management practitioners:

- Behaviours play a big part in decision-making
- Irrational decisions do have an explanation
- Behaviours are the enabler to better outcomes

CHAPTER 2 | AN OVERVIEW OF NON-TECHNICAL SKILLS (THE THINGS WE ALREADY KNOW AND USE)

In recognition of the fact that there are a number of pre-existing and more widely known tools and techniques, it is appropriate that I set out these in summary for completeness for you the reader. Equally, it sets into context the quantum of competences that are currently used and taught today in most graduate level qualifications.

2.1 Am I hearing you right?

The age-old saying that *"we have one mouth and two ears and should use them in that ratio"* is indeed a very wise statement. Most people are acutely aware, particularly when things go wrong, that the intended communication has not been received as intended. This is often where problems occur in relationships, reaching agreement and much more.

Setting aside the formal report writing and more "formulaic styles" of communication, the written and oral forms of communication in the relationships we form and hold are critical – and even more so the communication that exists between us. Crucially, the way we communicate has, from the beginning of humankind, been one of the most critical skills we use and possess during our daily lives, both socially and in business.

However, at times we do not observe or recognise that we have not communicated either correctly or effectively. This is especially critical at the outset of a communication, from which subsequent communication relies – the first communication is, therefore, arguably the most important.

Generally speaking, within a business transaction, people buy from people; moreover, when there is a strong relationship between people, an opportunity exists to correct things before any misunderstanding or other "damage" may be done. Therefore, mastering the art of communication has and will continue to be recognised as a key skill in business – a fact that is unlikely to change even with the advent of new technologies such as AI, digital applications and more.

In light of this we need to observe a few of our actions – CAPRICI – which translates as the following:

- Clarify – ensure that you are clear, that you are communicating the right messages before you begin. Managing expectations is a key ingredient in any recipe for success!
- Adaptability – adapt and change where necessary. Tailor what you wish to communicate to suit the audience (or the individuals) you are working with, as this will significantly improve your chances of communicating effectively, and get things right first time. Recognise that a generic or standard approach is simply not good enough if you want to engage multiple parties on a single topic.
- Preparation – particular for key meetings, critical exchanges and of course negotiations (as part of the planning).
- Realism – ensure what you're delivering is realistic and deliverable, with no false promises; remember trust is hard to win but easy to lose!
- Interpretation – consider the different ways in which your statements might be misconstrued or fundamentally changed, even to the extreme examples, and then consider how you might rephrase things to mitigate such outcomes.
- Checking – ensure the other party has truly understood and recognised what you intended to say versus how it may have been transcribed or understood.
- Identification – ensure you understand who you are communicating with as this will help you highlight and emphasise those points that are salient and relevant to the person or parties you are communicating.

Adapting YOUR style and approach is one of the key considerations in communication or persuasion. Often the reason we communicate is either to share some information, to seek confirmation/agreement, or gain approval, but seldom other than in a social context, to precipitate an action of some kind. Furthermore, you as the communicator will know your subject and the details behind it far and beyond the person receiving it, therefore your behaviour should be focused on them and not yourself!

Some of the most impactful pieces of communication stand out because they are memorable and create visual images or simple impactful statements that resonate long after the first point of communication.

Additionally, consider some of the following to test what you are seeking to communicate:

- Concise (and to the point)
- Energising
- Passionate
- Creates a vision/picture

- Humility (delivered with)
- Easy/Simple (especially when the subject is complicated)
- Memorable
- Purposeful
- Be Receptive

In behavioural terms, the single biggest communication no-no is miscommunication or ineffective communication that subsequently leads to a downward spiral where relationships and/or desired outcomes put up with risk, or worse still end in conflict. I have witnessed far too many situations where an intended positive communication has been interpreted negatively by the other party, and where usually in a rapid sequence events turn very ugly.

In the scenario which follows we can explore the above. I have set up a case where a simple statement gets misinterpreted from the outset.

Consider the following:

"Well of course you will have to comply fully with all the legislation, both State and Federal, if you want to do business here."

There are two ways in which this can be interpreted:

Positively: "Do you need our help in interpreting what is needed, as we know it can be a hard to interpret on occasions?"

Negatively: "We don't think you have the capability and skills within the organisation to discharge your responsibilities under the contract."

A legitimate response would be to test this statement in a balanced and objective way to establish what was meant, giving each party the opportunity to clarify or correct a belief based on incorrect information, historical circumstances, etc.

This should enable a more collaborative relationship from the outset. This is just one simple example, but in essence these competences, once mastered, become the enablers to deal with everyday situations such as the above.

What I have observed and recognised over my career across many countries and continents is that despite our job titles, including sales, marketing, business development, CRM, etc. all of the different functions need to be really good at communication to be effective and ultimately successful. Sales and Marketing are not the enemy, they just have a different interest to those who are doing the procuring, contract management, etc. So, ensure you understand those interests, objectives, timescales or whatever it may be as part of your pre-research.

A breakdown in communication is one thing; leaving it to fester is another. Extreme examples of miscommunication can result in literally life-changing events, such as those within the medical and surgical profession where incorrect procedures are performed with disastrous consequences. Thankfully, we are not practicing medical professionals, but there are many occasions and industries where the impacts can be just as critical to success or catastrophe.

2.2 Are we in touch? (Emotional Intelligence)

Emotional Intelligence (EI), or Emotional Quotient (EQ) as it is sometimes known, was first introduced into the business lexicon by two psychologists Peter Salovey and John D. Mayer in 1995. However, the concept of Emotional Intelligence dates back to the 1920s. This has been refined and developed well into the early-2000 by the likes of Daniel Goleman, a world authority on EI. A full chronology of the evolution and its contributors can be seen at the end of this chapter.

Emotional Intelligence has come to the attention of the business world relatively recently and now represents a significant aspect of corporate ethos and practice in many organisations. For the purposes of clarity, Salovey and Meyer[1], the people responsible for coining the term *Emotional Intelligence* defined it as:

> *"The capability of individuals to recognise their own and other people's emotions, discern between different feelings and label them appropriately, use emotional information to guide thinking and behaviour, and manage and/or adjust emotions to adapt to environments or achieve one's goal(s)."*

Today there is an abundance of EI models offered for our consideration. So, for the purposes of clarity and simplicity I have chosen to adopt the domains and competences as defined Goleman's model, which is shown in the list below and is very useful and easily accessible. It reflects the 5 elements of EI/EQ:

1. Self-Awareness
2. Self-Regulation
3. Motivation
4. Empathy
5. Social Skills

A diagramatic representation of the domains and competences appeared in the *Harvard Business Review* in February 2017.[2] The basic principles of the

---

1. Salovey, P. and Mayer, J.D. (1990). *Emotional intelligence. Imagination, Cognition and Personality*, in Sage Journal Vol. 9:3, pp.185-211.
2. Goleman, Daniel and Boyatzis. (2017). "Emotional Intelligence Has 12 Elements. Which Do You Need to Work On?" in *Harvard Business Review* 6th February 2017. Graphics by More Than Sound, LLC, 2017. Accessed at https://hbr.org/2017/02/emotional-intelligence-has-12-elements-which-do-you-need-to-work-on

above must become second nature to us if we are to operate successfully in contemporary business.

As procurement and related disciplines work across the whole organisation, it is important that we assimilate what we do and how we do it in the same way, and that the business community as whole recognises EQ. EQ is a non-intellectual ability, but finding the balance between this and other more formal aspects of cognition is a critical skill in all aspects of procurement. The outward demonstration of your skills and abilities to handle your emotions and indeed those of others is a mark of those that have understood and recognised the benefits and possibilities of incorporating EQ into the more formal and structured practices we use.

Goleman identifies a number of key competences which are not always included in more recent works on EQ. They include:

- The ability to read your own emotions and recognise their impacts.
- Knowing your strengths and limitations (being honest about them to yourself).
- Knowing your true capabilities (I have often seen professionals assess their abilities and capabilities above and beyond their true level of operation and this is where I would suggest a true sense of realism as this will allow you to accurately assess, evaluate and indeed control the situations you will find yourselves in).
- Identifying and controlling disruptive emotions and impulses.
- Transparency: honesty and integrity; trustworthiness
- Adaptability: flexibility in adapting to changing situations or overcoming obstacles.
- Achievement: drive to improve performance to meet inner standards of excellence.
- Initiative: readiness to act and sees opportunities.
- Optimism: seeing the upside in events and portraying them as such.
- Change catalyst: initiating, managing, and leading in a new direction.
- Building bonds: cultivating and maintaining a web of relationships both internally and externally, as well as being an ambassador for the profession.

This area of psychology is relatively young and will clearly develop further over time. There are many models and tests such as MSCEIT, ESCI360, etc. available in this area, which I expect to be further developed and integrated into more comprehensive assessments, particularly where they relate to larger programmes or more complex arrangements.

Behavioural assessments are already being adopted in a number of major sectors such as construction, utilities, professional services and other areas.

With the call for behavioural assessments to become part of bid criteria, ranging from 20-40% of the overall evaluation score, the professional understanding and use of this is key if we are to play an integral or leading role. Further, the introduction of ISO10667 introduces an effective benchmark that supersedes other commercially available tests.

Some professionals operating in this area believe that high levels of EQ in people may be detrimental, with negative effects including counterproductive work behaviours, psychopathy and stress proclivity. Further, this may impair areas such as:

- Creativity
- Innovation
- Giving and receiving feedback
- Reluctance to be disruptive, even to achieve critical outcomes.
- Aversion to risk
- Manipulative (which is not sustainable)

What this tells us, or confirms, is that the approach needs to be balanced with no tendency to lean towards any particular style or method.

2.3 Stakeholder Management

Stakeholder management exists at many levels and can be seen to operate between individuals or groups, as well as between internal stakeholders such as sponsors, budget owners, team members, a diversity of internal roles – and also between companies and their suppliers. It is this latter context that most attracts attention and focus as this is most often where most value is created.

However, just as critical to a project's success is team stakeholder management and with that internal stakeholder management. The principles of managing stakeholders at multiple levels is nevertheless broadly the same – adapting for situation, circumstance and the people involved.

A structured approach leads to the identification, analysis, planning and implementation of actions designed to engage with stakeholders at all levels. Each stakeholder will have an interest in the project or programme, but their influences may vary from being extremely positive to extremely negative – therefore assessing their interests, influences (both within and outside of the project or programme), their prior experiences and much more are all part of the "profiling" of individuals in the first instance.

This profiling of individuals, as well as organisations, takes the form of the following:

- Formal research
- Brainstorming
- Networking
- Interviewing
- Prior projects and programmes evaluated
- Checklists
- Lessons learnt

This has traditionally been evaluated in terms of high, medium and low interests and influences, which we will begin to explore in the areas of heuristics and biases. However this is simply inadequate for evaluating more complex and multi-layered projects and programmes, as well as cultural diversities, etc.

Below is an often-used stakeholder management matrix:

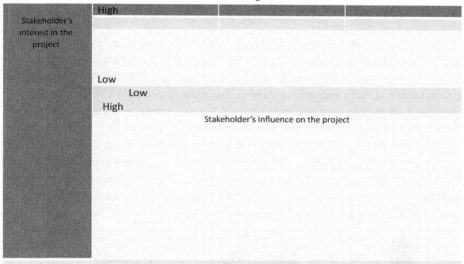

Figure 2.2. Generic standard category management stakeholder matrix

In the stakeholder matrix individuals are mapped by size of balloon to indicate position and relative influence. The portfolio management team needs to be satisfied that appropriate approaches to stakeholder management are being taken by all projects, programmes and areas of business-as-usual within the portfolio. They must also own and monitor a portfolio-wide stakeholder management plan.

The project/programme lead is responsible for the quality of the stakeholder management approach and effectiveness of execution, which then manifests as a series of "issues" being identified and escalated, and risks being reported/mitigated. This approach also takes into account that over the duration of the project people's perceptions, positions and understanding of the outcomes may change. A further consideration should always be that some individuals or groups may be adversely affected by the outcomes, and as such need to be appropriately handled. Therefore, considering a more formal approach may call for the following:

- An overall stakeholder management policy, including key stakeholder groups and interfaces.
- How the stakeholder management policy will be monitored.
- Dealing with perceived weaknesses in stakeholder management at project and programme level.
- Gathering and publicising executive support for the project processes and approach/methodology, e.g. Category Management.
- The overall change can be undermined if there are significant areas of an organisation with poor stakeholder commitment – this may need sponsor intervention to address this.

Continuous maintenance of the stakeholder documentation is seen as a critical task and needs a single owner. This is also linked to the communications plan. It will provide guidance to projects and programmes on stakeholder management and will audit stakeholder management throughout the project's duration.

Whilst the above sounds very simple, it is actually very complex, mainly because relationship strategies are only one dimension of a much more sophisticated management system. Figure 2.3 sets out a view that focuses on the supply chain strategy from my perspective. While some of the attributes have been written about before, the business dynamics have advanced and will continue to change. Therefore, we must continually review what the key attributes are that we must observe to deliver an optimal supply chain strategy.

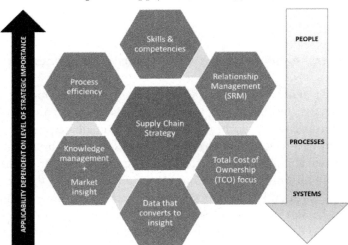

Figure 2.3. Supply Chain Strategy Dynamics (SCSD) Matrix (Loseby 2018)

As can be seen in Figure 2.3, the strategic importance of a supplier should drive the approach, but not at the expense of the total supply chain. The salience and interdependence of the of the key attributes to a supply chain strategy should flex depending on the external and internal factors, as well as the people, processes in place and the systems being used. The extent to which relationship management is needed – and Supplier Relationship Management for the truly very small number of suppliers/service providers – is part of the choice architecture that is inherent in the SCSD matrix, to maintain an alignment of corporate and supply policies. However, a number of salient factors come into play when "real world" situations are evaluated, for example:

- Awareness or understanding of organisational objectives and policies.
- Strategic goals.
- Corporate Social Responsibility (CSR), Modern Day Slavery Act (MDSA), Environmental policies, etc. (this is also true where an organisation wants to have a "passive" position on these matters rather than an active approach, as I have witnessed and experienced).
- Short-termism (where cost is the only driver).
- Market changes/innovations that turn assets into liabilities!
- Size versus differentiation mentality.
- Liquidity and cash flow, including working capital in the organisation.
- Collaborative long-term approaches, with asset sharing and leverage with the supply base.
- Collaborative design/patents, etc. with exclusivity periods to drive competitive advantage.
- Risk/reward in partnership.
- Joint ventures.

In short, a differentiation approach versus cost-cutting short-termism requires resource investment and a much longer-term view of business, as well as the need to have effective and supported relationship management at its core. This is where true competitive advantage is driven from.

My own experiences and applying the insight gained from a global survey of CPOs, academics and Supply Chain specialists led me to create a visual model of how collaboration models vary. They can be characterised by various collaborative states – from those invoked by circumstance (tactical and enforced) to those by choice and design (project and strategic). This model is a reflection of current day responses to the interaction of the market and internal stakeholders, shown in Figure 2.4 overleaf:

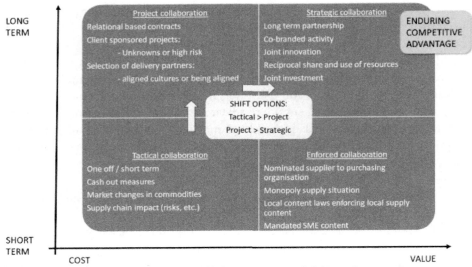

Figure 2.4. The Four States of Collaboration model (Loseby 2017)

Strategic collaborations are concerned with aligning the customer requirements with the supplier, the sharing of technological processes and products to enhance offerings to existing and new customers which may lead to new product development activities. Furthermore, this type of collaboration will also focus on sharing production engineering resources, developing joint capital investment and expenditure plans.

These are typically in the shape of risk- and reward-sharing agreements between the buyer and supplier. Firms that have a differentiation focus will require supply to align its approach to achieve the various goals and objectives outlined above.

Clearly the risk is for organisations to default to type and destroy the trust that has been built, with usually an immediate retrenchment to a tactical approach. The impact of bounded rationality will impact the ability of people and organisations to achieve a truly strategic collaborative state.

Most purchasing professionals tend to think of a relationship as an activity or process (a thing) – they will often refer to "the relationship that exists between us and Supplier X." Often in discussion with purchasing professionals they talk in terms of "managing" the suppliers rather than "developing relationships" as a building block to developing trust or achieving a collaborative way of working.

Developing the skills for effective relationship management is embodied in what behavioural procurement has to offer, as these skills relate to a greater focus and understanding of oneself, as well as other parties in a far more complex way, as demonstrated in Behavioural Economics. Developing an approach that is appropriate to the DNA of the organisation and the desired outcomes is critical to the adopted approach.

In research and through experience we have learned that this is truly complex and will change and evolve – the reality is that we should not rely upon fixed models, but be agile and flexible in how we manage relationships. The variables are endless if we want to truly extrapolate them all, but in the end we have to have mechanisms to cope with this and make it simpler, not more complex.

As such we must begin to group similar areas and impacts (positive and negative), etc. in order to "make sense and translate" this into something others as well as we can assimilate, thereby optimising the information and what we choose to do with it. Mari Sako (1992) developed four contractual mechanisms to help deal with the complexity from adversarial to collaborative to give 4 levels of certainty:

1. Contractual
2. Competence
3. Goodwill
4. Political

This in turn helped to develop a more useful Strategic Relationship Context Model that aids the interplay between external and self-factors. The recognition of trust and collaboration has an inflection point where – due to weaknesses or strengths – relationships will either endure or implode depending on whether the point of strength in the relationship has been achieved or not.

I have not been able to find any definitive research on this subject but what I present is derived from the surveys and interviews I conducted in November and December 2017. What is clear, is that considering the strengths and/or values of each of the primary attributes (circles) and secondary attributes (boxes), the relationship complexity dynamics will be conducive. That is to say, conducive towards creating fast, agile routes to innovation and competitive advantage for all parties.

To have some of these factors missing or as a weakness will significantly impact the relationship, which directly correlates to value creation.

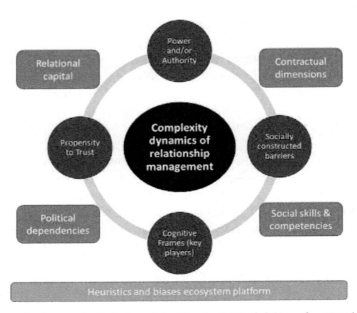

Figure 2.5. Strategic Relationship Context Model (Loseby 2017)

The cautionary tale comes when we consider how people and organisations are incentivised, as the model of reward may not be fully aligned or worse still contradictory to the desired outcomes! This messy reality is often caused by the need for corporates or public bodies to default to the short-term measures by which they are made accountable and measured as an entire entity either traditionally or politically. Hence, they are significant in behavioural terms and something to be considered as we turn to the subject of heuristics and biases!

Above all, relationship management executed well is not a tickbox exercise, but something that imbues a focus and understanding on outcomes. Alignment to the values and indeed the core values and behavioural signature of the organisation will be a key determinant in the success of all parties. Dealing with mismatches of inter-departmental objectives or cross-company objectives, etc. is an early pre-requisite, even if this means that you come to a personal compromise and realignment of what is realistic, achievable and deliverable. Without this, the constant friction and dissonance of such a matter is not sustainable in the medium- to long-term.

For me, the complexity of areas that need to be considered simultaneously will not only increase and evolve over time, but will revert to the fundamentals of trust and collaboration at a base level. In essence, relationships are part of a systematic process that drives or facilitates necessary changes in behaviour. From this it can lead to looking at what compromises and decisions are needed to ameliorate the potential conflicts and tensions between organisation, teams, suppliers, etc. There is a range of tools available for this, generally employing Analytical Hierarchy Processing (AHP)[3] which is a weighting and scoring system. Having selected and collectively taken ownership of this approach, it is essential that this is clearly set out in a transparent way either as project/ programme document that is signed off, business case, etc., to ensure total alignment of direction.

In summary it is:

- Complicated.
- Endlessly changing.
- Not formulaic.
- It needs to add value/competitive advantage and be quantifiable.
- It can't just be purely "jam tomorrow".
- And fundamentally it's behavioural.

AHP is a structured technique for organising and analysing complex decisions based on mathematics and psychology. Since it was developed it has been extensively studied and refined. It has particular application in group decision-making, and is used around the world in a wide variety of decision situations.

Rather than prescribing a "correct" decision, AHP helps decision-makers find one that best suits their goal and their understanding of the problem. It provides a comprehensive and rational framework for structuring a decision-based problem, for representing and quantifying its elements, for relating those elements to overall goals and for evaluating alternative solutions.

Users of AHP first deconstruct their decision problem into a hierarchy of more easily comprehended sub-problems, each of which can be analysed independently. The elements of the hierarchy can relate to any aspect of the decision problem – tangible or intangible, carefully measured or roughly estimated, well or poorly understood – anything at all that applies to the decision at hand.

Once the hierarchy is built, the decision-makers systematically evaluate its various elements by comparing them to each other two at a time, with respect to their impact on an element above them in the hierarchy. In making the comparisons, the decision-makers can use concrete data about the elements, but they typically use their judgments about the elements' relative meaning and importance. It is the essence of AHP that human judgments, and not just the underlying information, can be used in performing the evaluations.

AHP converts these evaluations to numerical values that can be processed and compared over the entire range of the problem. A numerical weight or

3. Saaty, Thomas L. (1980). *The Analytic Hierarchy Process: Planning, Priority Setting, Resource Allocation.* McGraw-Hill.

priority is derived for each element of the hierarchy, allowing diverse and often incommensurable elements to be compared to one another in a rational and consistent way. This capability distinguishes AHP from other decision-making techniques.

In the final step of the process, numerical priorities are calculated for each of the decision alternatives. These numbers represent the alternatives' relative ability to achieve the decision goal, so they allow a straightforward consideration of the various courses of action.

2.4 Active Listening Skills

The well-used saying *"We have two ears and one mouth, and we should use them in that proportion"* is simple but true in this case! In the context where there are a number of key things to consider far and above what might be considered the ability and the patience to attentively listen to another person speaking I would consider this to be a critical soft skill.

I will focus upon this for the purposes of meaningful engagement – for a practitioner seeking to deliver a specific outcome and/or effect a change, especially where this occurs in complex situations, this must become more of a conscious competency rather than a passive non-engaged state of mind. Some of the following other things that I would actively encourage you to consider before commencing any form of engagement that demands a critical outcome include:

- The context and environment with which this will take place:
    - Do you know the person?
    - Have you already formed a working relationship?
    - Will there be distractions? (phone, laptops, etc.)
    - Is this a formal or informal engagement?
    - Is this a one-time opportunity?
    - Do you need to consider a neutral meeting point?
    - Have non-attributed issues been brought into the room that could distract either party?

In this process of active listening, even when you have a very clear understanding of your goals and objectives for the exchange, you should see this as an opportunity to try and leverage from the other party information over and above what you already know.

A cautionary note, having been there and fallen foul of thinking you are better than you are, your self-assessment may be different to others! This will clearly help you to formulate your strategy and approach towards achieving your goal, recognising that you may have to adapt or amend your approach as the discussion proceeds.

There are number of techniques and approaches that have been documented, but in essence these come down to the following key competences and attributes:

1. Understand what you want to say and the response that you expect and ensure it cannot be misconstrued, be delivered ambiguously, or be framed in a negative context if this is not what is intended.
2. Learn to recognise body language.
3. Ensure you maintain eye contact at all times.
4. Make sure that your pitch and tone are appropriate for the situation when you respond.
5. Demonstrate empathy.
6. Ensure you are non-judgemental.
7. Build trust.
8. Be genuine.
9. Ask open-ended questions (i.e. questions that require an answer more complex than just 'yes' or 'no'.
10. At critical points consider giving back brief verbal affirmation.
11. Consider paraphrasing to show that you have understood.
12. Capture non-verbal exchanges in the conversation too, such as a nod, gesture, leaning forward, etc.
13. Avoid barriers to active listening such as; tiredness, thirst, hunger, etc. as well as situations where people are not working in their native language (take translators into account).
14. Don't assume statements are fact; ensure that they are verified.
15. Has the other party finished speaking? Don't interrupt as a rule.
16. Signal that you have heard and understood the points being made.
17. Have you: helped the other person gain in confidence, self-esteem, worth? Have you understood, helped, taken the discussion to a deeper level, explored other options in a positive way?
18. Extending ideas or options is a positive approach.
19. Understand the emotions and behaviours of the person.
20. Remove any prior misconceptions or misalignment before you start!

This is merely a "shopping list" of all I have observed! The four-sides model (also known as communication square or four-ears model) is a communication model developed by Friedemann Schulz von Thun. According to this model every message has four facets – see the diagram overleaf – though not the same emphasis might be put on each. The four sides of the message are fact, self-revealing, relationship, and appeal.

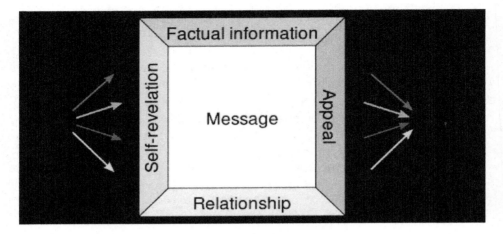

Figure 2.6. Four sides of the communication square[4]

The communication square describes the multi-layered structure of human utterance. It combines the postulate (second axiom) of Paul Watzlawick, that every communication has a content and a relationship aspect, with the three sides of the Organon Model – developed by Karl Bühler – which postulates that every piece of information contains something about the matter, the sender and the receiver. Such models are familiar in the linguistic models of speech.

The four sides of communication are explained as follows:

- The Matter layer contains statements which are matter of fact, like data and the news.
- In the Self-revealing or Self-disclosure layer, the speaker – consciously or not – tells something about themselves, their motives, values, emotions etc.
- The Relationship layer is expressed as respect received – how the sender gets along with the receiver and what they think of them.
- The Appeal layer contains the desire, advice, instruction and effects that the speaker is seeking.

Every layer can be misunderstood individually. The classic example is of Schulz von Thun as the front-seat passenger, as he tells the driver: "Hey, the traffic lights are green".

The driver will understand different things about the statement: on the Matter layer he will understand the "fact" that the traffic lights are green. He could also understand it as a command: "Come on, drive!", or on the Relationship level

---

4. Friedemann Schulz von Thun enlarges the Watzlawick Model of communication by adding two more layers: The Self Revealing Layer and the Appeal Layer. These four Layers shape the Square of Communication (Kommunikationsquadrat):

could hear a plea like "I want to help you...or I am in a hurry" in which case it reveals part of yourself.

The emphasis on the four layers can have different interpretations. Consequently, the sender can stress the appeal of the statement and the receiver can mainly receive the relationship part of the message. This is one of the main reasons for misunderstandings.

In summary, effective and good listening is really a healthy two-way dialogue, not a monologue!

Development and Chronology of Contributors to the Theory of Emotional Intelligence

1920: Thorndike, E.L. Intelligence and its uses. *Harper's Magazine*, 140, 227-235.

1937: Thorndike, R.L., and Stern, S. An evaluation of the attempts to measure social intelligence. *Psychological Bulletin*, 34, 275-284.

1952: Wechsler, David. *The range of human capacities*. New York: Hafner.

1962: Kuhn, T. *The structure of scientific revolutions*. Chicago: University of Chicago Press.

1983: Gardner, H. *Frames of mind: The theory of multiple intelligences*. New York: Basic Books.

1990: Salovey, P. and Mayer, J.D. *Emotional Intelligence. Imagination, Cognition and Personality*, 9, 185-211.

1995: Goleman, D. (a). *Emotional Intelligence*. New York: Bantam Books. (b). What's your Emotional Intelligence quotient? You'll soon find out. *Utne Reader*, November/December.

1997: Mayer, J.D. and Salovey, P. "What is Emotional Intelligence?" In P. Salovey and D. Sluyter (Eds.), *Emotional development and Emotional Intelligence: Implications for educators* (pp. 3-31). New York: Basic.

1998: Goleman, D. (a). *Working with Emotional Intelligence*. New York: Bantam Books. (b). What makes a leader? *Harvard Business Review*, November/December.

2000: Goleman, D. (a). Emotional Intelligence. In Sadock, B. and Sadock, V. (Eds.), *Comprehensive textbook of psychiatry*, seventh edition. Philadelphia: Lippincott Williams and Wilkins. (b) Leadership that gets results. *Harvard Business Review*, March/April. (c) Mayer, John. Presentation at Linkage Emotional Intelligence Conference, London, May 18. (d) Mayer, J.D., Caruso, D., and Salovey, P. (e). Emotional Intelligence meets traditional standards for an intelligence. *Intelligence*, 27(4), 267-298. Bar-On, R. (f). Emotional and social intelligence: Insights from the emotional quotient inventory. In R. Bar-On and J.D.A. Parker (Eds.), *Handbook of Emotional Intelligence*. San Francisco: Jossey-Bass. Boyatzis, R., Goleman, D., and Rhee, K. (g). Clustering competence in Emotional Intelligence: Insights from the emotional competence inventory (ECI). In R. Bar-On and J.D.A. Parker (Eds.), *Handbook of Emotional Intelligence*. San Francisco: Jossey-Bass. Cherniss, C. and Adler, M. (h). *Promoting Emotional Intelligence in Organisations*. Alexandria, Virginia: ASTD. Mayer, J.D., Salovey, P., and Caruso, D. (i). Competing models of Emotional Intelligence. In R.J. Sternberg (Ed.), *Handbook of human intelligence*, second edition (pp.396-420). New York: Cambridge University Press.

CHAPTER 3 | SOFT SKILLS (BEHAVIOURAL COMPETENCES)

A more generalist way of describing people skills has been to refer to them as "soft skills". However, this has been a loose collection of different attributes and competences and therefore often means different things to different people. By the end of the book I hope to show that the people skills we need can be defined from what we already know in a structured and considered way. These known competences, combined with Behavioural Sciences, bring together everything that can collectively be regarded as Behavioural Procurement and provides the bridge from current to new approaches discussed in this book.

3.1 The As and Bs of Professionalism (Attitudes and Behaviours)

To be truly professional, adopting and displaying the right attitudes and behaviours is an essential ingredient. Recognising that this may be an elusive concept, it is necessary to define Attitudes and Behaviours in the context of Purchasing and Supply Chain Management, in addition to any professional codes of conduct that we may observe through various professional bodies.

The As and Bs are a quintessential part of how we define the way we conduct ourselves as practitioners or academics. Many professional bodies have embarked upon a journey to define 'professionalism' – some require members to attain chartered status, licenses to practice, codes of conduct and so on in an attempt to establish what expertise and professional values are needed to practice in their field or discipline. In this reference to being a "professional" we are looking to signal that others can bestow their trust in us, respect us for what we do and the knowledge that we bring. Many organisations, professional bodies, consulting practices and other bodies have attempted to define professionalism. For example, in the public sector The Organisation for Economic Co-operation and Development (OECD) defines professionalism as:

> "Building professionalism among procurement officials with a common set *of professional and ethical standards is equally important. Survey results highlighted that public procurement is a significant factor for successfully managing public resources and should therefore be considered as a strategic profession rather than simply an administrative function".*[1]

1. OECD. (2007). *Integrity in public procurement: good practice from A-Z*. London.

Their definition highlights the key factors they consider necessary to ensure value for money:

- Rationalised and efficient units to deliver procurement.
- Comprehensive tools and techniques.
- Better planning.
- Better data and information.
- Communication technologies.
- Risk management.
- Qualifications and standards.
- Contract Management skills (recognising post contract value).
- Project Management skills in a procurement context.
- Ethical guidance and avoidance of conflicts of interest.

The report supports and reinforces the need for appropriate attitudes and behaviours that underpin organisational/public interest above self-interest, and that display the values, beliefs, behaviours and attitudes that meet public expectations of probity. In essence, an expectation is placed by others upon us as practitioners to essentially "do the right thing" in any given circumstance.

The origins of this definitive position were derived from the area of Social Sciences in the 1950s and 1960s, and were based upon the possession of certain characteristics which were set out in Dana Perkurson Hammer's paper "*Professional Attitudes and Behaviours: As and Bs of Professionalism*".[2]

She identifies the structural attributes of professions and professionals as having:

- Specialised body of knowledge and skills.
- Unique socialisation of student members.
- License/certification.
- Professional associations.
- Governance by peers.
- Social prestige.
- Vital service to society.
- Code of ethics.
- Autonomy.
- Equivalence of members.
- Special relationship with clients.

Attitudinal attributes of professionals were described as:

---

2. Hammer, Dana. P. (2000). "Professional Attitudes and Behaviors: The "As and Bs" of Professionalism" in *American Journal of Pharmaceutical Education* Vol. 64, Winter 2000. Pp 455-464

- Use of the professional organisation as a major reference, i.e. using professional colleagues as the major source of professional ideas and judgments in practice.
- Belief in service to the public, i.e. one's professional practice is indispensable to society and benefits the public.
- Belief in self-regulation – one's peers are the best qualified to judge one's work.
- sense of calling to the field, i.e. dedication to the profession regardless of extrinsic rewards.
- Autonomy, i.e. one can make professional decisions without external pressures from clients, non-professionals, and employers.

From this I have derived what I believe represents how we can understand and provide examples of professional attitudes and their corresponding behaviours as they relate to Procurement and Supply Management. Table 3.1 below describes these attitudes and behaviours.

ATTITUDE	BEHAVIOUR
Accountability	Takes ownership and responsibility for their actions.
Diversity	Fair treatment of all people regardless of ethnicity, background, demographics, etc.
Open-minded	Increased receptiveness to new ways of working, techniques and approaches.
CPD	Recognises that their status as professional means that are not fulfilling a job but a career.
Respect	Considers input from all levels and areas of the team equally without bias.
Fairness	Transparent approach, but maintains confidentiality where needed and appropriate.
Governance	Upholds the codes of conduct and ethical practices.

Table 3.1. Attitudes and Behaviours of Purchasing and Supply Chain Management Professionals

The above reflect how attitudes and behaviours can change perception and responses from an assumed negative to a demonstrable positive. For example, if we take the proposition 'we have a problem', it can be read two ways:

NEGATIVE: "We have a problem" >>> "I'm not even going to try and fix it."
POSITIVE: "We have a problem" >>> "Let's try and find a solution before we go any further."

As a leader one must establish demonstrable behaviours in advance of dealing with any given situation. This becomes the greatest influence we have to offer as professionals and leaders. Jack Welsh (ex-CEO of GEC) once said on witnessing board members who had agreed to do one thing differently but ultimately made no change in the end, of providing merely "superficial congeniality". In other words, they had not taken accountability nor ownership – and ultimately responsibility – for their actions.

Looking at the impact of good or positive attitudes and behaviours within an organisation, we can link them to how this translates into driving competitive advantage through ownership, accountability and responsibility. Looking at the broader classifications of attitudes, in a positive context, as defined by Daniel Katz, we can see how they might appear:

1. Utilitarian: Utilitarian refers to an individual's attitude as derived from self or community interest. An example could be getting a raise. As a raise means more disposable income, employees will have a positive attitude about getting a raise, which may positively affect their behaviour in some circumstances.

2. Knowledge: Logic, or rationalising, is another means by which people form attitudes. When an organisation appeals to people's logic and explains why it is assigning tasks or pursuing a strategy, it can generate a more positive disposition towards that task or strategy (and vice versa, if the employee does not recognise why a task is logical).

3. Ego-defensive: People have a tendency to use attitudes to protect their ego, resulting in a common negative attitude. If a manager criticizes employees' work without offering suggestions for improvement, employees may form a negative attitude and subsequently dismiss the manager as foolish in an effort to defend their work. Managers must therefore carefully manage criticism and offer solutions, not simply identify problems.

4. Value-expressive: People develop central values over time. These values are not always explicit or simple. Managers should always be aware of what is important to their employees from a values perspective (that is, what do they stand for? Why do they do what they do?). Having such an awareness can the manager/leader seek to align organisational vision with individual values, thereby generating passion among the workforce.

Clearly attitudes influence behaviour and where different people have different attitudes, this can often result in conflict – as such, needs to be addressed. This should never be underestimated as it is often not a simple solution; but identifying the differences and various unique characteristics – people's beliefs or values, what their motivators are etc., how to reward or recognise them – are a good starting point. However, my focus will remain within behavioural spectrum, not address the area of attitudes in this book.

3.2 Working together (Positive Indicators of Collaboration)

In 3.1 I established what I believe are the positive attributes needed in this area in order to put a framework and context to what needs to be considered in everyday practice. The whole concept of working together, being more effective than a solo effort, should not come as a complete revolution to those engaged in the context of professional procurement or Contract Management.

Aristotle wisely stated that "the whole is greater than the sum of the parts" but that requires motivation and desire from all parties to be truly effective in their collaborations if they are to achieve major success. Hence, recognising and staying true to the positive indicators of collaboration requires the more conscious parts of our brain at times to be actively engaged and charged with this in front of mind.

I will now develop this idea and set out what I consider to be the positive indicators of collaborative behaviour below, highlighting Trust and Fairness as the most critical of all:

- **Fairness**
- **Trust**
- Transparency
- Integrity
- Promotion of reciprocity
- Motivation
- Passion
- Empathy
- Cooperation
- Consistency
- Balance
- Realistic
- Constructive

- Mindfulness
- Selfless
- Active listening
- Open minded
- Creating the right environment
- Displaying the right attitudes to elicit the right behaviours
- Professional

I was recently reminded not to "just stick these up on the wall as a poster"; one needs to live and breathe them every day. For me there are the critical ones – if these are not evident or are weak, the rest are simply irrelevant. Therefore, I have bolded Trust and Fairness as "must have" as I can recall many situations where the other attributes were present, but collaboration couldn't be achieved as they were effectively the blockers to this.

This list is not exhaustive, but covers the major attributes and relates to the whole team, and their playing their part to the best of their ability so that one's goal is reached. There is an emerging pattern and connectedness to many of the facets shown above, which will become more of a re-occurring theme as we progress into the areas of Behavioural Science.

The importance of collaboration and the delivery of a minimum consistent standard should be the concern of any medium or large organisation to ensure it is operating optimally. This has culminated in the development (and publication) of a recognised International Standard ISO44001 (replacing British Standard for Collaborative Business Relationships BS11000). Since its publication it has been adopted mainly in the construction and infrastructure sectors. However, there is now evidence of its further momentum into other sectors.

This standard attempts to bring order and structure to collaboration in multiple environments and as such can only be regarded as a core platform. This core platform provides the groundwork which enables organisations to adapt and modify this to suit their needs, just like any other operating system. Keeping the approach simple and as a structured framework to begin with allows organisations to become familiar with the principles and intended outcomes. Clearly as familiarisation, skills competences and individual organisational needs are developed, the framework approach will allow appropriate customisation to suit the organisation and environment over time.

Hence, the emergence of ISO 44001 has given rise to debate among practitioners as to its reach and impact alongside established collaborative delivery models. However, now having an international standard for a strategic framework through which organisations can develop, implement and sustain their approach to collaborative business relationships is established.

This is essentially a high-level model that supports a variety of collaborative contracting arrangements, with flexibility as a key advantage in the modern business environment.

The essence of ISO44001 is that productive collaborative working requires appropriate behaviours together with supporting processes, collective leadership and contracting arrangements that do not constrain collaboration, but actively facilitate it via the alignment of objectives and creation of incentives.

This has spawned a number of organisations who specialise in this area, such as the Institute for Collaborative Working (ICW), who set out their aims as follows:

- To be recognised and acknowledged as the thought leader on business collaborative working.
- To carry out research to further develop collaborative working principles, practises and processes.
- To ensure the widespread development of collaborative working skills through training and development.
- To progressively build a global collaborative working knowledge sharing community.

This has led their leadership to develop their "CRAFT" (Collaborative, Relationship, Assessment, Fulfilment, Transformation) methodology from the collective experience of the Institute's Executive Knowledge Network, with many similarities and parallels for procurement of capital related goods and services and/or projects as you will see from their approach.

This continues to reinforce that the procurement and allied professions cannot sustain an approach that sits in a vacuum, but must constantly seek other collateral and information that has parallel or dual applicability in order to stay current and relevant.

3.3 What goes around comes around (Relationship Lifecycle Management)

Relationship Lifecycle Management is an approach that concerns itself with *relationship management* with customers in the context of customer relationship management. Both Procurement and Sales collectively need to consider relationship lifecycles and how they are managed to maximise commercial outcomes.

Relationships truly do matter in business, and it should come as no surprise to us that investing time in managing those relationships should be a critical priority, especially when we consider that we need to build trust first and foremost.

The paradigm shift for me is that we need to be more cognitive and comprehensive when it comes to the business of managing stakeholders and/or people, not simply focusing on cost alone. Therefore, relationship life-cycle management is the logical evolution of stakeholder management.

Much in the same way that salespeople can consider a cycle where they move customers from a position of awareness, consideration, purchase, customer retention, up-selling, cross-selling and cross-business referrals, we should consider a similar cycle like the following:

Step 1: Educate and build awareness of what procurement is.

Step 2: Market and promote our diverse skill set.

Step 3: Offer potential options and solutions to deliver stated business needs/outcomes (Strategy + Objectives).

Step 4: Engage the relevant parts of the business and form a cross-functional team and take them through a structured process to deliver a business outcome.

Step 5: Ensure effective handover.

Step 6: Contract Management through to full Supplier Relationship Management.

Step 7: Enagage in other projects/programmes.

Step 8: Become the trusted business advisor and "go to" point for all things commercial.

This whole process becomes cyclical, whereby we identify stakeholders, build awareness of what we do as a function and create a value proposition that drives their interest and engagement in us as a function that effectively turns them into customers of procurement.

Developing trust through this process enables us to retain those customers just in the same way that any sales department would, by gaining their loyalty and affiliation with us as a professional practitioner that proactively manages the relationship even when we are not fully engaged in a project or programme.

Again, be conscious that we are not there to constantly distract the business, but to ensure that we are on hand, especially in the early phases of new and different projects and programmes to help shape the direction and approaches that will deliver the best outcomes both for the organisation and for them as individuals groups and functions.

Retaining and developing the trust and relationship with internal and external stakeholders is key to future transactions. Equally they will be advocates of what you can deliver and hence feed the next generation of projects or programmes. In other words, rather than needing to try and seek out where the new projects and programmes are, internal stakeholders come to you early on in the process where significant value can be added, ahead of any formal procurement process.

Adapting the tools, competences and practices to problem solve in the organisation is essential to the whole relationship cycle, even if this does not directly translate to immediate and measurable savings or cost avoidance. This is the way we build trust and respect that leads to deep and meaningful relationships across organisations. This is parallel to what we do in our social lives – we do not necessarily do things because we believe there is a gain or benefit to be had out of a particular relationship, but we do it because we believe it's the right thing to do and that it will engender a deeper trust and a sustainable relationship way beyond the first encounter.

Understanding ourselves and others, and developing a deeper and greater understanding of the relationship lifecycle in its entirety is fundamental to achieving the full potential of relationship life-cycle management. Clearly this level of investment would not be warranted for one-off short duration types of activity.

In looking at the different tools and techniques available, there are many proprietary approaches to this that effectively profile and indeed define us as a specific type, and describe our compatibility within a team or a group. One such example is the Enneagram[3] developed by Oscar Ichazo. Ichazo was born in Bolivia and raised in Peru, but as a young man moved to Buenos Aires, Argentina, where he learned many of the things that now form part of the Enneagram.

After many years of developing his ideas, he created the Arica School[4] as a vehicle for disseminating the knowledge that he had received, teaching in Chile in the late 1960s and early '70s before moving to the United States.

In 1970, when Ichazo was still living in South America, a group of Americans, including noted psychologists and writers Claudio Naranjo and John Lilly, went to Arica to study with Ichazo and to experience first-hand the methods for attaining self-realization that he had developed.

Detailed as follows are the Nine Enneagram Type Descriptions developed by Ichazo:

---

3. The Enneagram of Personality, or simply the Enneagram meaning something written or drawn, is a model of the human psyche which is principally understood and taught as a typology of nine interconnected personality types.

4. The Arica School, also known as the Arica Institute or simply as Arica, is a human potential movement group founded in 1968 by Bolivian-born philosopher Oscar Ichazo (born 1931). The school is named after the city of Arica, Chile, where Ichazo once lived and where he led an intensive months-long training. Headquartered in the USA since 1971.

1. **THE REFORMER:** The Rational, Idealistic Type: Principled, Purposeful, Self-Controlled, and Perfectionistic.

2. **THE HELPER:** The Caring, Interpersonal Type: Demonstrative, Generous, People-Pleasing, and Possessive.

3. **THE ACHIEVER:** The Success-Oriented, Pragmatic Type: Adaptive, Excelling, Driven, and Image-Conscious.

4. **THE INDIVIDUALIST:** The Sensitive, Withdrawn Type: Expressive, Dramatic, Self-Absorbed, and Temperamental.

5. **THE INVESTIGATOR:** The Intense, Cerebral Type: Perceptive, Innovative, Secretive, and Isolated.

6. **THE LOYALIST:** The Committed, Security-Oriented Type: Engaging, Responsible, Anxious, and Suspicious.

7. **THE ENTHUSIAST:** The Busy, Fun-Loving Type: Spontaneous, Versatile, Distractible, and Scattered.

8. **THE CHALLENGER:** The Powerful, Dominating Type: Self-Confident, Decisive, Wilful, and Confrontational.

9. **THE PEACEMAKER:** The Easy going, Self-Effacing Type: Receptive, Reassuring, Agreeable, and Complacent.

Broadly speaking, the nine descriptions encompass and represent similar other commercial systems, but provide a reference point and a means by which to establish the process of evaluating and assembling relationship models or constructs.

In summary, the cyclical nature of relationships outlasts singular contracts as we move across organisations through our entire career. Perhaps, like all good marriages, it requires effort, empathy, compromise, etc. on an ongoing basis and not purely for fleeting moments.

3.4 Have you got my back covered? (Developing Trust and Reciprocity)

Trust is fundamental as a positive building block on which any successful organisation depends. Lamentably there are too many organisations where a universal level of trust is simply not there to the required level and indeed in certain organisations this lack of trust has devalued the business in the eyes of the investor community.

"Trust is a commodity that is acquired over time, but cannot be traded or exchanged with others, being unique to its owner".

The Edelman Trust Barometer[5], which is used on a global basis, is a good indicator of the rise and fall of a company's fortune. At a company level people respond to a lack of trust or a trust inequality by not buying the company's products, selling their shares in this company, negative press and so forth.

Businesses and indeed all the commercial activities carried out by the procurement functions around the world need to understand how trust is built, supported and in certain cases a recovered competency.

Previous examples of how trust has been defined can be found from respected luminaries such as Rousseau[6] and her colleagues who offer the following definition:

"Trust is a psychological state comprising the intention to accept vulnerability based upon positive expectations of the intentions or behaviour of another."

Similarly, Lewicki[7] and his colleagues describe trust as:

"An individual's belief in, and willingness to act on the basis of, the words, actions, and decisions of another."

As we can see from the Edelman Barometer, and research that I will set out in Chapter 16, there is a direct link with how organisations embrace and discharge the ethical values and commitments. Further, many organisations and indeed individuals can spend a great deal of effort building trust and the reputation that goes with that and thus to lose this trust, which can happen so quickly, determines that this is a very fragile but precious commodity.

Trustworthy conduct has been described as a core principle in ethics by many professional and international bodies – simply to be ethical is to be trustworthy. The many common values or themes such as integrity, deeds matching words, fulfilling commitments, genuine concern and fairness are clear to see.

In discussion with many fellow practitioners and new entrants to the profession, and central to many lectures I have delivered across the world, trust has become a recognisable attribute. This attribute of trust was one millennial's key determinant for joining an organisation over another. This I believe will become ever more critical as a criterion to attract and retain talent in organisations employment strategies in the future.

---

5. Edelman Trust Barometer: Conducted by the privately owned Edelman Intelligence (research), based in the USA, is a global communications and marketing organisation that conducts an annual online survey in 28 countries, with33,000+ respondents, using data collected over 17 years to determine levels of trust by their own metrics.

6. Rousseau, D. M., Sitkin, S. B., Burt, R. S., and Camerer, C. (1998). "Not so Different After All: A Cross-Discipline View of Trust" in *Academy of Management Review,* 23, 393-404.

7. Lewicki, R. J., McAllister, D. J., and Bies, R. J. (1998). "Trust and distrust: New relationships and realities" in *Academy of Management Review,* 23, 438-458.

The Institute of Business Ethics finds the most common model of trust way in which we judge other party's trustworthiness along three dimensions:

1.   Ability (i.e. technical competence)
2.   Benevolence (i.e. their motives and interests) and
3.   Integrity (i.e. honesty and fair treatment).

If the person we are seeking to work with or influence is considered to be ethical, then this increases our willingness to take a risk in our dealings with that entity or individual and therefore to trust them. This trusting act might involve buying an organisation's products and services, all the way through to investing in them as an organisation or an employee.

However, should any of these attributes fall seriously into question, this makes us wary and reluctant to engage in any risk-taking. Such distrust can hamper collaboration, exacerbate the inefficiencies of monitoring, stifle innovation and damage relationships.

Lewicki and Tomlinson in their paper *"Trust and Trust building"*[8] say that:

"Trust has been identified as a key element of successful conflict resolution (including negotiation and mediation). This is not surprising insofar as trust is associated with enhanced cooperation, information sharing, and problem-solving.

They went on to assert that the origins and development of trust come from:

*   Being able to explain the differences in the individual propensity to trust;
*   Understanding the dimensions of trustworthy behaviour, and;
*   Suggesting levels of trust development

Trust is generally stable over the longer term, with some people having higher levels of trust than others. However, research has shown that this can be improved. Most importantly, the paper offered three dimensions of trust as being the most important of observed attributes. These include Ability, Integrity and Benevolence. This can be considered in a commercial context as seen in figure 3.2:

---

8. Lewicki, Roy J. and Edward C. Tomlinson. "Trust and Trust Building." Beyond Intractability. Eds. Guy Burgess and Heidi Burgess. Conflict Information Consortium, University of Colorado, Boulder. Posted: December 2003: http://www.beyondintractability.org/essay/trust-building

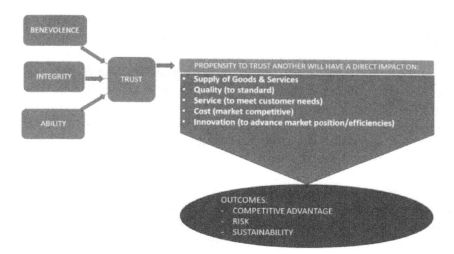

Table 3.2. The impact of propensity to trust (Loseby 2018)

Although these three dimensions are likely to be linked to each other, they each contribute separately to influence the level of trust in another within a relationship. However, ability and integrity are likely to be most influential early in a relationship, as information on one's benevolence needs more time to emerge. The effect of benevolence will increase as the relationship between the parties grows closer.

Reciprocity has implications for procurement in terms of what it can potentially open up through the simple act of "kindness". Reciprocity is a social norm that involves in-kind exchanges between people – responding to another's action with another equivalent action. It is usually positive (e.g. returning a favour), but it can also be negative (e.g. punishing a negative action)[9].

Reciprocity is an interesting concept from the perspective of Behavioural Science, because it does not necessarily involve an economic exchange, and it has been studied by means of experimental games (see Game Theory).

A simple example in business could be setting up a meeting with another party or company, and a few days prior to the meeting at your office you make a phone call to offer help in getting to the office (sending a map), checking whether they need a car parking space, greeting them in reception. There is no cost attached to this, but the payback can be seen as they move towards you as an individual or company they want to do business with.

Charities often take advantage of reciprocity when including small gifts in solicitation letters, while supermarkets try to get people to buy by offering free samples. Reciprocity is also used as a social influence tool in the form

---

9. Fehr, E., and Gächter, S. (2000). Fairness and retaliation: The economics of reciprocity. *Journal of Economic Perspectives,* 14, 159-181.

of 'reciprocal concessions', an approach also known as the 'door-in-the-face' technique, which occurs when a person makes an initially large request (e.g. to buy an expensive product), followed up by a smaller request (e.g. a less expensive option) if the initial request is denied by the responder. The responder then feels obligated to 'return the favour' by agreeing to the conceded request.[10]

Being the first party to offer something to another party as an act of kindness, without it necessarily being solicited, may be the first move to open up something more tangible in value in negotiation, without behaving in an unethical way e.g. the simple act of offering someone a cup of coffee before a meeting could be said to be such an action.

Having established the right attitudes and behaviours, collaborated, developed trust and made efforts to engage the other party with an act of reciprocity, the foundations are built to take things to the next level. Before doing this, a short overview of human psychology will help you understand how this functionality is delivered in ourselves in the next chapter, after which we can begin to look at behaviours and Behavioural Science in more detail.

10. Cialdini, R. B., Vincent, J. E., Lewis, S. K., Catalan, J., Wheeler, D., and Darby, B. L. (1975). Reciprocal concessions procedure for inducing compliance: The door-in-the-face technique. *Journal of Personality and Social Psychology*, 31, 206-215.

CHAPTER 4 | OVERVIEW OF PSYCHOLOGY

In this chapter, I will confine my commentary and observations to the area of cognitive psychology, social psychology, behavioural psychology and personality psychology – the other branches of psychology I have chosen to ignore for the purposes of simplicity and the peripheral impact they have as applied to commercial elements.

4.1 Human Nature and Society

Given the above, I will take each of the aspects of psychology mentioned above and address them as we progress through the chapter.

Cognitive psychology is primarily concerned with the science of how people think, learn, and remember, and was established in the 1960s.
Social psychology is primarily concerned with the study of topics such as group behaviour, social perception, nonverbal behaviour, conformity, aggression and prejudice. Social influences on behaviour are primarily centred around how people perceive and interact with others.
Behavioural psychology (also known as behaviourism) is primarily concerned with the theory of learning based upon the idea that all behaviours are acquired through conditioning. Conditioning occurs through interaction with the environment. Behaviourists believe that our responses to environmental stimuli shape our actions. According to this school of thought, behaviour can be studied in a systematic and observable manner regardless of internal mental states.

Behaviourism was formally established with the 1913 publication of John B. Watson's paper *Psychology as the Behaviourist Views It*.[1] Simply put, strict behaviourists believe that *all behaviours are the result of experience.* Any person, regardless of his or her background, can be trained to act in a particular manner given the right conditioning.

There are two major types of conditioning:

Classical conditioning is a technique frequently used in behavioural training in which a neutral stimulus is paired with a naturally occurring stimulus. Eventually, the neutral stimulus comes to evoke the same response as the naturally occurring stimulus, even without the naturally

---

1. Watson, John. B. (1913). Psychology as the Behaviorist Views it. First published in *Psychological Review*, 20, 158-177

occurring stimulus presenting itself. The associated stimulus is now known as the conditioned stimulus and the learned behaviour is known as the conditioned response.

Operant conditioning (sometimes referred to as instrumental conditioning) is a method of learning that occurs through reinforcements and punishments. Through operant conditioning, an association is made between a behaviour and a consequence for that behaviour. When a desirable result follows an action, the behaviour becomes more likely to occur again in the future. Responses followed by adverse outcomes, on the other hand, become less likely to happen again in the future

Personality psychology is primarily concerned with the branch of psychology that focuses on the study of the thought patterns, feelings, and behaviours that make each individual unique. Classic theories of personality include Freud's psychoanalytic theory of personality and Erikson's theory of psychosocial development. In this form, different factors such as genetics, parenting, and social experiences influence how personality develops and changes.

The evolutionary process of human nature and the way it impacts how we operate as a society can be traced back through many centuries, even to the point of the animal kingdom and how certain aspects such as basic survival needs, hierarchy, etc. still have an ever-present influence and control on how we socialise and interact today. A simple example such as how and why we try and be healthy, but statistically fail more often than not is part of our ancestral heuristic. Why? Because physiologically we are still "wired" like our ancestors to eat plenty when food is available, and the signal from the stomach to the brain that tells us we are full takes probably 20 minutes to register is still within us. So why is this relevant?

The simple fact is that there are aspects about how we "operate" that are often in our subconscious and have a profound effect on how we interact in many situations, including those that impact our daily lives at work. Therefore, understanding them and how, why, where and when they occur is important to know, to allow us to avoid conflict, maximise our opportunities and so forth. Recently a colleague remarked, "I often wonder how I managed to make all those important decisions without knowing what I know today, it's scary!" The inference is that decisions are and have been made, but almost in a state of unconscious thinking.

Having the perspective of how we view and judge others also happens in reverse, a fact that should not come as a surprise, but often does! The biggest challenge we often face is the uncomfortable truth about ourselves – how we behave within society and how we are judged.

My earlier references to Adam Smith's book *The Theory of Moral Sentiments*, a man whose vocation was in part to help shape economics as we know it, wrote as a precursor to his most famous book *The Wealth of Nations* in 1776 about human behaviour and its impact! The salience of this is that the founder of modern economics recognised that human behaviour was just as important to the process of how decisions, markets and investments were governed not by pure rational and logical attributes, but the science of human behaviour first and foremost.

More recently Daniel Kahneman remarked, "The idea of human nature with inherent flaws was consistent with a tragic view of the human condition and it's a part of being human that we have to live with that tragically". Clearly, we have the ability to overcome some of our limitations as humans through education, collaborations with others, new experiences and so forth, but fundamentally we are still left with flaws. The extent to which these flaws will impede our effectiveness and that of society will hopefully diminish over time, but I don't believe there are any magic one-day cures available.

In summary, the way we conduct our business and behave within society is of critical importance, perhaps more so than the Four Box Matrices that have governed our approach and training thus far. The way we present ourselves and our ideas and approaches is probably more fundamental than the idea itself in order to gain traction with others. As I've said before and will say again, the approach that results from translation and making sense to the various audiences is a mantra we should all practice whoever we are, or think we are!

4.2 The unthinkable can happen! (Black Swan Events)

The concept of 'Black Swan Events' was developed by Nassim Nicholas Taleb in his book *Black Swan*. A Black Swan Event must have the following three attributes.

1. It is an outlier, beyond the realm of regular expectations, because experience can't point to its possibility.
2. It carries an extreme impact.
3. After the fact we produce explanations for its occurrence, making it explainable and predictable.

So, in summary *extreme impact, and retrospective predictability*. Taleb's Black Swan Concept is in fact a metaphor; as Taleb explains to Europeans, all swans are white. However, when the first Europeans saw black swans in Australia the event was a complete surprise (to the observer) and had a major impact on them. After the fact, the event is explainable.

So, a Black Swan Event must have the following characteristics according to Taleb:

- The event is a surprise (to the observer).
- The event has a major impact.
- The event is rationalized by hindsight, as if it could have been expected (e.g., the relevant data were available but not accounted for).

Here are some examples:

- The Tacoma Bridge collapse in moderate winds (1940).
- The Chernobyl nuclear explosion during a safety exercise (1986).
- The terrorist attack on the World Trade Centre in New York (2001).

I hope the relevance of this as a form of risk that should be part of our considerations when looking at supply chains will be obvious, especially as much of our more efficient manufacturing relies upon many Just In Time (JIT) principles. Therefore, the impact of any significant event will be immediate and will put many manufacturing businesses in a severe position.

Psychologically it is the "unexpected" element that is intrinsically important to recognise, as is how we might consider constructing contingency and mitigation plans that are both reasonable and proportionate.

Psychology, and in particular heuristics – our historical "pre-wiring" as part of our original survival mechanisms – has taught us that human behaviour relies a lot on the past in terms of how we shape our behaviours and thinking, and hence we cannot afford to "sleep walk" into the future based on our *bounded rationality.*[2]

Our thinking and behaviours generally lead us away from such thoughts, but we need to be prepared to think the unthinkable, even if we subsequently have no plan to deal with it now, as we may have in the future.

The recent shift in politics and/or economics that affect us all, such as Brexit, has implications far and wide, many of which we cannot yet imagine. Such events appear to be occurring with a greater level of frequency than history has shown to date, and therefore the stability we have enjoyed for many decades cannot be relied upon. What this should tell us is that the behaviours and

2. Bounded rationality: the term was coined in Simon, Herbert. (1957). "A Behavioural Model of Rational Choice" in *Models of Man, Social and Rational: Mathematical Essays on Rational Human Behaviour in a Social Setting.* New York: Wiley, 1957. Simon points out that most people are only partly rational, and are irrational in the remaining part of their actions. He also states "boundedly rational agents experience limits in formulating and solving complex problems and in processing (receiving, storing, retrieving, transmitting) information". Simon describes a number of dimensions along which "classical" models of rationality can be made somewhat more realistic.

norms we have developed need to be broken and reshaped to fit the future, not the past.

4.3 Did I get the right deal in the end? (Fairness)

My belief and that of many others is that the definition of human fairness will be different for each and every single person, especially when you take into account the vast range of complex factors and external forces in any given situation.

The evolution of human fairness has been covered in some depth by Debove[3] and in principle sets out that different explanations for the evolution of fairness coexist. Debove reviewed 36 theoretical models of the evolution of human fairness, and identified 6 categories into which they can all be broadly classified:

- Alternating role-based models.
- Reputation-based models.
- Noise-based models.
- Spite based models.
- Spatial population structure models.
- Empathy-based models.

Debove then summarised this by saying that *the variety of models shows that there is no current consensus in the scientific community as to where fairness could come from. There is also no consensus as to what type of evolution led to fairness: biological, cultural or learning-based.* In essence this confirms that each individual's system or attribution of fairness is unique to themselves, although there may be broad groups into which we could place individuals if we had the need to do so and this was critical to the project in hand.

Pragmatically, this is highly unlikely and actually simply checking with another party what they consider fair and reasonable and why might be the simplest solution. Past economic models incorporated altruism or the fact that people may care not only about their own well-being, but also about the well-being of others. However, evidence indicates that pure altruism does not occur often; contrarily most altruistic behaviour demonstrates three facts (as defined by Rabin[4]) and these facts are proven by past events. Due to the existence of these three facts, Rabin created a utility function that incorporates fairness:

3. Debove, S. The evolutionary origins of human fairness. *Psychology.* Universite Sorbonne Paris Cite, 2015. English. NNT: 2015USPCB017

4. Rabin, Matthew. (1993). "Incorporating Fairness Into Game Theory and Economics." *The American Economic Review.* 83, 1281-1302

i. People are willing to sacrifice their own material well-being to help those who are being kind.

ii. The attempt to provide public goods without coercion departs from pure self-interest.

iii. Experiments show that people cooperate to contribute toward a public good to a degree greater than would be implied by pure self-interest. Individually, optimal contribution rates as defined by the standard utility model are close to 0%.

However, data shows that deciders are willing to punish any unfair offer and proposers tend to make fair offers. Finally, in Rabin's experiments both motivations i) and ii) have a greater effect on behaviour as the material cost of sacrificing becomes smaller.

Fairness is also a sign of the way in which we maintain cooperative relationships with large numbers of unrelated and often unfamiliar people. Therefore, from the very beginning of an encounter in business we are immediately making judgements about the fairness, as developed in our psychological foundations, along with social norms.

As fairness is a complex concept that can be applied across many social contexts, the focus for studies both theoretical and empirical – as we can observe from the work of Rabin and Debove in particular – has been around the principles governing the allocation of resources, so-called distributive justice[2]. The reality is that different people will respond in different ways to what they perceive as being fair, and thus the outcomes from encounters in business can differ, none more so than in negotiations and the delivery of decisions such as business cases, stage reviews, personal reviews etc.

Other aspects that can be observed in the pursuit of fairness is where people want to compensate for disadvantageous events or inequality (disadvantageous inequity aversion)[5]. This can also manifest itself as a "punishment" or overcompensation for something that they believe to be unfair. This can also be observed when one party's behaviour is seen as being either fair or unfair in the situation, irrespective of whether they are directly or indirectly involved. Whilst

5. Barone, M. J., and Tirthankar, R. (2010). Does exclusivity always pay off? Exclusive price promotions and consumer response. *Journal of Marketing*, 74(2), 121-132.

Fehr, E., and Schmidt, K. M. (1999). A theory of fairness, competition, and cooperation. *The Quarterly Journal of Economics*, 114, 817-868.

Human resistance to inequitable outcomes is known as 'inequity aversion', which occurs when people prefer fairness and resist inequalities. In some instances, inequity aversion is disadvantageous, as people are willing to forego a gain, in order to prevent another person from receiving a superior reward. Inequity aversion has been studied through experimental games, such as dictator, ultimatum, and trust games (Fehr and Schmidt, 1999), and the concept has been applied in business and marketing, including research on customer responses to exclusive price promotions (Barone and Tirthankar, 2010).

the figure below is a simplified version of what we may see in modern business, the principles and applications are just as relevant.

Our fairness system is developed in childhood and progresses through modification and refinement[6] and essentially builds into the complex layers that make each of us unique in terms of our system of fairness. This emerges into adolescence and then adulthood, as observed in figure 4.1 below:

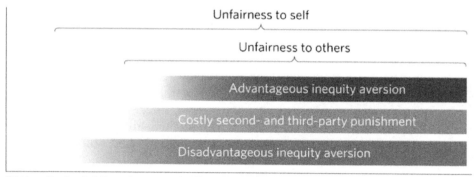

Figure 4.1. The emergence of fairness behaviours in childhood to adolescence

The process of capturing and processing the way we develop our unique sense of fairness can be represented by how and where this occurs in the brain as illustrated below:

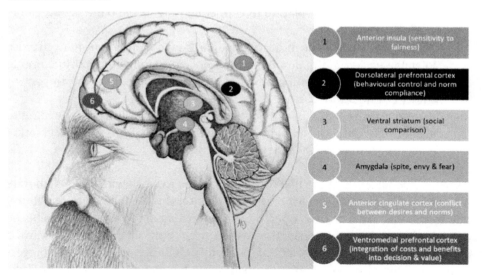

Figure 4.2. Primary inner brain areas diagrammatic (sectional illustration by Angela Loseby-Jackson)

From a pure psychology point of view, the Ventromedial prefrontal cortex activity is truly the shaping of social norms and the demonstration of a balanced behaviour. This is where the activity we witness plays out in many business-related activities and, as outlined earlier, has its origins of formation very early in a person's life. Perhaps the most relevant way of explaining the existence and relevance of fairness comes from Fehr and Schmidt:

- There are situations in which the standard self-interest model is unambiguously refuted.
- However, in other situations the model predictions seem very accurate.
- The vast majority of the subjects behaves in a "fair" and "cooperative" manner although the self-interest model predicts very "unfair" and "non-co-operative" behaviour.
- Market games or public good games without punishment, in which the vast majority of the subjects behaves in a rather "unfair" and "non-cooperative" way – as predicted by the self-interest model.
- A main insight of our analysis is that there is an important interaction between the distribution of preferences in a given population and the strategic environment.
- There are environments in which the behaviour of a minority of purely selfish people forces the majority of fair-minded people to behave in a completely selfish manner, too.
- Yet, we have also shown that a minority of fair-minded players can force a big majority of selfish players to cooperate fully in the public good game, with punishment.
- The gift exchange game indicates that fairness considerations may give rise to stable wage rigidity despite the presence of strong competition among the workers. Thus, competition may or may not nullify the impact of equity considerations.
- If, despite the presence of competition, single individuals have opportunities to affect the relative material payoffs, equity considerations will affect market outcomes even in very competitive environments.

On a personal level, I have had the good fortune to work with and collaborate with many sales teams and business development teams over the years, and found that by treating them fairly is often a most rewarding approach. This was borne out a few years ago in a negotiation with a monopoly supplier who rewarded the company that I was representing not only a 20% discount over our biggest competitor, but also a marketing campaign worth tens of thousands of pounds, simply because in their words *"We had treated their people and their teams fairly and with respect during the course of negotiations that had lasted several months"*.

This dispelled the myth that even if we have laws they are powerless if people believe they are unfair[6], or a company that has a dominant or monopolistic position is not sufficient in itself to sustain and gain competitive advantage in the long term. Human fairness as derived by the person exacting what is deemed to be fair or unfair (and maybe reasonable), and is a powerful behavioural/psychological aspect that can and has derailed many commercial activities and relationships.

4.4 Functions and Systems of the Human Brain

There are two hemispheres of the brain which control different parts of our body, senses and thinking. That is a fact. However, there is no such thing as left and right brain thinking – in that the left is 'artistic' and the right 'scientific'. Sorry!

However, here are some facts about the human brain before we get going, as I know we all like to have a handy list of these ready for the next quiz night:

- The human brain is the largest brain of all vertebrates, relative to body size.
- It weighs about 1.5 kilograms.
- The brain makes up about 2% of a human's body weight.
- The cerebrum makes up 85% of the brain's weight.
- It contains about 86 billion nerve cells (neurons) – the "gray matter".
- It contains billions of nerve fibres (axons and dendrites) – the "white matter".
- These neurons are linked by approximately 300 trillion connections, or synapses (de Courten-Myers, 1999).
- The cortex contains 20 billion nerve cells.
- It took 40 minutes with the combined muscle of 82,944 processors in Riken's K Computer to get just 1 second of biological brain processing time. While running, the simulation ate up about 1PB of system memory as each synapse was modelled individually.
- The brain changes as a function of experience and potential damage in a process known as (neuro)plasticity.

The brain has two hemispheres (left and right) and they are divided into four lobes, separated by folds, known as fissures. In the diagram overleaf – taken from the front of the brain (the cortex) – we can see the frontal lobe, primarily responsible for thinking, planning, memory and judgement. The parietal lobe, is responsible for processing touch. Occipital lobe processes visual information and finally the temporal lobe is for sound.

6. Luther King, Jr., "Letter from a Birmingham Jail", April 16, 1963. African Studies Centre, University of Pennsylvania: "One has not only a legal but a moral responsibility to obey just laws. Conversely, one has a moral responsibility to disobey unjust laws."

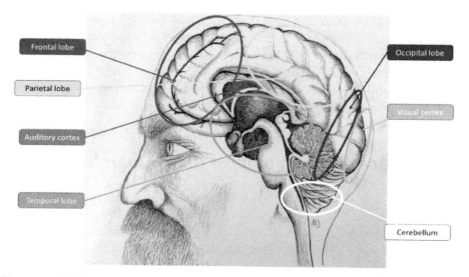

Figure 4.3. Primary Exterior brain areas diagrammatic (sectional illustration by Angela Loseby-Jackson)

For the purposes of the area of commercial and relational activities, we need to concern ourselves with the limbic part of the brain, which is largely responsible for the memory and emotions we possess. Our limbic system is located between the brain stem and the two cerebral hemispheres. Of particular interest to us are the amygdala, the hypothalamus, and hippocampus.

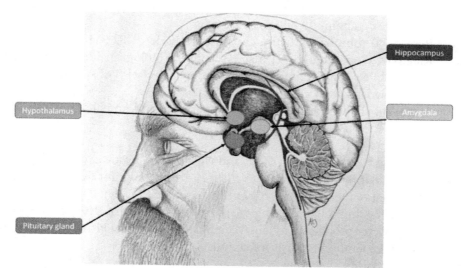

Figure 4.4. Inner brain key areas (sectional illustration by Angela Loseby-Jackson)

The amygdala is primarily responsible for regulating our perceptions of, and reactions to aggression and fear. The amygdala has connections to other systems in our body related to fear, including the sympathetic nervous system, facial responses (which perceive and express emotions), the processing of smells, and the release of neurotransmitters related to stress and aggression (Best, 2009).

In addition to helping us experience fear, the amygdala also helps us learn from situations that create fear. When we experience events that are dangerous, the amygdala stimulates the brain to remember the details of the situation so that we learn to avoid it in the future (Sigurdsson, Doyère, Cain, and LeDoux, 2007).

The hypothalamus helps regulate body temperature, hunger, thirst, and sex-drive, and responds to the satisfaction of our needs by creating feelings of pleasure. Olds and Milner (1954) discovered these reward centres.

The hippocampus is important in that it stores information in our long-term memory. If the hippocampus is damaged, a person cannot build new memories, living instead in a strange world where everything he or she experiences just fades away, even while older memories from the time before the damage remain unaffected. Interestingly it is this part of the brain which enables London taxi drivers to do 'The Knowledge'. They are required to learn by heart the complex maze of streets, landmarks and cut-throughs of London's sprawl. Research has shown that drivers who have passed the examinations to gain The Knowledge have a much larger (physically) hippocampus than say a bus driver, who drives the same route daily.

As all the parts of our brains are interconnected, including the areas of the brain that are responsible for memory, emotion and fear, it should not come as a surprise that decisions or judgements based on pure logic are pretty rare. In conclusion, we need to be aware that the biases we possess as individuals are bound to have an impact on our decisions, as well as the decisions we expect to see. In tandem with this, our hardwiring in the brain ensures that some aspects that trigger primal senses such as fear, survival, etc. will always be prevalent too.

4.5 Are we wired the right way? (Neuroscience and how it supports the understanding of behaviours)

Neuroscience can support and improve the way Behavioural Science is understood and used in two main areas. Firstly, it can offer an efficient framework for rationalising the growing list of behavioural biases quickly and efficiently. Secondly it can increase our understanding of people's behaviour and our ability to predict it. Later I will argue that the most effective way to change behaviour may actually be to change the brain's functioning.

Neuroscience has the potential to help behavioural scientists to categorise and make more sense of our cognitive biases by aligning them to different areas and functions of the brain, especially as Behavioural Science is at an early stage of evolution.

This is particularly significant when we consider that there are nearly 200 biases already, with the likelihood of more to follow. The result of a neuroscientific approach will allow us to provide a simpler and more effective framework within which to work. As we have already learned, the brain changes as a result of experiences and/or damage to the brain itself over time, and the brain in each of us matures at a different rate. Generally speaking takes between 12 and 17 years for the brain to fully mature.

Recent developments have shown that it is possible to use neural indexes, which are brain signatures to specific behaviours, to understand and identify behavioural biases in different populations. In essence the human brain and its neural circuits have not changed since prehistoric ages where we forged a "survival of the fittest" mentality – hence the vast majority of people have the same basic "wiring". Therefore, the neurological struggle that we have is that our genetics are being outpaced by the technological environmental changes over each generation.

In conclusion, we need to recognise that neuroscience will help the behavioural agenda at some point, but probably not in the foreseeable future. The principal reasons are that Behavioural Science is still in its infancy relative to other scientific disciplines, and neuroscience as an ongoing area of research and collaboration between the two areas has only been established fully in the last few decades.

PART B

//

THE APPLICATION OF BEHAVIOURAL SCIENCE IN PURCHASING AND SUPPLY CHAIN MANAGEMENT

CHAPTER 5 | THE APPLICATION OF BEHAVIOURAL SCIENCE IN PURCHASING AND SUPPLY CHAIN MANAGEMENT

In Part A the focus was on what already exists and is widely known within the profession of Purchasing and Supply Chain Management, as well as the evolution of Behavioural Science from its beginnings in the 18th century. In this section we shall build on that and begin to explore how and where Behavioural Science, Social Science, Decision Sciences and Cognition fit into the wider people skills needed. To begin, it might be useful to define some of the terms used in the application of Behavioural Science.

5.1 Overview of the Behavioural Landscape

In starting this journey into the area of Behavioural Science, all the history and competences that have gone before are not separate to the subsequent chapters in this section and following sections, but are additive and in some cases a lead or complementary to the overall behavioural landscape. To set the scene here are a few short definitions of what is meant by heuristics and biases.

Heuristics
Generally taken as being the "rule of thumb" or the procedure that helps find an adequate, though often imperfect, answer to difficult questions. A form of shortcut in some cases to help us quickly make judgements or decisions. I will elaborate on this more in subsequent chapters. This is often comprised of all the many "layers" of experience(s) we have had in our lives, even from childhood.

Biases
These can be said to be the influencing factors or prejudices based on known limits of knowledge, experience, etc. Sometimes people see this as a way of changing what some may see as a more logical, rational or expected outcome. Often the changes we experience in ourselves and that of others can be explained by such biases.

The behavioural landscape is a collage of many sciences and branches of psychology, as well as a number of other relevant competences such as active listening, communication skills, emotional intelligence and others that I have referred to in Part A. As we dig deeper into this area we should not be surprised at the range and complexity of factors that are truly at play, and realise that it is not that surprising that things don't always turn out the way we expect. Considering the number of variable factors that might have an impact on a decision or an outcome, we could express the number of permutations to that outcome as follows:

Number of employees involved in the decision-making process X Number of life experiences (heuristics) X number of biases (188+) X number of projects X market forces (political and economic) = ∞ (infinity!)

For the practical application of the above in Purchasing and Supply Chain Management we need to focus on the commercial outcomes of these processes. This means understanding and taking into account our own and those of other parties' cognitive biases and their tendency to drive our thinking away from making purely rational decisions. This is especially important when we take into account the myriad processes and huge data sets that drive Purchasing and Supply Chain Management. If we likened this to the four-legged 'bar stool' analogy, three legs of the stool represent processes, systems and data, and the fourth leg people.

We have a tendency to put great store in the use of processes and data, but for some reason fail to take people into our equation, particularly when we consider that processes and data can be delegated to others, but not the people aspects. Moreover, when looking at the people aspect we must ensure that when we use the term 'people' that we include (a better understanding of) ourselves in this context, as our own behaviours have an impact.

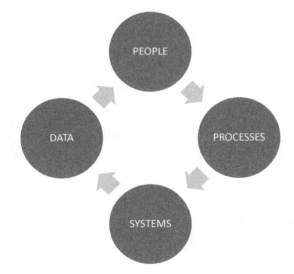

Figure 5.1. Bar Stool Analogy

Modern businesses have "lakes"[1] of data and more systems than we can shake a stick at. For example, modern category management process has countless templates, tools and associated processes, and yet the people aspect represents few competences. People are the single biggest enabler here, so why do we pay so little attention to this aspect?

Clearly experienced Purchasing and Supply Chain Management practitioners will recognise some biases and take them into account when developing strategies, business cases, stage reviews and other key milestones. This might be something as simple as accounting for someone's over optimism when presenting the benefits, or a timeline in which the project may be delivered.

However, research and personal empirical observation suggests that these corrections are too inaccurate and limited to be helpful. Taking the biases out of a decision-making process is hugely difficult and complex. Equally a senior manager or leader/executive who delivers a business case with high levels of confidence and enthusiasm is more likely to gain approval than someone who sets out precisely all the risks and potential issues of a project.

Probably one of the most respected psychologists in this field, Daniel Kahneman, pointed out that the odds of defeating biases in a group setting actually rise when discussion of them is widespread. In addition to this, to have familiarity alone isn't enough to ensure unbiased decision-making, so as we begin to discuss each family of biases, set out below, we also need to consider examples of practices that can help counteract those biases effectively too.

For the purposes of looking at biases in the context of Purchasing and Supply Chain Management I have listed the biases we need to focus on:

- Self-biases
- Group biases
- Societal biases
- Institutional biases

This grouping is intended to help to pinpoint and orientate the practitioner to an understanding of where and when certain biases may be most prevalent and therefore require consideration. As we will see in the subsequent chapters, there are different ways of creating groups and families of biases, but ultimately as you become familiar with them you will properly create your own ways understanding where, when, and how these may impact work that you are undertaking.

If we consider that there are currently 188 cognitive biases, added to our experiences (heuristics), we begin to see that we need to find both efficient and

---

1. Loseby, David, 2016: I used the term "lakes of data" to refer to every growing collection of data companies have that is so large it starts to become indefinable and unmanageable just in the same way as a large lake has a large surface area and is very deep.

optimal ways to group them; notwithstanding the fact that we must also consider their impacts (positively and negatively) at key points in any decision-making process.

A key takeaway learning for me has been to refer to things in the third person or as objective rather than aiming references at the person themselves, as this has the effect of countering social biases and sources of conflict, particularly in delicate or difficult negotiations.

It is also worth pointing out that investing time in understanding a stakeholder's approach that recognises the impact of behaviours needs to be the reserve of key and/or critical decisions, strategies, acceptance milestones etc., and is not intended for day-to-day type activities *per se*. Furthermore, it is more likely that our biases will become the sources of conflict or the delivery of decisions and outcomes that do not meet our personal expectations in a given situation, such as business case approvals, change of supplier, etc. This has led to them being referred to as irrational or unpredictable decisions and outcomes, as they do not align with the view or the prediction we place upon outcomes.

Detailed below is a selection of biases which I feel are most pertinent to Purchasing and Supply Chain Management:

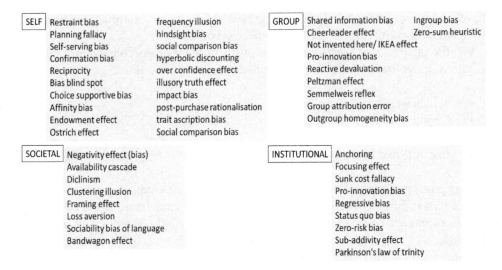

Figure 5.2. Selection of biases, by prevalence, in Procurement

The UK Government recognised that cognitive biases were pivotal to the adoption of changes to policy for public good and generally ensuring that decisions within the population, especially where decisions that every adult needed a considered and conscious effort to make, as it was most likely to impact their future life in terms of wealth and health. This then needed the UK Government's Behavioural Insights Team (BIT), sometimes referred to as the "Nudge Unit", because of what they do in nudging the UK public into better decisions (more of this later).

As part of BIT's contribution to assisting policymakers and behavioural scientists to approach their work in a consistent and sustainable manner, they developed a framework called MINDSPACE, was aimed at helping behavioural scientists develop a checklist of influences on our behaviour for use when making policy. However, based on my years of experience in many and diverse organisations, I believe this is equally valid for how we look at approaching the design towards communication and engagement commercially.

With this in mind, BIT set out nine of the most robust (non-coercive) influences on our behaviour, captured in a simple mnemonic – MINDSPACE – which can be used as a quick checklist when making policy.

Messenger: we are heavily influenced by who communicates information
Incentives: our responses to incentives are shaped by predictable mental shortcuts such as strongly avoiding losses
Norms: we are strongly influenced by what others do
Defaults: we "go with the flow" of pre-set options
Salience: our attention is drawn to what is novel and seems relevant to us
Priming: our acts are often influenced by sub-conscious cues
Affect: our emotional associations can powerfully shape our actions
Commitments: we seek to be consistent with our public promises, and reciprocate acts
Ego: we act in ways that make us feel better about ourselves

In addition to this, from the same BIT document we can look at the approach to policy-making and understand that the benefits of this give structure to policy-making in a commercial context too, for example, when seeking approval for investment in business cases.

Figure 5.3. The 6 Es framework for applying MINDSPACE (p 49)
Source: https://www.instituteforgovernment.org.uk/sites/default/files/
publications/MINDSPACE.pdf

5.2 Heuristics

As stated earlier in the introduction, heuristics are generally taken as being the "rule of thumb" or the procedure that helps find an adequate, though often imperfect, answer to difficult questions; a form of shortcut in some cases to help us quickly make judgements or decisions. This is often comprised of all the many "layers" of experience(s) we have had in our lives, even from childhood. Therefore, this relies upon using readily accessible, though loosely applicable, information to manage problem-solving ourselves. The primary heuristic is trial and error, which can be used in everything from matching invoices to payments, energy values to sites, etc.

Here are a few other commonly-used heuristics from George Pólya's 1945 book, *How to Solve It*[2]:

- If you are having difficulty understanding a problem, try drawing a picture.
- If you can't find a solution, try assuming that you have a solution and seeing what you can derive from that ("working backward").

---

2. Pólya, George. (1945). *How to Solve It: A New Aspect of Mathematical Method.* Princeton, NJ: Princeton University Press.

- If the problem is abstract, try examining a concrete example.
- Try solving a more general problem first (the "inventor's paradox": the more ambitious plan may have more chances of success).

In psychology, heuristics are simple, efficient rules – learned or hard-coded by evolutionary processes – that have been proposed to explain how people make decisions, come to judgments, and solve problems typically when facing complex problems or incomplete information. Researchers test if people use their heuristic "shortcuts" or rules by applying scientifically-recognised methods of research to identify and validate these. These rules work well under most circumstances, but in certain cases lead to systematic errors or cognitive biases (which we will look at in more detail later in the book).

In essence a heuristic technique or approach, using previous experiences or knowledge, enables us to shortcut the route to making an evaluation or decision. Clearly it does not guarantee an optimal or perfect solution, but it is practical and quick. Heuristics can ease the cognitive load of making a decision. Examples of heuristics (approach to decision-making) can be described as using a rule of thumb, an educated guess, an intuitive judgment, guesstimate, stereotyping, profiling, or just plain old common sense.

The study of heuristics in human decision-making was developed in the 1970s and 80s by Israeli psychologists Amos Tversky and Daniel Kahneman, although the concept was originally introduced by Herbert A. Simon. (Simon's original, primary object of research was problem-solving, which showed that we operate within what he called bounded rationality). This leads to a situation where people seek solutions or accept choices or judgments that are "good enough" for their purposes, but could be better.

Heuristics, through greater refinement and research, have begun to be applied to other theories, or be explained by them. For example: The Cognitive-Experiential Self-Theory (CEST) is an adaptive view of heuristic processing. CEST breaks down two systems that process information. Sometimes, roughly speaking, individuals consider issues rationally, systematically, logically, deliberately, effortfully, and verbally. On other occasions, individuals consider issues intuitively, effortlessly, globally, and emotionally. From this perspective, heuristics are part of a larger experiential processing system that is often adaptive, but vulnerable to error in situations that require a more logical analysis.

Clearly heuristics can be considered to reduce the complexity of judgements and decisions, especially when time is of the essence. This goes some way to explain how senior executives rely heavily on their previous roles and or situations, which then spill over into their biases. This often cuts across rational and factual information in favour of what they see as their "better judgement" and can be a source of conflict for this reason.

Looking at some of the better known heuristics, we can see how they might play out in real life situations when applied to the activities in Purchasing and Supply Chain Management:

- **Anchoring and adjustment** – Describes the common human tendency to rely too heavily on the first piece of information offered (the "anchor") when making decisions. For example, in a negotiation a supplier or buyer might suggest a price when there are no other relative benchmarks to attribute cost to a product or service, and this then becomes the anchor from which negotiations commence.
- **Availability heuristic** – A mental shortcut that occurs when people make judgments about the probability of events by the ease with which examples come to mind. For example, when we think about developing a Supplier code of conduct, it is easy and acceptable to most people to base it on something from the United Nations (UN) – this being the UNGP (United Nations Global Compact) as a start point, as this uses 10 principles that are readily available across multiple geographies.
- **Representativeness heuristic** – A mental shortcut used when making judgments about the probability of an event under uncertainty. Or, judging a situation based on how similar the prospects are to the prototypes the person holds in his or her mind. For example, the CFO will always look at the numbers and spreadsheets first when evaluating a business case and the CFO is not likely to be a creative type of person. The likelihood of two events cannot be greater than that of either of the two events individually.
- **Naïve diversification** – When asked to make several choices at once, people tend to diversify more than when making the same type of decision sequentially.
- **Escalation of commitment** – Describes the phenomenon where people justify increased investment in a decision, based on the cumulative prior investment, despite new evidence suggesting that the cost, starting today, of continuing the decision outweighs the expected benefit. This is related to the sunken cost fallacy.
- **Familiarity heuristic** – A mental shortcut applied to various situations in which individuals assume that the circumstances underlying the past behaviour still hold true for the present situation, and that the past behaviour thus can be correctly applied to the new situation. Especially prevalent when the individual experiences a high cognitive load.

I have detailed some of the heuristics which are of a lesser importance to Purchasing and Supply Chain Management, for completeness, but I don't intend to go into great detail for the purposes of commercial activity.

- Affect heuristic
- Contagion heuristic
- Effort heuristic
- Fluency heuristic
- Gaze heuristic
- Peak–end rule
- Recognition heuristic
- Scarcity heuristic
- Similarity heuristic
- Simulation heuristic
- Social proof
- Take-the-best heuristic

In designing an approach to deliver a presentation or some information to a group, even a simple matter of how we present numbers may be significant, as the ability to remember just a few digits, i.e. 3 or 4, versus say 6 or 7 is significantly more complex. Even by breaking large numbers down to smaller blocks can impact the way people read and remember the numbers! This is true when you look at how telephone numbers are visually presented in communications, business cards or the like.

We have probably long known it, but giving people really concise and to-the-point information or "factoids" as they are known, helps us with our heuristic skills and abilities to assimilate the information and remember it, recall it and use it, etc.

This can sometimes be referred to "bite sized" chunks of information, i.e. something we can put in our mouths chew and digest as opposed to a whole plate of food or whole piece of fish, meat or vegetable. So, confine those detailed spreadsheets to the appendices or one-to-one discussions with the analyst!

In researching and reviewing this area and conceiving ways of conveying information to audiences, it is imperative that we do the hard work to "make sense and translate" so it is easier for others to process it. Even within the task of implementing a new way of working or a new system, we need to construct or design simple rules of thumb and instructions as this will improve the way people use and adopt these new ways and systems. This may only be 10% or 20% better, but that may be the difference between the margin of failure and adoption/acceptance!

5.3 System 1 and System 2 Judgements

In this section, I will move beyond heuristics and begin to develop an understanding of how we tend make judgements and decisions. I have made provision for those who want to explore the subject further by developing a list of references at the end of the chapter.

In simple terms, we make judgements in two ways: intuitive and simple decisions (System 1), and more complex decisions that require research or greater effort (System 2).[3]

In everyday terms, we might use the following to identify this dual system: the "Do I want a cup of coffee or tea?" (System 1). "Which pension plan should I choose?" (System 2). If we take the primary attributes of each, the table below sets out in some detail how we go about these processes:

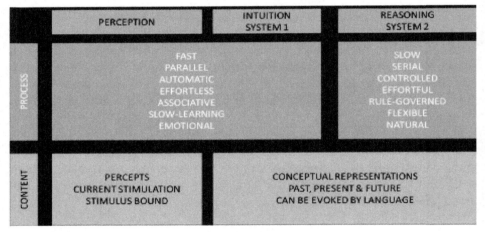

Figure 5.4. Process and content in two cognitive systems
©2003. American Psychological Association. *American Psychologist 697, Vol. 58*, No. 9, 697–720 DOI: 10.1037/0003-066X.58.9.697

As can be seen, System 1 thinking relies heavily on situational cues, salient memories and heuristic thinking to arrive quickly and confidently at judgements, particularly when situations are familiar and immediate action is required. This may be something as simple as putting in place a nondisclosure agreement prior to releasing sensitive information to third party.

Therefore, good decisions emerging from System 1 thinking often feel intuitive. These decisions are often seen to take place when a highly experienced and capable practitioner uses all the expertise, training and practice to exercise

---

3. Kahneman, D. (2012.) *System 1 and 2 Judgements: Thinking fast and slow.* Penguin Books.

good judgement. However, if we are confronted with a situation that is quite extreme, for instance when a supplier in a public procurement process, as a result of losing the tender, launches a legal action to prevent the award of the contract, our natural instincts of "fight or flight" will automatically kick in.

Even if another member of the department reassures you that the supplier will withdraw its claim at some future date, your natural instinct will be to rebuff the action by the supplier.

When it comes to System 2 thinking we are looking at making decisions regarding unfamiliar situations, or perhaps for processing abstract concepts, with the luxury of time for planning a more comprehensive consideration. We may use these heuristic manoeuvres in System 2 thinking as part of the integrated components of logical arguments. Therefore, an argument is often part of the inference and deliberation process when making System 2 decisions. When we subsequently share our reflective interpretations, analysis, evaluations and/or inferences we are in fact offering explanations. Because of this, critical thinking is self-regulated System 2 thinking, focused on resolving the problem at hand and at the same time monitoring and self-correcting your own process of thinking about that specific problem.

This approach must not be confused by the simple but false dichotomy such as the psychological effect on "emotion versus reason" and "head versus heart", etc. The decision-making process is not as simplistic or superficial as these false and popularised expressions. Generally speaking System 1 judgements operate in the background. However, the two systems of judgement can override each other. This is where we get the situation where people see facts and data presented to support a decision where somebody states that their "gut reaction" overrides something more considered and rational.

This then produces a situation where you might observe a contrary decision. This is probably the simplest way of illustrating the point that emotion rules over rationality. Clearly when we look at both systems of judgement there will be times when we can point to errors in both systems, either because we have overestimated or underestimated the benefits, the time to deliver the project, the resources required, etc.

As stated earlier, we need to reflect on our own capabilities and competences to make judgements and decisions, as we are (at least) equally vulnerable to making errors as anybody else. Perhaps the salient point to make here is when considering how we make judgements, particularly those that are System 1 judgements, the risk is that we may stereotype part of a mental shortcut in the process, something which we then later realise was the root cause of our error(s).

As we have read earlier, there are 188 biases – they are laid out for you in figure 5.5, to see another way of how they have been classified. As set out earlier in the beginning of part B, I have chosen the most pertinent and relevant biases that relate to the commercial areas. However, this does not mean that other biases may have an impact of equal or greater magnitude, as it is always a question of the variable factors that are relevant to each situation. Each chapter in part B will explore the primary biases I have chosen. However, for transparency I have shown them all, and how others have chosen to set them out as per the algorithmic set in figure 5.5 opposite.

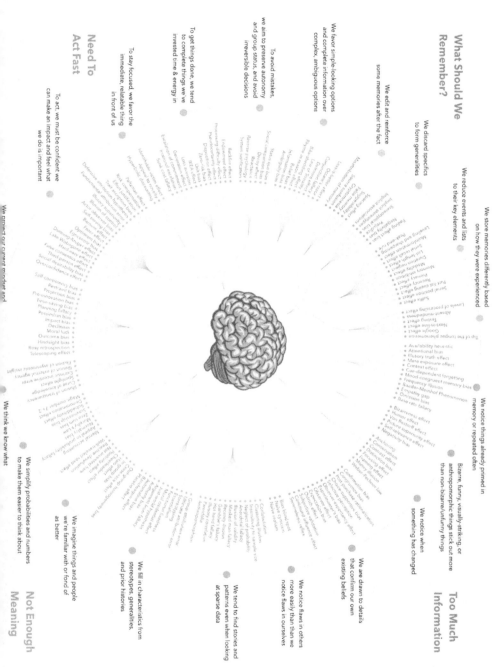

Figure 5.5. All the biases we possess (Cognitive Bias Codex, 2016)[4]

4. Manodgian III, John and Buster Benson categorisation. Design by JM3; deep research by Wikipedia Far + Wide: algorithmic layout of Cognitive biases: CODEX of Cognitive biases 2016)

CHAPTER 6 | SELF BIASES

6.1 Overview

In this chapter, I will deal with the biases which are self-centric in nature. There are many factors than can hinder success, which I will explore across all the behavioural biases and heuristics in particular, including lack of trust between supply chain partners, the intervention of internal stakeholders, the poor alignment of incentives and objectives and a tendency toward risk aversion.

The behaviours of everyone in the business have the potential – indirectly and directly – to impact the delivery of outcomes, including those attributed to you yourself. Perhaps the most salient question here is, to what extent will that impact be? Currently there are no models or recognised ways to calculate the effect of peoples' behaviours on a project, and much of the impact will not be evident or uncovered until the latter stages or post-project, which is of course too late.

Importantly, these behavioural impacts are not exclusively confined to the activities of Purchasing and Supply Chain Management; they span across the whole organisation and supply chain. Furthermore, each situation is likely to be different and have its own unique set of factors for those involved to consider, so we need to avoid generalisation.

In developing a metric which will be of use to the organisation, we must focus on and find optimal ways in which we can group issues and develop approaches that are both practical and impactful. The reality is that we can use certain measures to help manage and ameliorate self-biases, but we cannot fully eradicate them. Therefore, recognising what we can and can't manage or influence is equally key as we explore the nature of biases.

In considering self-biases, Table 6.1 below shows my view of some of the more common and impactful biases that we need to consider.

Restraint bias	frequency illusion
Planning fallacy	hindsight bias
Self-serving bias	social comparison bias
Confirmation bias	hyperbolic discounting
Reciprocity	over confidence effect
Bias blind spot	illusory truth effect
Choice supportive bias	impact bias
Affinity bias	post-purchase rationalisation
Endowment effect	trait ascription bias
Ostrich effect	Social comparison bias

Table 6.1. Self-biases

There are many case studies (e.g. Nadler 1979, Sasone 1986, Sarin and Weber 1993, Kluger and DeNisi 1996, Gelfland and Realo 1999, Bachrach 2001, Katok and Roth 2004, Bolton et al 2004, Kwasnica 2005, et al) that demonstrate how human motivation is linked to feedback, especially when projects find themselves in a situation where there are overruns, cost pressures, benefits erosion, etc.

In a recent paper by Bendoly et al[1], the authors examine the assumptions of the 'decision-maker' in procurement, and whether they were acting objectively or whether in reality prior experience would significantly influence choice behaviour. They conclude that if the savings splits between buyer and supplier were not equitable/fair, then this would likely lead to adversity and potential loss of control.

I find this conclusion interesting, as in my experience one of the single biggest contributors to project/ programme dynamics is the influence of the person leading the procurement – where the project lead's influence becomes perhaps the single biggest contributor to the behaviours in the whole end-to-end activity. Therefore, I feel that it is incumbent on me to shoulder the blame for some of the behaviours and biases that I have brought to the projects and programmes I have managed across a variety of sectors and geographic regions.

Firstly, let's explore some of the principal biases and effects, common to all of us, but clearly to different degrees in each individual; then we can examine how to look practically to mitigate and manage these biases, if possible.

In providing an overview and definition, hopefully you'll begin to understand and recognise some of these behaviours in relation to yourself and others, in real-world situations:

- Planning Fallacy.
- Self-serving bias.
- Confirmation bias.
- Reciprocity.
- Bias blind spot.
- Affinity bias.
- Endowment effect.
- Frequency illusion.
- Hindsight bias.
- Hyperbolic discounting.
- Illusory truth effect.

We will now explore this list in some detail to enable us to work with them in our own organisations.

---

1. Bendoly, E., Donohue, K. and Schultz, K.L. (2005). Behavior in operations management: Assessing recent findings and revisiting old assumptions, in *Journal of Operations Management*, 24 (6), 737-752, 2006. 432, 2006. Elsevier.

Planning Fallacy – first proposed by Daniel Kahneman and Amos Tversky in 1979, this is a bias in which predictions about how much time will be needed to complete a future task are optimistic, and generally underestimate the time needed.

This occurs regardless of the individual's knowledge, relative to past tasks of a similar nature and how long they have taken to complete than the original estimate or plan. The bias only affects predictions about one's own tasks; when outside observers predict task completion times, they show a pessimistic bias, overestimating the time needed. The Planning Fallacy requires that predictions of current tasks' completion times are more optimistic than the beliefs about past completion times for similar projects, and that predictions of the current tasks' completion times are more optimistic than the actual time needed to complete the tasks.

Subsequently in 2003, Dan Lovallo and Kahneman proposed an expanded definition of this bias, as the tendency to underestimate the time, costs, and risks of future actions (and at the same time) overestimate the benefits of the same actions.

According to this new definition, the Planning Fallacy results not only in time overruns, but also cost overruns and benefit shortfalls. This, from previous experience, is more realistic given the projects and programmes I have seen – hence why an accurate method of benefits management is important in tempering this type of bias.

Self-serving bias – is a consequence of any thought or perception on the part of the individual that alters and enhances as consequence the value or worth of one's own ability. It is the belief that individuals tend to ascribe success to their own abilities and efforts, but ascribe failure to other people or external factors.

Furthermore, when individuals reject any objective negative feedback, but continue to reference their own strengths and achievements as well as overlooking their faults and failures, fail to take ownership for their failures, or fail to recognise the contribution of others, these are clear signs of this bias.

In a project or programme situation they might maximise the contributions they have made or claim poor advice from another as being the reason they did not properly attribute a benefit in a business case. You may have heard the terms such as "Mr Teflon" or having "sloping shoulders" as a way of referring to people who exhibit overt signs of this bias, given that no criticism that is just is ever accepted. Critically, trust is lost, relationships break down and the team soon become dysfunctional.

Both motivational processes (i.e. self-enhancement, self-presentation) and cognitive processes (i.e. loss of control or self-esteem) influence the self-serving bias. There are both cross-cultural (i.e. individualistic and collectivistic culture differences) considerations within the bias too.

Confirmation bias – also called confirmatory bias or 'my-side' bias, is the tendency to search for, interpret, favour, and recall information in a way that confirms one's own or an individual's pre-existing view or outcome. It is a type of cognitive bias and a systematic error of inductive reasoning. Sometimes people have referred to it as selective or convenient memory, referring to the omission of all the salient facts or information. The effect is likely to be stronger for emotionally charged projects, personal or company issues and for deeply entrenched beliefs.

People also tend to interpret ambiguous statements, views and factual statements as supporting their pre-existing position. A biased memory and interpretation are at play in the attitude polarisation (when a disagreement becomes more extreme even though the different parties are exposed to the same evidence), belief perseverance (when beliefs persist after the evidence for them is shown to be false), the irrational primacy effect (a greater reliance on information encountered early in a series) and illusory correlation (when people falsely perceive an association between two events or situations).

There is much scientific evidence that supports the "one-sided" view that focuses on the pre-existing belief of someone which allows them to ignore alternatives. One explanation is that people show confirmation bias because they are weighing up the costs of being wrong, rather than investigating in a neutral, scientific way. Confirmation biases contribute to overconfidence in personal beliefs and can maintain or strengthen beliefs in the face of contrary evidence. Poor decisions due to these biases have been found in many organisations.

Reciprocity – to be clear this is not a bias as such, but a self-generated action that is intended to yield a positive response in return from another individual or group. This is something that relates to the notion that "one good deed deserves another"; an act of kindness that may not have any cost attached to it, but is valued by the other party. My experience in using this in engaging with suppliers, is that by offering something they value highly, such as the use of your company name or reference to help them secure a good name and reputation for their business or activity in a sector, is important to them.

Bias blind spot – is a common cognitive bias in most people, which is recognising the impact of biases on the decisions and judgements made by others, while at the same time failing to see the impact of any bias on your own judgment.

The term was coined by Emily Pronin, Daniel Lin and Lee Ross. Interestingly it appears to be a stable individual difference that is measurable (this can be found by referring to the scales produced by Scopelliti et al in 2015). It has been scientifically proven that everyone believes that they are less biased than they actually are.

Probably the most common and everyday example of this is the reference to the self-evaluation of driving skills and abilities versus those actually observed.[2] However, bias blind spots may be caused by a variety of other biases and self-deceptions. As we saw earlier, having a self-serving bias does not mean the person is aware that they have the bias, and hence people tend to think of their own perceptions and judgments as being rational, accurate and free of bias.

The self-enhancement bias also applies when analysing our own decisions, in that people are likely to think of themselves as better decision-makers than others. We only have to look at the statements they make about their own driving abilities versus those of others to see how wide the gap is! In reality, the only way to show some biases is to record video meetings and other activities to be able to play back and show people such open manifestations of their biases, if we are to change them.

Affinity bias – this leads us to favour and select those people who are like us, especially when recruiting teams and new hires, etc. On the surface it seems to be common sense that we tend to like people who are like we are, and we have a natural propensity to be associated with people who we can relate to, who share certain values, and who we are comfortable around.

This tendency to surround ourselves with like-minded people is a bias and can have drawbacks. In certain cases, it can lead to favouritism, based on unrelated criteria to the role in question such as gender, educational background, social class and so on.

The flip side to this is where we tend to notice the faults of others who do not have these affinities with us, and overlook other more critical factors in those we are drawn towards. Research shows that this occurs far more frequently than we allow ourselves to believe. A famous study in 1999 by Steinpres et al[3] found that recruiters showed a preference for male applicants, when in reality they had all been sent exactly the same CV, with half being sent a CV apparently from an applicant with a traditionally 'male' name and half from an applicant with a traditionally 'female' name.

The recruiters reported the male applicants as better qualified and more likely to be offered a job. Similar studies have found even more dramatic preferences for job applicants with traditionally British-sounding names, over applicants

---

2. Pronin, E., Lin, D. Y. and Ross, L. (2002). "The Bias Blind Spot: Perceptions of Bias in Self Versus Others" in *Personality and Social Psychology Bulletin.* 28 (3): 369–381. doi:10.1177/0146167202286008.
3. Steinpreis, R.E., Anders, K.A. & Ritzke, D. (1999). *Sex Roles.* 41: 509. https://doi.org/10.1023/A:1018839203698

with names that do not sound traditionally British; and yet further studies have found recruiter preferences for younger candidates over older ones. So, beware of the pitfalls, as we need good cognitive diversity to have high performing teams.

Endowment effect – is the hypothesis that people ascribe more value to things merely because they own them. For example, to elicit the endowment effect is the ownership paradigm, primarily used in experiments in psychology, marketing, and organisational behaviour. In this paradigm, people who are randomly assigned to receive goods ("owners") evaluate it more positively than people who are not randomly assigned to receive the goods ("controls").

The endowment effect can be equated to the behavioural model Willingness to Accept or Pay (WTAP), a formula sometimes used to find out how much a consumer or person is willing to put up with or lose for different outcomes. This will play out in scenarios where people are looking to dispose of used assets, such as fleet, and ascribe a higher value to something they own and believe is better than what is offered in the market, even though it may be similar or better.

Hence you are biased in the belief that your asset has a greater value than the other person's, even though it may be the same. However this cannot be confused with market forces in terms of who is willing to pay for what at any given time as there will be other factors at play such as scarcity or over-provision, etc.

Frequency illusion – the frequency illusion (also known as the Baader-Meinhof phenomenon) is the phenomenon in which people who just learn or notice something then start seeing it everywhere. For instance, a person who just realised the introduction of a new piece of legislation that they were previously unaware of suddenly begins to recognise conferences, courses, bulletins, etc. that would have previously gone unnoticed.

Hindsight bias – also known as the knew-it-all-along effect or creeping determinism, this is the inclination, after an event has occurred, to see the event as having been predictable, despite there having been little or no objective basis for predicting it. It can present itself at different stages of a project or programme as well as in different contexts. Hindsight bias may cause memory distortion, where the recollection and reconstruction of content can lead to false and sometimes theoretical outcomes.

It has been suggested that the effect can cause extreme methodological problems while trying to analyse, understand, and interpret results in complex financial analysis. A basic example of the hindsight bias is when, after viewing the outcome of a potentially unforeseeable event, a person believes he or she "knew it all along". Such examples are present in the writings of historians describing outcomes of battles, physicians recalling clinical trials, and judicial systems trying to attribute responsibility and predictability of accidents.

This can occur where we might evaluate a long list of suppliers, and in the evaluation and weighting and subsequent scoring when we are presented with a result we don't expect, and either discount the outcome and overrule it, or worse still re-work an objective process to give the answer we want, which is clearly unethical.

Hyperbolic discounting – in economics, hyperbolic discounting is a time-inconsistent model of discounting. It is one of the cornerstones of Behavioural Economics. The discounted utility approach states that Intertemporal choices[4] are no different from other choices, except that some consequences are delayed and hence must be anticipated and discounted (i.e. reweighted to take into account the delay).

Put into the context of Purchasing and Supply Chain Management, this is where we look for the "quick wins". We have a tendency to show a preference for a positive outcome that arrives sooner rather than later. People are said to discount the value of the later reward, by a factor that increases with the length of the delay – hence the benefits case that spans over multiple years dissipates.

This process is traditionally modelled in the form of exponential discounting, a time-consistent model of discounting. A large number of studies have since demonstrated deviations from the constant discount rate assumed in exponential discounting. Hyperbolic discounting is an alternative mathematical model that accounts for these deviations. It is not linear, but time-relevant adjusted.

The most important feature of hyperbolic discounting is that it creates temporary preferences for smaller rewards that occur sooner over larger rewards that occur later, although they are still considered part of an overall business case. Individuals using hyperbolic discounting reveal a strong tendency to make choices that are inconsistent over time – they make choices today that their future self would prefer not to have made, despite knowing the same information.

This dynamic inconsistency happens because hyperbolas (a part of your brain, which we explored earlier in chapter 4) distort the relative value of options, with a fixed difference in delays in proportion to how far the choice-maker is from those options.

---

4. Intertemporal choice is the study of how people make choices about what and how much to do at various points in time, when choices at one time influence the possibilities available at other points in time. These choices are influenced by the relative value people assign to two or more payoffs at different points in time. Most choices require decision-makers to trade off costs and benefits at different points in time. These decisions may be about savings, work effort, education, etc.

Illusory truth effect – also known as the truth effect, the illusion-of-truth effect, the reiteration effect, the validity effect, and the frequency-validity relationship, is the tendency to believe information to be correct after repeated exposure to the same piece of information, irrespective of its validity. In practical terms, if a statement or outcome is repeated many times over in a variety forms and forums, people begin to believe that it will happen.

A personal example of this was an ERP programme that over time discounted risks and issues, slimmed down the testing and skipped activities to assure senior management it would reach the intended milestone, only to fail on the due date! This was a sad case that had far-reaching implications in the organisation, simply because the sponsor and others did not want to take full account of the true risks and activity needed to deliver the stated outcome.

A practical way to counter some of the aspects of behavioural impact can be to carry out what is referred to a "pre-mortem" (the opposite of a post mortem). Clearly this will only be necessary for more major projects/programmes and/ or investments, as it is an investment in time and resource upfront of the work to be undertaken. The term or approach was first developed by Gary Klein, (and first introduced in 2007, based on the technique from research in the topic of prospective hindsight) – in essence a pre-mortem requires the decision-makers, and project team(s) to imagine that the project has failed and then work backwards to conceive all the possible reasons why this might have happened.

The pre-mortem can be designed to minimise the effect of collective behaviours (GroupThink) simply following and agreeing with influential and senior stakeholders (cheerleader effect), as they may not wish to challenge if they are junior or less articulate or introverted members of a team.

The aim is to require everyone to consider the risks and scenarios independently and then discuss them anonymously. This produces a better quality of understanding and impact of risks, as well as how to mitigate them. Clearly there are other measures that assist, such as better quality data, effective but not bureaucratic governance, etc. Since introducing the pre-mortem approach, Klein has gone on to introduce an approach called the pro-mortem, looking at the scenario that the project or programme is a real triumph and success too.

A very readable paper produced by the Behavioural Insights Team titled *"An exploration of potential behavioural biases in project delivery in the department for transport"*[5] is a good reference for further reading, which I have summarised as a case study at the end of this book.

---

5. Behavioural Insights Team (BIT). (2017). *An exploration of potential behavioural biases in project delivery in the department for transport.* Commissioned by the Department for Transport's Governance Division. Accessed at www.behaviouralinsights.co.uk/publications/ an-exploration-of-potential-behavioural-biases-in-project-delivery-in-the-department-for-transport

6.2 Predictions and Forecasts

I have personally encountered many senior players who look for certainty in an uncertain world, even to the point where they are looking for the nirvana of zero risk. I recognise that this is my perspective and I may be biased in that view. However, the tendency for greater certainty is diametrically opposed to a world that is "speeding up" and becoming more complex – technology is moving at a faster pace than human development, all of which makes the process of predictions and forecasts more inherently risky.

This, coupled with the pursuit of economic models and techniques that rely upon a rigid system of logic and rationale that does not yield to human behaviour, leaves too many predictions and forecasts fundamentally flawed.

This is particularly true in the public domain when we see that the Brexit vote in the UK was not the predicted outcome, the American presidential election never envisaged Donald Trump winning, and France's new president and subsequent government was based on a party founded by French President Emmanuel Macron's centrist La Republique En Marche (LREM) that didn't exist 12 months before the election. So, that predictability is for fools and theorists and has little to do with real life could be the new normal!?

While the world of Purchasing and Supply Chain Management is far less spectacular than the world of politics, it is nevertheless clear that we need a different approach to the rigid models and processes that can leave us with the need to "adjust" those outcomes in the future. The question will always be, what degree will a behavioural impact have on the logic and rationale of linear decision-making, and what then becomes material to that outcome? Detailed in figure 6.2 overleaf is a model I developed in 2016 to illustrate this visually:

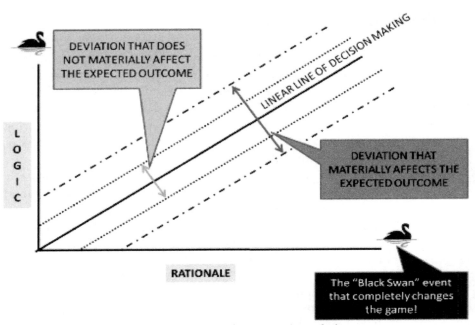

Figure 6.2. Behavioural deviation to the norm (Loseby)

As managers it is our responsibility to determine those events and actions/ behaviours that will either materially affect (or not) the outcomes that are planned, based upon our logical and rational approaches.

This is where strategic projects benefit from use of the pre-mortem (or pro-mortem). We can enhance the impact of this approach by coupling this and extending the approaches to combine and modify what we already know – for example combining a PESTLE approach with SWOT analysis, and extending our methods of identifying stakeholders, so that they reflect the behavioural influences in our approach.

A tangible example of this is where a senior decision-maker has been involved, who will bring with their experiences (heuristics) and personal biases into a new organisation. These can either be used positively to avoid and/or mitigate a common issue, or negatively where they impose their heuristics and biases to such an extent that they alter the objective and rational decision-making that changes the desired outcome.

I have seen this occur in a number of organisations – it can on occasion be effectively managed but sometimes not, due to the seniority of the individual, much to the detriment of the company – with collateral impact on the team involved in the project. However knowing that this might happen, and very much in the "materially adverse" segment of the decision line, helps avoid conflict and manage the team around you to minimise the collateral impact.

This predication or forecast is more realistic and hence you are better positioned to manage this in the outcome and the team.

So, if we take the factors and try and set them out as to what the influencing factors may be, we end up looking at something like the following, but the situational element will be specific to the organisation and people involved:

Item	Category area	Example	Impact
1	Informational issues	a) Ambiguity aversion, particularly those that are anchored in data/finance b) Anecdotal evidence	Deferred decisions and loss of confidence in the team lead
2	Heuristics and biases	a) Heuristics – all b) Status quo bias c) Confirmation bias d) Not invented here bias	Distorts the path of rational and objective data and changes the outcome to some or a significant extent
3	Intertemporal choice	a) Self-control b) Procrastination c) Hyperbolic discounting d) Emotions	Project loses pace and focus and may ultimately be rejected or ignored over other priorities
4	Decision context	a) Reference dependence b) Choice bracketing c) Framing effects d) Choice architecture	Things may be unfairly evaluated against past or current events that are unrelated and unknown by the team and change the course of the outcome or context
5	People dynamics	a) Lack of cognitive diversity b) Group think c) Cheerleader effect	The project is railroaded into something that is destined to fail and has no ownership

While this all looks quite negative, it is possible to look at the opposite spectrum; this positive outlook can also be mapped out. In conclusion this allows us to predict and/or forecast outcomes in the context of behavioural impacts. This in turn is the Soft Skills for Hard Business aspect which can help mitigate the effect on projects or allow you to prioritise and/or approach things in an entirely different way!

The deployment of a behavioural approach regarding predictions and forecast can be both rewarding and risky at the same time. However, I would argue that the traditional approach that simply relies on what we currently know or is based on what historically has happened is flawed. Start to think about asking some more open questions to begin with: stakeholders, budget owners, decision-makers might just give more of an insight and allow us to do the "make sense and translate" exercise needed. Questions can include:

- Have you ever been involved in anything similar and what was the outcome?
- If you have experience in this before, what things would you do differently and why?
- Do you think the company is more likely to look at a leading edge solution or play safe?
- How high is this on your priority list?
- Do you have any thoughts about what the outcome might look like?

One can explore where the issues and traps might lie. This may include registering your own biases too, which needs to be equally honest, focusing on de-biasing predictions and forecasts in the way you are with others.

6.3 Dealing with the Self Biases and Overconfidence

Not recognising one's own biases and heuristics is a serious error of judgement. Striving for objectivity is the perfect state, and in reality, the question is how close can we get to achieving this? Therefore, it is important to recognise that we all hold our own subjective world-views and are influenced and shaped by our experiences, beliefs, values, education, family, friends, peers and others. Being aware of self-biases is vital to both personal well-being and professional success.

People and professionals who have a high degree of self-awareness are likely to be more adept in one of the most critical competences: people skills (not soft skills) and hence should be more objective and ethical as practitioners. Understanding and realising what your personal biases are, which might or already do contribute to less objective and rational outcomes, allows you to manage them effectively.

Consider it a navigational necessity to do this, and if you're like me you need time to reflect on how you have or will evaluate a situation – this is a necessary step. We are human and therefore fallible, no exceptions.

A negative or unfavourable bias could be any arbitrary factor not directly related to the situation or circumstance in question, and is therefore less obvious to others.

I acknowledge that my bias in expecting others to be able to perform the same tasks in the same order and at the same speed is unrealistic. The fact that I operate and evaluate situations the way I do should not be an expectation for how others will perform a similar task.

There are many factors at play here, so defining those that are indirect to the central question of bias awareness is the most important objective.

Consider the following practical tips when constructing the project, in terms of resources, objectives, the team, evaluation criteria, etc.:

- Get regular feedback from colleagues – formal (e.g., part of a 180- or 360-degree assessment) or informal (e.g., conversations with supervisors, peers or direct reports). Be careful to ensure that peers and subordinates feel safe in giving this feedback. If this is not handled carefully and respectfully the consequences for all can be quite serious.
- Pause and reflect. Study yourself and your reactions. How do you react to change? What do you feel when something doesn't go the way you expected it to? Take notes.
- Confide in someone you really, really trust like your partner, wife, soul mate, etc. – someone who you trust who realises that their relationship with you won't change as a consequence of honest reflection and feedback. It's particularly important you relay any scenario back honestly and with the right context or the feedback will not be of value to you.
- Expand your horizons. Proactively look for new experiences to discover more about yourself and your reactions to unfamiliar situations. Engage with the other side, as some refer to it, like the sales, marketing, etc. They really don't bite!
- Learn to know yourself. This may be most challenging, but find time for solitude and to relax. It's amazing what you learn about yourself when you sit with your thoughts. Some find meditation helpful, others like me just need quality time and space to declutter our brain activity and indulge in some "me time".
- Observe others who you respect, and reflect on and internalise how they deal with parallel and similar situations. Also consider how they may deal with a situation you have not observed, but need to address.
- Reflect on a time when things went really well and the outcome exceeded expectations, and ask what led to this situation and what behaviours you observed, as well as the relativity to new or forthcoming scenarios.

In the final analysis, the maxim "know thyself" it is a profound and useful mantra that we need to observe if we are to be effective. In summary, we are all biased to some extent – the question for us all is "Which biases am I prone to? And how do they affect my objective judgements and decisions?"

6.4 Cognitive Framing

I recently had the privilege of collaborating with Professor Lutz Preuss (Psychology) and Professor Andrew Fearne (Value Management) to consider the aspect of cognitive framing from the perspective of Purchasing and Supply Chain Management.

The term cognitive framing was introduced in 1974 by Erving Goffman in *"Frame Analysis: An Essay on the Organisation of Experience"*, which introduces the concept of *cognitive frames* to the field of sociology. Goffman's ideas start with the concept of primary frameworks, which are perspectives that help us make sense of the chaotic world around us.

He wrote: *"Each primary framework allows its user to locate, perceive, identify, and label a* see*mingly infinite number of concrete occurrences,"* allowing the user to interpret and understand the meaning of the occurrences according to the frame. Most people are completely unaware of the frames at work in their brains and would probably not be able to describe their frames, but have absolutely no problem in applying them in practical ways every day of their lives.

Once these frames are part of our cognition (way of thinking), they are effectively automatically enabled and function without the person even being conscious of this happening. This supports the fact of our brain's ability to operate unconsciously, thus enabling many things in our life to work quickly and efficiently.

In childhood we develop some primary circuitry through repeated activity/ use and form ways that "frame" how we see things and effectively make sense of them. These then become spontaneous and no longer a conscious activity. i.e. we see snow and feel cold. This invokes physical actions, such as shivering, etc. – again no conscious thought is needed for this.

While cognitive frames are integral to how our brains work and allow us to function in the world, the embodied nature of the frames can present limitations as well. For example, we can develop frames based on incorrect information or dangerous ideas that we may find difficult to shed in later life. The same process works for more complicated frames based on cultural, gender or other substantive issues which can hijack our thinking. Typically, people have competing and contradictory frames in their brains at all times, and through complex interactions with the social and physical environment, different frames can take precedence at different times, places, and/or situations.

The mechanism which switches the brain from one dominant frame to another is called a social or primer cue. In real life, switching from one cue to another does not immediately seem an issue. However, responding to continuous inputs from mass media, social interactions, and the physical environment all have an impact. Because switching is automatic, people may not be aware of what is affecting their perceptions, and cultural biases can find their way into perceptions without intention or consciousness.

Daniel Kahneman[6] describes the two systems in the brain that work together.

System 1 is the automatic system that controls impressions, perceptions, feelings, and reactions.

System 2 is the system that "allocates attention to the effortful mental activities that demand it."

However, the two systems do not operate independently. One of the greatest implications of Kahneman's work is that people are bad at making predictions and estimations and, therefore, they are bad at making decisions based on having to make a prediction about something in the process of decision-making. Foundational to this is the paper *Prospect Theory: An Analysis of Theory Under Risk*[7].

Having set out in some detail the notion of *cognitive framing*, let us now place it in the context of Purchasing and Supply Chain Management. My collaboration with Lutz Preuss and Andy Fearne, and building on the three cognitive frames outlined by Preuss stimulated my thinking to how this is applied in the "real world".

Preuss built upon previous work (Suedfeld and Tetlock, 1977; Tetlock et al., 1993), and his recent work *Consequences of Unidimensional, Hierarchical and Paradoxical Frames* was my cue to look at what this meant in terms of the cognitive frames for Procurement and Supply Chain Managers. By looking at the process of evolution of skills and experience, it occurred to me the following cycle was evident, as shown in figure 6.3 overleaf.

5. Kahneman, D. (2012.) *System 1 and 2 Judgements: Thinking fast and slow.* Penguin Books.
7. Kahneman, D. and Tversky, A. (1979.) Prospect Theory: An Analysis of Decision under Risk in *Econometrica*, Vol. 47, No. 2. (Mar., 1979), pp. 263-292.

Figure 6.3. Evolution of skills to develop higher cognitive frames (Loseby)

The next challenge was to set that into context and dispel some logic without bias, which meant taking a different look as to how we define higher skills and competences, that are non-traditional. This lead me to define and set out what constituted the there levels of cognitive frames for the Procurement profession.

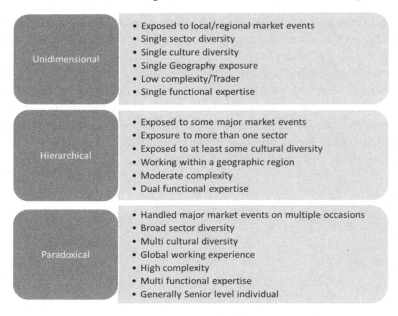

Figure 6.4. Unidimensional, Hierarchical and Paradoxical frames (Loseby)

It can also be said that factors that are the antecedents are inter-related and are dynamic when related to the individual as defined in the three types.

Therefore, a combination of any or all, and the quantum of influence will have a direct bearing on the cognitive frames of individuals which is likely to be expressed as "algorithm of cognition" and not a simple linear expression. The interplaying factors can be selected with any one of a number of headings NOT directly related to the individual.

Figure 6.6. Factors relating to the algorithm of cognition (Loseby)

In conclusion, Cognitive Frames are proportional to the ability of the individual to manage and deliver competitive advantage, while simultaneously managing and mitigating risk and other key factors. Equally, the dynamic perspective is and will become increasingly key to cognitive frames in individuals and how they impact on social relations in the supply chain to beneficial effect.

Given the complexity of the subject area, I decided to set this into context from personal experience to illustrate the three cognitive frames:

Unidimensional: Consider the scenario: a food buyer that has never worked outside of the catering food sector, despite having a senior/head of procurement role, with 20+ years' experience can fall into this category. How might this be so?

The food buyer's objectives are to reduce the cost of the raw ingredients to produce a range of dishes that form part of a menu on rotation or as part of a core menu. In this scenario a core meal would appear as "fish and chips", with the prime ingredient being white fish that has solid texture, that flakes and can be deep fried, etc.

However several years ago a very senior procurement manager offered up a fish substitute that mirrored the specification, yet was either tasteless or worse still of a poor taste profile. To overcome this alternative to cod (pengasious) I organised a blind taste test with senior directors to sample all the meal ranges, including this one.

The ensuing result was to responsibly source cod as the alternative, despite the fact that the cheaper alternative would generate greater savings. Consequently, the brand and superior quality and sourcing of the fish would be a clear differentiator to be "marketed" over the competition (and the margin required was still achieved with no loss of consumption/volume).

The food buyer (unidimensional) had merely looked at maximising the savings, whereas as a CPO (paradoxical) I had considered the brand, the quality, reputation, marketing opportunities, as well as cost savings.

Hierarchical: the scenario in this instance involves a Head of Procurement with extensive experience in the Travel and Events Sector, limited International experience, but with 20+ years of procurement experience. They agreed to build and champion a new travel policy and subsequent contract provision. The experience at interfacing with Executive stakeholders was new and was part of the development opportunity.

In agreeing the new travel policy, the head had consulted the sponsor (Group HR Director), but not all of the Executive (Board), relying upon the sponsor to do this. Despite being well prepared and having all the facts in the presentation for agreement at the Executive Board meeting, the Head of Procurement had failed to recognise the different cognitive frames of the board members and indeed that the "one-size-fits-all style of presentation did not engage everyone.

The proposal was in part accepted, but did not allow the project to proceed. Subsequently the project was re-presented and the Executive Board were counselled one by one on their support. This change of approach recognised their cognitive frames and specific interests geographically, allowing a much shorter presentation 6 months later which went on to be approved.

In summary, the project proceeded but had skipped a financial year and had a much slower than designed implementation. Not a total loss, but a severe setback.

Paradoxical: In this case a seasoned Interim Chief Procurement Officer (CPO) was charged with organising an e-auction for Energy provision of a retail organisation with over 300 outlets in the UK. No other members of the team had any experience of the market or the use of e-auction tools/portals, lot structures, etc. The CPO did have this experience, and had worked in many sectors and across many international markets and had over 20 years' experience lead the project.

The CPO set about defining all the data sets, lot structures, auction timing, bidders, supplier training on the portal and so on, and proceeded to agree a timeframe to ensure that the contract could be awarded in good time before any current contracts expired.

On return of the bids, the revised proposals offered a significant reduction to current pricing (over 15% reduction for a 2 year term) and exceeded original estimates with a cluster of providers within a narrow range of £45,000 to each other. However, on further analysis there was an opportunity to collaborate with an Energy provider who had a considerable domestic and commercial footprint in the UK. This collaboration provided an opportunity to use the energy provider's customer database. Therefore, in the context of a narrow spread of £45,000 on an overall cost of energy in excess of £2-million; giving up £30,000 of that narrow spread was not material on a saving of over £300,000, especially when access to a customer database of 1.8-million contacts was on offer. The deal was signed off within 24 hours by the CFO and CEO.

6.5 Reciprocity

This is a subject I touched upon in more detail in Chapter 3.4, which I have summarised here for completeness.

Consider the simple act of reciprocity, i.e. the giving of something of value to another without being prompted or required to do so. Remember that this action will in itself engender a sense of commitment, trust and high likelihood that they too will reward you with something you value, without great effort on your part, usually with little or no cost attached.

In concluding this chapter, you will now recognise the importance and impact of your own behaviours and biases. Recognising that this is in addition to the following 3 chapters on group, institutional and societal biases hopefully brings into focus the complexity and importance of the people skills needed.

As you reflect upon your cognitive frame and how you can improve it through diversity of roles and experiences, to simply being able to recognise your biases more readily is essential. Also, reflect on who that objective peer or friend is that will help you reflect more accurately on your own behavioural profile.

CHAPTER 7 | GROUP BIASES

7.1 Overview

In this section, I will deal with all those aspects that I believe are generally attributed to situations where there is a group dynamic, which builds on the self-biases in the previous chapter – recognising of course that some of the biases are not confined to group situations alone, but are simply more evident in these types of scenarios.

This moves away from the self-centric approach and begins to build a picture across more than one dimension. This continues in subsequent chapters to expose the rich tapestry of biases that could all be evident in one event or a series of events. This approach I believe will help you assimilate and digest what you would otherwise see as a very complex multi-layered conversion of biases.

This is what I believe we need to consider for groups when we are looking at bias management:

Shared information bias
Cheerleader effect
Not invented here/ IKEA effect
Pro-innovation bias
Reactive devaluation
Peltzman effect
Semmelweis reflex
Group attribution error
Outgroup homogeneity bias
Zero sum heuristic
Ingroup bias

Table 7.1. Bias Management considerations

As you will have gleaned in the previous chapter, the effect of biases is significant and in the group context it is no less impactful, but from a different perspective. Trust remains one of the core aspects, as it interplays between the individuals across the team or teams, in both internal and external contexts.

In providing an overview and definitions of the group biases, you'll begin to understand, recognise and adapt some of these behaviours to your team, or simply observe them for future reference and mitigation. Let's explore some of these group biases in a little more detail:

Group attribution error refers to people's tendency to believe either that the characteristics of an individual group member are reflective of the group as a whole, or that a group's decision outcome must reflect the preferences of individual group members, even when information is available that suggests otherwise.

The fundamentals of the attribution error are similar in that it refers to the tendency to believe that an individual's actions are representative of the individual's preferences, even when available information suggests that an individual's actions were as a consequence of other non-personal influences. It is accepted that there are two forms of group attribution error.

In the first instance the group attribution error (proposed by Ruth Hamill, Richard E. Nisbett, and Timothy DeCamp Wilson in 1980[1]) people associate a perspective based on non-related evidence of the occurrence of a group attributable error; and in the second case people tend to assume incorrectly that group decisions reflect group members' attitudes (proposed by Scott T. Allison and David Messick in 1985[2]). Subsequently, Corneille et al[3] conducted further studies that suggest that threatening groups are viewed as being both more extreme and more homogeneous.

In essence, the fundamental group attribution error results when you see the behaviour of a single person, and immediately project that person's traits to the entire group. For example, at a meeting you might see a group of people having an informal discussion in open forum, where one of them is particularly obnoxious, loud and vocal. This could potentially cause you and the rest of the people in the same meeting to assume that the entire group is similarly "aggressive", rather than just the one individual, as you might "generalise" or group one person's behaviour as representative of the whole group.

The bottom line for most of these biases is that you shouldn't take anything at face value, or trust your instincts too much. Most of your instincts are based on evolutionarily advantageous cognitive functions, which means when it comes to the logic and rational elements, our minds can't be trusted. So, buyer be aware!

1. Hamill, Ruth; Wilson, Timothy D.; Nisbett, Richard E. (1980). "Insensitivity to sample bias: Generalizing from atypical cases" in *Journal of Personality and Social Psychology 39* (4): 578–589. doi:10.1037/0022-3514.39.4.578.

2. Allison, Scott T; Messick, David M. (1985). "The group attribution error" in *Journal of Experimental Social Psychology 21* (6): 563–579. doi:10.1016/0022-1031(85)90025-3

3. Corneille, Olivier; Yzerbyt, Vincent Y.; Rogier, Anouk; Buidin, Genevieve. (2001). "Threat and the Group Attribution Error: When Threat Elicits Judgments of Extremity and Homogeneity" in *Personality and Social Psychology Bulletin 27* (4): 437–446. doi:10.1177/0146167201274005.

Semmelweis reflex or "Semmelweis effect" is a metaphor for the reflex-like tendency to reject new evidence or new knowledge because it contradicts established ways of working, or the usual "how things work around here" and is not the norm or belief held by others in the group.

The term originated from the story of Ignaz Semmelweis, who discovered that childbed fever mortality rates reduced ten-fold when doctors washed their hands with a chlorine solution between patients and, most particularly, after an autopsy (at the institution where Semmelweis worked, a university hospital, surgeons/doctors performed autopsies on every deceased patient).

Semmelweis's decision stopped the ongoing contamination of patients. His hand-washing suggestions were rejected by doctors of his time, often for non-medical reasons. For instance, some doctors refused to believe that a gentleman's hands could transmit disease! Clearly, we now know better than this, and more besides.

In an everyday situation there are similarities with the "not invented here" effect, but we have all been in situations where – as a new person in a company – we face a wall of culture that simply repeats what has gone before, rejecting any suggestion of new ideas, even in the face of evidence which suggests otherwise.

Pro-innovation bias – in diffusion of innovation theory, a pro-innovation bias is the belief that an innovation should be adopted by the whole society without the need for any alteration. The innovation's "champion" has such strong bias in favour of the innovation, that the innovator themselves cannot or may not see its limitations or weaknesses, and despite all of these continues to promote.

Often, in looking at different options and alternatives to deliver the functionality needed by a business, many ideas may be generated and sometimes people can get carried away with what they see as a good idea, despite the fact that it is obvious to the wider group there are either better ideas, or that the proposed idea has too many flaws to be viable.

(Not invented here)/IKEA effect means that you can put a disproportionally higher value on something you personally work on over and above that which may have come from another team member.

In reality this can mean that you become too attached to something or an approach that is not delivering, or is unlikely to succeed. This results in the classic "not invented here" type of rejection, as well as disregarding the ideas of others in favour of your own failing ones!

Cheerleader effect – People and their ideas can be seen as more attractive when they're part of a group than when they're alone. This is supported by research developed in this area, published in *Psychological Science*, a journal of the

Association for Psychological Science. This phenomenon – first dubbed the "cheerleader effect" by lady killer Barney Stinson on the popular TV show *How I Met Your Mother* – suggests that having a few friends around might be an easy way to boost perceived attractiveness.

According to Drew Walker and Edward Vul[4] of the University of California, people tend to "average out" the features of faces in a group, thereby perceiving an individual's face as more average than they would be otherwise.

While being average-looking might seem like a bad thing, research suggests that's not necessarily the case for attractiveness:

"Average faces are more attractive, likely due to the averaging out of unattractive idiosyncrasies… perhaps it's like Tolstoy's families: Beautiful people are all alike, but every unattractive person is unattractive in their own way."

Walker and Vul suspected that the attractiveness of average faces coupled with the tendency to encode groups of objects as an "ensemble" might actually support the cheerleader effect.

In several experiments, Walker and Vul discovered that the pictures don't need to be from a cohesive group portrait to obtain this effect. When participants were asked to rate the attractiveness of one person out of a collage of 4, 9, and 16 pictures, the "group" picture was still rated more highly than when an individual's picture was presented alone.

To quote Walker and Vul: *"If the average is more attractive because unattractive idiosyncrasies tend to be averaged out, then individuals with complimentary facial features – one person with narrow eyes and one person with wide eyes, for example – would enjoy a greater boost in perceived attractiveness when seen together, as compared to groups comprised of individuals who have more similar features."*

We tend to judge (teams and companies) by how we perceive the group as well as the individuals we interact with. It follows then that a friendly set of faces to work with, who are open and engaged, makes a big difference to how we respond in both a social and a business context. This notion supports the adage or sentiment that "people buy from people". We need a connection as well as trust and other attributes such as empathy, being treated fairly, etc. to make a positive impact.

Ingroup bias - This simple but powerful concept impacts people, groups and perhaps society as a whole. Ingroup bias is simply our tendency to favour a group with which one feels a sense of affinity and belonging.

This refers to any group with whom one associates with at a particular time. So, for example, if you work with a Specific Interest Group (SIG) on Corporate Social Responsibility (CSR) then you will have an affinity with that group. Or,

4. D. Walker, E. Vul. (2013). "Hierarchical Encoding Makes Individuals in a Group Seem More Attractive" in *Psychological Science, 2013*; DOI: 10.1177/0956797613497969

perhaps you might be working on something larger, perhaps on an international scale. Affinities can occur between different professional bodies, alliances or approaches advocated by such groups, and can impact, for example, which codes or standards they collectively recognise or not.

Zero-sum heuristic (also known as zero-sum bias) – here the behaviour reflects something approaching a zero-sum game. The mindset is 'one person's gain would be another person's loss'.

The term, as its name suggests, is derived from Game Theory (see chapter 10). However, unlike the Game Theory concept, zero-sum thinking refers to a psychological construct in which a person's subjective interpretation of a situation is captured "your gain is my loss" (or conversely, "your loss is my gain"). This was more recently defined in 2015 by Rozycka-Tran et al as zero-sum thinking:

> "A general belief system about the antagonistic nature of social relations, shared by people in a society or culture and based on the implicit assumption that a finite amount of goods exists in the world, in which one person's winning makes others the losers, and vice versa. Hence, a relatively permanent and general conviction that social relations are like a zero-sum game. People who share this conviction believe that success, especially economic success, is possible only at the expense of other people's failures."

This is clearly an overly simplistic way of thinking, and if observed can be seen as a very aggressive or hostile style or approach, particularly in negotiations.

Here are some examples of the concept of zero-sum thinking:

- In a negotiation when one negotiator thinks that they can only gain at the expense of the other party (i.e. that mutual gain is not possible).
- Jack of all trades, master of none: the idea that having more skills means having less aptitude (also known as compensatory reasoning). This belies the reference to generalists versus specialists and how this is perceived in society as a whole.
- Regarding copyright infringement, the idea that every download is a lost sale.
- Group membership is sometimes treated as zero-sum, such that stronger membership in one group is seen as weaker membership in another.

The zero-sum bias can be seen from two perspectives:
Firstly, in terms of ultimate causation, zero-sum thinking might be a legacy

of human evolution. Specifically, it might be understood to be a psychological adaptation that facilitated successful resource competition in the environment of ancestral humans, where resources like mates, status, and food were perpetually scarce.

Secondly, zero-sum thinking can also be understood in terms of proximate causation, which refers to the developmental history of individuals within their own lifetime. The proximate causes of zero-sum thinking include the experiences that individuals have with resource allocations, as well as their beliefs about specific situations, or their beliefs about the world in general.

More recently, Rozycka-Tran et al (2015) conducted a cross-cultural study that compared the responses of individuals in 37 nations to a scale of zero-sum beliefs. This scale asked individuals to report their agreement with statements that measured zero-sum thinking. For example, the "Successes of some people are usually failures of others". Rozycka-Tran found that individuals in countries with lower Gross Domestic Product showed stronger zero-sum beliefs on average, suggesting that "the belief in zero-sum game seems to arise in countries with lower income, where resources are scarce". Similarly, Rozycka-Tran found that individuals with lower socioeconomic status displayed stronger zero-sum beliefs.

When individuals think that a situation is zero-sum, they are more likely to act competitively (or less cooperatively) towards others, because they will see others as a competitive threat – for example, when suppliers are being assessed against fixed and rigid criteria for a selection of work packages, which calls for collaboration between them (or a range of suppliers) they are less likely to be open to the option of divided work packages rather than a single award, as this the divided package represents a loss in total terms.

7.2 Planning Fallacy and GroupThink

A number of the group-related biases we have explored so far can have negative consequences of a far greater magnitude (rather than positive outcomes). This is especially true when compared to the impact in an identical situation or scenario between two individuals. Furthermore, in addition to this, Planning Fallacy and GroupThink perhaps have the greatest significance and detrimental impact of all on organisations, given the propensity and potential when combined. In a similar way to chapter 7.1, I will provide an overview, with some related examples.

The Planning Fallacy is the tendency of individuals to underestimate the duration that is needed to complete most tasks (see Kahneman and Tversky,

1979). For example, if individuals predict they will complete a task within three weeks, the activity might actually require a month or more. Several factors reduce this Planning Fallacy. For example, individuals are less likely to underestimate the time that needs to be devoted to tasks after they consider three obstacles or more that could potentially affect negatively the progress of a task, project or programme. Additionally, the Planning Fallacy is increased in team settings too. In essence the Planning Fallacy is an issue as individuals do not set themselves enough time to complete key tasks, exacerbating pressure and stress.

Conversely, in some instances, the Planning Fallacy can accelerate progress, when individuals estimate they will complete a task within a short period, they generally deliver the outcomes in shorter time periods, the caveat being that this only applies to activities that are a one-off single session exercise, not a whole programme.

There are several possible factors that this may be attributed to:

1. Focalism – people end up focusing too much on the task in hand and as a consequence lose sight of the overall time needed to complete the whole outcome or project/programme. The task in hand is seen as unique and not something more general or doesn't accurately relate similar tasks from previous exercises – looking at things through "rose-tinted glasses" and as a consequence underestimating due optimism bias and ignoring the difficulties they encountered, revealing only the positive aspects of what happened.

2. Secondly, when they construct plans that have best possible outcomes and neglect to consider real alternatives or options and have no plan 'B'. They might, therefore, underrate the likelihood of unexpected but plausible complications and obstacles.

3. Thirdly, other factors such as bonuses and incentives, established as part of the pay structure of a person, amplify the Planning Fallacy in the manager's attempt to deliver quickly and secure their bonus. Again, if this is related to a single one-off task then the converse would be true. However, this is unlikely in most projects or programmes due to the nature of multiple activities, etc.

4. Another factor that tends to distort outcomes is the perceived (or perhaps real) power derived from leading or managing a group. The incumbents can amplify this effect especially if they are new to the role and are eager to impress. They fall prey to lack of consideration for the broader issues and end up focusing inordinately on the principal goals, disregarding other peripheral sources of information.

Getting into the detail and ensuring that there are robust and early reviews of a programme or plan will help alleviate these pitfalls and bring a sense of realism to the team. Equally, breaking things down into "smaller" tasks that can be assimilated more easily, as well as bringing a sense of sequence and prioritisation of tasks will help too.

Finally getting people to agree to what and when they can deliver, reminding them of pre-existing tasks and priorities and bring a sense of realism to the task(s) in hand can pay dividends. A difficult task provokes a sense of unease, usually interpreted as a problem or complication, diminishing optimism and offsetting the Planning Fallacy.

The Planning Fallacy has been well researched and overestimates of time can be quite substantial. Nevertheless, when the task is completed over an extended time, this fallacy is especially pronounced and as a consequence infuriating to stakeholders and manages in equal measure.

GroupThink – a term coined by social psychologist Irving Janis (1972)[5], occurs when a group makes faulty (sub-optimal) decisions based on 'group' pressures, which lead to a deterioration of "mental efficiency", resulting in poor evaluations and inappropriate benchmarks and perhaps even a lack of moral judgment.

GroupThink is likely when the members are from a similar background (creating poor cognitive diversity), rendering the group insulated from disparate opinion, which leads to fuddled principles and rules for decision-making.

Janis has documented eight 'symptoms' of GroupThink, which are set out below:

1. Illusion of invulnerability – Creates excessive optimism that encourages taking extreme risks.
2. Collective rationalization – Members discount warnings and do not reconsider their assumptions.
3. Belief in inherent morality – Members believe in the rightness of their cause and therefore ignore the ethical or moral consequences of their decisions.

5. Janis, Irving L. (1972). *Victims of GroupThink; a psychological study of foreign-policy decisions and fiascos.* Boston: Houghton, Mifflin. ISBN 0-395-14002-1.
Additionally:
Janis, Irving L. (1982). *GroupThink: Psychological Studies of Policy Decisions and Fiascos. Second Edition.* New York: Houghton Mifflin.
Hart, P. (1994). *Government: A study of small groups and policy failure.* Baltimore: The John Hopkins University Press
Ahlfinger, N. R. and Esser, J. K. (2001). Testing the GroupThink model: Effects of promotional leadership and conformity predisposition. *Social Behaviour and Personality: An International Journal, 29(1),* 31-42.

4. Stereotyped views of out-groups – Negative views of "enemy" make effective responses to conflict seem unnecessary.
5. Direct pressure on dissenters – Members are under pressure not to express arguments against any of the group's views.
6. Self-censorship – Doubts and deviations from the perceived group consensus are not expressed.
7. Illusion of unanimity – The majority view and judgments are assumed to be unanimous.
8. Self-appointed 'mind-guards' – Members protect the group and the leader from information that is problematic or contradictory to the group's cohesiveness, view, and/or decisions.

Where these symptoms exist, consortium is likely to fall into the GroupThink modus. GroupThink occurs when groups are highly cohesive and where they are under considerable pressure to make a decision. When pressures for unanimity seem overwhelming, members are less motivated to realistically appraise the alternative courses of action available to them.

These group pressures lead to carelessness and irrational thinking since GroupThink by its very nature fails to consider alternatives in their effort to maintain unanimity. It goes without saying that these decisions have a low probability of achieving successful outcomes.

Group think can be notably seen to exist in situations like the decisions of governments to go to war; Iraq and Afghanistan in recent times are probably the most notable examples. In corporate terms, this may relate to a decision to pursue a decision or project that is a course or a direction, such as buying a small business that is not core, but is something that becomes the pet project of a board member – however nobody can truly make the case under "normal rules" to proceed with the purchase.

Janis compiled a 'warning' signs list to help eliminate the pitfalls of GroupThink:

a) An incomplete survey of alternatives.
b) An incomplete survey of objectives.
c) Failure to examine risks of preferred choice.
d) Failure to reappraise initially rejected alternatives.
e) Poor information search.
f) Selective bias in processing the information at hand.
g) Failure to work out contingency plans.
h) Low probability of successful outcome.

Appended below are a series of approaches that can help avoid the trap of GroupThink:

- The leader should assign the role of critical evaluator to each member.
- The leader should avoid stating preferences and expectations at the outset.
- Each member of the group should routinely discuss the groups' deliberations with a trusted associate and report back to the group on the associate's reactions.
- One or more experts should be invited to each meeting on a staggered basis. The outside experts should be encouraged to challenge views of the members.
- At least one articulate and knowledgeable member should be given the role of devil's advocate (to question assumptions and plans).
- The leader should make sure that a sizeable block of time is set aside to survey warning signals from rivals; leader and group construct alternative scenarios of rivals' intentions.

7.3 Peltzman Effect (Risk Compensation)

The significant reference in the context of this risk related attribute is set out by economist Sam Peltzman[6]. Peltzman's 1975 work is the seminal text regarding *risk compensation,* where he focused on the impact of *'feeling safer'.* Using the example of the legislation regarding drivers and passengers wearing seat belts, he showed that if people believe they can "afford" to drive more recklessly as a result of wearing them, they will.

The illusion of safety afforded by the "Peltzman effect" reflects the behaviour of people who believe a risk has been mitigated by intervention (and do not revisit it or monitor the risk) and then close their minds to it.

From personal experience, the only parallel I can draw to this is when I have seen team members pass a large problem or issue across from one group to another, or to the sponsor, in the belief that they can fix it. The intention here is to mitigate any risk that they perceived, given that they have a belief that this action would avoid any potential derailing of the project.

Risk allocation can often be assigned on a "deal with it" basis by senior management. The senior managers then observe the programme's progress from afar, whilst allowing themselves the luxury of the 'not-my-problem' standpoint in the hope that somebody else will mitigate the risk to ensure the success of their project. This may be a form of naivety, but not a conclusive outcome, nevertheless.

---

6. Peltzman, Sam (1975). "The Effects of Automobile Safety Regulation". *Journal of Political Economy. 83* (4): 677–726. doi:10.1086/260352. JSTOR 1830396.

7.4 Bringing it all together

Perhaps the most pernicious of all biases and most difficult to overcome is the "not invented here" mind-set. In polite company these people are to referred to as 'traditionalists'. They tend to be people who have been in the same industry, sector or role for a substantial period of time and whilst they have been successful for one reason or another, they cannot accommodate the potential of alternative points of view.

Consequently, these established groups or networks hold onto what is 'known' in favour of something new or better, and are characterised by their fundamental distrust of change. This resistance to a change in routine, to "everyday" work patterns, will be a recurring theme in this book; but as you will begin to see there are reasonable scientific markers that make this mind-set prevalent, and to some acceptable.

The power of a group who arrive at the same decision point for the wrong reason can be a difficult one to assuage, but with careful planning prior to any meeting this can be successfully challenged with the use of techniques such as those highlighted in chapter 15 e.g. pre-mortems, face-to-face pre-meetings on a 1-2-1 basis and so forth, pre-circulation of relevant alternatives that have been adopted successfully by the competition, etc. – these can all add to re-balancing of the situation.

We also need to recognise that people will "defend" and idea or an approach, especially if it has been *in situ* for some time. This can be for a plethora of reasons and I have detailed some below:

a)   We were doing it wrong or inefficiently before now.
b)   I was here and part of the previous group that agreed that this was 'best practice' at the time.
c)   I like the way things are done and understand it.
d)   It's not broken so why fix it? (not invented here).
e)   This is embarrassing – why didn't I spot there was a better way of doing things?

The list above is not exhaustive, but clearly the reality of 'challenge' to the *status quo* can and will be interpreted "negatively", so the language and/or approach must be sensitised to take account of this – a fact that can be overlooked by even the most seasoned professional. This sometimes only becomes clear when you step back from the situation.

And yet when you are part of a group or interfacing with a group of people, objectivity is often lost in the pursuit of logic and rational thoughts that demonstrate a different way of working., especially when the proximity to the original situation is distant.

The not-so-simple task of understanding the origins of an approach or arrangement, or indeed the 'who and how', can go a long way to designing an approach that recognises this and helps shape the approach and the desired change.

From a practical point of view, leaders need to realise the impact they have on the dynamics of the group. They must weigh-up how "dominant" they may appear to other members, even if this is not their intention. Sometimes leaders need to be overtly aware of the impact they have on teams and groups and take action to mitigate it.

Simple things like stepping out of the room after having framed an issue allows others to openly debate the options. Allow people to report back anonymously or instil a sense of trust in the team and enable others to develop and become more capable as a consequence of their candour and overt involvement.

Finally, the dynamics of diverse cultures and social norms can also be a factor – that requires consideration too.

In summary, we can recognise that the increased risk(s) associated with the approaches towards risk management that follow a formulaic, non-dynamic approach is that they are largely ineffective. Equally, we can be fooled into thinking that because we have carried out a prescribed task, without real consideration of "logical" and "rational" as a consequence of action, there can be no further consequence.

This false sense of security is scientifically misplaced. Furthermore the fact that as a group or team, because we have "collaborated" (albeit in a biased way), we have again ensured project success, is also misplaced. It is, I believe, these misplaced mental comforts that create the greatest threats and surprises to outcomes.

CHAPTER 8 | SOCIETAL BIASES

8.1 Overview and the Significance of Trust

In this chapter, I will deal with those aspects that I believe are generally attributed to situations where there is a wider societal impact and/or attribution, which builds on the self-biases and group biases in the previous chapters. Within this, I do recognise, of course, that some of the biases are not confined to these types of situations alone, but are just generally more evident in this context.

This moves away from the self-centric or smaller group environments and moves into a wider public domain, thus continuing to build a picture across more dimensions. I will then conclude with what I refer to as Institutional Biases, to complete the most relevant and/or prevalent of biases in a commercial context.

This approach I believe will help you to continue to assimilate and digest what would otherwise be seen as a very complex multi-layered conversion of biases.

In this chapter I also set out why I believe trust is a fundamental element of everything, as a prerequisite.

This is what I believe we need to consider for groups when we are looking at bias management, across society as a whole:

Negativity effect (bias)
Availability cascade
Diclinism
Clustering illusion
Framing effect
Loss aversion
Sociability bias of language
Bandwagon effect

Table 8.1. Societal biases

In attempting to address the biases that operate across society at large, we need to recognise the influences and biases that affect us all, as well as the ways in which they presented to us. Some common examples include:

- Website pop-up ads (nudging)
- The Media
- Sponsorship of "white papers" on matters pertaining to the area of interest to the sponsor.
- Proportionality of information on particular topics.
- Professional opinions or advice e.g. regarding suppliers or service provision.

Looking at some of the more specific biases we will again see that there is a "layering" of biases and effects that distort our objectivity or rationality, and as such we need to be aware of these factors. I will pick out what I believe to be the most salient from a Purchasing and Supply Chain Management perspective.

I have detailed below the topics identified above as they relate to specific biases, and provided some detail regarding their impact.

The Negativity effect – Why do insults, offensive statements or inflammatory remarks, once levelled against us, stick with us for an inordinate period of time? Perhaps the answer is quite simple. The more negative/offensive the comment/ remark, the bigger the impact it has in our minds and our concept of 'self'. Take for example the saying, "Bad news sells better than good news every time" – this is a phenomenon that relates to our own "negativity bias"; i.e. our brains respond with far greater sensitivity upon hearing unpleasant news. The bias is automatic and inbuilt, and has been detected in humans at the earliest stage of the brain's information processing.

Illustrating this with a few examples will help set the principles. Imagine you are asked to view three sets of images:

- The first set contains things known to arouse positive feelings (say, a sports car, or a favourite meal).
- The second set containing images known to stimulate negative feelings (a mutilated face or dead animal).
- The third set contains images known to produce neutral feelings (a plate, a hair dryer).

In a study carried out by Dr John T. Cacioppo at the University of Chicago, he was able to record neural activity in the brain's cerebral cortex that reflected the magnitude of information processing taking place as each of the sets of images were viewed. What his study showed was that our brains will be more stimulated by the negative image, and less so by the more pleasant or neutral images.

Our capacity to evaluate negative inputs so heavily most likely evolved to keep us out of harm's way. From the dawn of human history, our very survival depended on our ability to avoid danger. The brain developed systems that would make it unavoidable for us not to notice danger and thus respond to it. We can consider this to be the early barometer of response.

I feel it is safe to assume our subconscious mind recognises the criticality in getting the ratio of good and bad news in place as soon as possible. In social partnerships, we usually operate at a ratio of 1:5 in terms of bad references to good references. It follows that there is a tipping point in (working) relationships and we need to understand this. As I have already alluded to in earlier chapters, we must ensure that any intended communication is phrased correctly, that it must not be misconstrued, misheard or misinterpreted from the outset. Therefore, thinking through what you are going to say and how it may be received by the other party, is of paramount importance.

I will use a recent example which occurred while writing this book, where a respected senior practitioner asked me to speak at a gathering of the "good and great" of a professional institute in London. All the planning was going well, with nothing out of the ordinary – they declared that they little knowledge about the subject in detail, and implied therefore that they were happy for me to proceed with my preparations without input from their side. Then, without warning, they suddenly demanded, with non-negotiable terms, that they needed to see my presentation prior to the delivery thereof.

On the face of this I could have taken it very negatively – making the assumption that they did not trust me to do a competent job. However, what transpired was that the organiser, in a number of presentations prior to mine, had fallen foul of heavy sales pitches rather than an appropriate level of insight and engagement on a professional level. Not wanting to fall foul of this again, this was the mechanism chosen to avoid the issue. Although this is understandable, the method for presenting this parameter could elicit a very negative reaction from prospective presenters!

However, had the organiser said, "Can I just clarify that there isn't any direct or indirect selling in your presentation, as previous presentations have suffered negative feedback as a consequence" coupled with "And I know you wouldn'twant that, given your professionalism", it's likely that the reaction would be different as the negative bias is avoided.

Clustering illusion – This is a cognitive bias, which occurs as a consequence of seeing a pattern where one does not actually exist. Sometimes when we see what is actually a random sequence of numbers or events, we misconstrue this to be pattern. It is a form of apophenia[1] related to the Gambler's Fallacy (see chapter 11).

---

1. The tendency to attribute meaning to perceived connections or patterns between seemingly unrelated things. Confirmation bias is a variation of apophenia. Conrad, Klaus .(1958). *The onset of schizophrenia: an attempt to form an analysis of delusion.* Stuttgart: Georg Thieme Verlag. OCLC 14620263.

A simple way to understand this illusion is to imagine casting one hundred coins of exactly the same denomination into a square meter space. Unless all of the coins fall in an exactly even distribution, which is extremely improbable, some coins will be closer to each other than others, and therefore appear to form a cluster or group despite their random distribution.

This phenomenon is sometimes called the "hot hand fallacy" due to the belief common among sports coaches, managers and/or players that it was best to use 'in form' players, those as they say are 'on a hot streak' – a term coined from this behaviour by coaches of American basketball teams. A study demonstrated that the 'hot hand' trend was in fact the result of the coaches selecting a short run of baskets scored from a much larger sequence that was more or less random. Randomness is not such an intuitive concept for humans. In addition to being poor at recognising random sequences for what they are, people are also bad at generating random numbers as a practice *per se*.

In the pursuit of analysing data, we can sometimes try to read too much into a small sample, perhaps because that's all we have. Consequently, we then draw false conclusions, claiming that a trend exists where better analysis would obviate the randomness that actually exists. We are unable to make any sound deductions or conclusions because we were looking for something that doesn't exist. The danger with this is, of course, that you build a plan or an approach based on a false set of assumptions or evaluations to find that you have to retract something. This is clearly more detrimental than simply calling it what it is: random!

Below I have set out a practical approach regarding this phenomenon, for example as would be applied when looking to award a contract.

Imagine we have developed a contract. As a given we have constructed it on appropriate criteria which meet the needs of the business; however central to the establishment of this arrangement we wish to develop it on the basis of the realisation of quality data.

We need this data to enable us to make an informed decision in the future, let's say for the sake of argument in 12 to 18 months. In taking this approach, we are looking to mitigate risk and facilitate a more effect decision-making process based on this better quality data we have obtained. One shouldn't feel the urge to simply act. There are many courses of action one may take and many of these are far more considered and productive than the knee-jerk reaction people can feel pressured into.

Bandwagon effect – This reflects what researchers have long identified as the impact of social conformity in shaping how people think and act. Along with explaining new trends in fashion or popular fads, this bandwagon effect can also influence how people would be likely to vote on important issues. This process of voting no different to the process of gaining votes for an agreement to a business case or decision, etc. – with the purpose of recognising and gaining support and momentum to shape an approach or new way of working in an organisation. This normally takes place at a leadership level or with key stakeholders. Similarly, where you are appealing to a wider stakeholder group, many voters often opt not to make an informed choice before agreeing to a change in vendor, system, etc. – invariably they simply choose who or which group/influencer to follow by adopting the behaviour of other more influential people.

The bandwagon effect follows the rules and principles developed in Social Impact Theory[2]. Social impact theory was created by Mariah Castonguay in 1981 and consists of four basic rules which consider how individuals can be "sources or targets of social influence", where social impact is the result of social forces including:

- The strength of the source of impact.
- The immediacy of the event.
- The number of sources exerting the impact.
- The more targets of impact that exist, the less impact each individual target has.

Social impact theory uses mathematical equations to predict the level of social impact created by specific social situations. The theory was further developed in 1981 by Bibb Latané. Latané described social impact as a phenomenon in which people affect one another in social situations through daily experiences such as embarrassment, persuasion, humour, and a many other experience, which can be seen by the number of situations that are governed by the presence and actions of others. The impact can not only be observed visually, it also alters 'forces' within the target such as thoughts, attitudes, incentives and physiological states. Latané noticed that social impact was governed by three laws that can be translated into mathematical equations.

Essentially these equations reflect Strength (influence, power, or intensity perceives the source to possess), Immediacy (how recent the event occurred and whether or not there were other intervening factors) and People (the number of people exerting social influence on the target).

Subsequent to the original research, Latané and his colleagues, in 1996, developed the Dynamic Social Impact Theory (DSIT)[3] as an extension of the Social Impact Theory (as it uses its basic principles). DSIT proposes that groups are complex systems that are constantly changing and never static, which I

2. Latané, B.; L' Herrou, T. (1996). "Spatial clustering in the conformity game: Dynamic social impact in electronic games" in *Journal of Personality and Social Psychology. 70:* 1218–1230. doi:10.1037/0022-3514.70.6.1218.

3. Latané, B. (1996a). "Dynamic social impact: The creation of culture by communication" in *Journal of Communication, 46,* 13–25

believe is more realistic and relevant to most, if not all, commercial situations. Groups that are spatially distributed and interact repeatedly organize and reorganize themselves in FOUR basic patterns (see below): consolidation, clustering, correlation, and continuing diversity. These patterns allow for group dynamics to operate and ideas to be diffused throughout the group.

1. Consolidation – as individuals interact with each other, over time, their actions, attitudes, and opinions become uniform. In this manner, opinions held by the majority of the group spread to the minority, which then decreases in size.
2. Clustering – individuals tend to interact with clusters of group members with similar opinions. Clusters are common when group members communicate more frequently with members in close proximity, and less frequently with members who are more distant. Minority group members are often shielded from majority influence due to clustering. Therefore, subgroups can emerge which may possess similar ideas to one another, but hold different beliefs than the majority population.
3. Correlation – over time, individual group members' opinions on a variety of issues converge and correlate with each other; this is true even of issues that are not discussed by the group.
4. Continuing Diversity – a degree of diversity can exist within a group if minority group members cluster together or minority members who communicate with majority members resist majority influence. However, if the majority is large or minority members are physically isolated from one another, this diversity drops.

Therefore, setting this into the context of an organisation: if a stakeholder or budget holder (owning a significant or larger slice of the budget to other divisions or departments) is seen as having majority support, he or she is seen in an "influencing light" more positively, and is more likely to get uncommitted or undecided followers' support. In essence, everybody likes to align with where the majority decision is headed.

8.2 Framing Effect

This is essentially the way in which an argument and/or proposal has been drafted to present choices to a recipient, and whether it has been couched as a potential loss or as a potential gain. In every scenario, individuals will react differently when a choice is presented to them as a loss, and a different reaction when that same choice is represented as a gain. Kahneman and Tversky's original experiment presented the problem of an impending outbreak in the United States of an unnamed disease that would kill 600 people, to illustrate how framing works. Two program options were presented to participants:

If Program A is adopted, 200 people will be saved. If Program B is adopted, there is a one-third probability that 600 people will be saved and a two-thirds probability that nobody will be saved.

Kahneman and Tversky found that respondents were risk averse in their decision-making, with 72% of respondents selecting program A and 28% selecting program B. In other words, you are more likely to avoid a risk when the framing is positive and more likely to take that same risk when the framing is negative. As expected, preferences are risk averse: with a clear majority of respondents preferring to save 200 lives for sure, over a gamble that offers a one-third chance of saving 600 lives.

Translating this into an everyday situation such as shopping, you might see the framing effect in advertising – supermarkets present potential customers with both a sale price and the higher comparison price. This provides the consumer with the expected gain of saving money on an item that they need (or maybe that they just really want). The framing of the price also plays a role in how it is interpreted. For example, offering "free" items with the purchase of one item can take the focus from the price of what is usually the more expensive item and shift it to the perceived special offer. Another example in retail are offers that give you free shipping or Buy One Get One Free (BOGOF).

Procurement professionals can use to effectively "frame" their communication and increase the effectiveness of acceptance by stakeholders. By communicating necessary courses of action as potential gains – for example how specific project will benefit the delivery of stated objectives or outcomes, rather than as a potential loss or neutral impact – they can improve stakeholder buy-in without removing the ethical and objective aspects of the project.

Another key part here is the tone or manner in which it is delivered. This resonates so much with some peers in the profession I know, who will be alert to a great approach, but their voice tone and physical body language can adversely affect the approach and in some cases, consign something really great to the grave.

As part of the approach, and as stated by the *Harvard Business Review*, framing also involves identifying potential problems in workflow prior to them actually occurring and offering solutions to them upfront. A leader skilled at framing anticipates what those obstacles will be and uses framing techniques to help team members involved in implementation and/or operation of the solution to navigate around them.

The leader begins by isolating the issue and framing it so everyone understands it and its relevance to their own work. Then the team leader needs to set out all the options for removing the obstacles, either by directly recommending courses of action or by posing questions that guide others to find them – often this is the better option as it drives ownership of the approach and encourages learning.

8.3 Loss Aversion

Loss aversion (see *also* Endowment Effect in self-biases) is a phenomenon that might be translated more commonly as "You don't know what you've got until it's gone".

In economics and decision theory, loss aversion refers to people's tendency to prefer avoiding losses as compared to acquiring equivalent gains: i.e. it's better to not lose €5 than to find €5. Some studies have suggested that losses are twice as powerful, psychologically, as gains – see Negativity Effect above. The term, *loss aversion* was first introduced in 1979 by Tversky and Kahneman in their seminal paper *Prospect Theory: An Analysis of Decision under Risk*[4], and has been researched and commented upon from many fields and people since then.

This leads to risk aversion when people evaluate an outcome comprising similar magnitudes of gains or losses. And, since people prefer avoiding losses to making gains, the choice moves to the avoidance of a loss. Hence, this implies that someone who loses €100 will suffer a greater loss in emotional terms than another person who gains satisfaction from a €100 windfall.

In marketing, the use of trial periods and rebates tries to take advantage of the buyer's tendency to value the good more highly, after the buyer incorporates it into the status quo. In past Behavioural Economics studies, users participate up until the threat of loss equals any incurred gains. Recent methods established by Botond Kőszegi and Matthew Rabin[5] in experimental economics illustrates the role of expectation, wherein an individual's belief about an outcome can create an instance of loss aversion, whether or not a tangible change of state has occurred.

Note that whether a transaction is framed as a loss or as a gain is very important to this calculation: would you rather get a €5 discount, or avoid a €5 surcharge? The same change in price framed differently has a significant effect on consumer behaviour. Though traditional economists consider this "endowment effect" and all other effects of loss aversion to be completely irrational, that is why it is so important to the fields of marketing, finance and indeed now procurement. The

---

4. Kahneman, Daniel and Tversky, Amos. (1979). "Prospect Theory: An Analysis of Decision under Risk" in *Econometrica 47*: 263-91. Prospect Theory is a behavioural economic theory that describes the way people choose between probabilistic alternatives that involve risk, where the probabilities of outcomes are known.
5. Kőszegi, B. and Rabin, M. (2006). "A Model of Reference-dependent Preferences" in *The Quarterly Journal of Economics, Vol. CXXI*: 4.

effect of loss aversion in a marketing setting was demonstrated in a study of consumer reaction to price changes to insurance policies.

The study found price increases had twice the effect on customer switching, compared to price decreases. Similarly, users in behavioural and experimental economics studies decided to cease participation in iterative money-making games when the threat of loss was close to the expenditure of effort, even when the user stood to further their gains.

Understanding that this is a tool to be used by marketers and sales teams in pursuit of contracts for/of services, products, licensing, etc. is of concern, and consequence as to how we objectively breakdown and evaluate these approaches. Equally, as humans we are likely to be hardwired to be loss averse due to asymmetric evolutionary pressure on gains and losses.

In several studies, it was demonstrated that the endowment effect could be explained by loss aversion but not the five alternatives, shown below, to ensure clarity of theory as presented:

1. Transaction costs.
2. Misunderstandings.
3. Habitual bargaining behaviours.
4. Income effects.
5. Trophy effects.

In each experiment, half of the subjects were randomly assigned an item and asked for the minimum amount they would be willing to sell it for, while the other half of the subjects were given nothing and asked for the maximum amount they would be willing to spend to buy the item. Since the value of the item is fixed and individual valuation of the item varies from this fixed value only due to sampling variation, the supply and demand curves should be perfect mirrors of each other and thus half the goods should be traded. The authors also ruled out the explanation that lack of experience with trading would lead to the endowment effect, by conducting repeated markets.

The first two alternative explanations – that under-trading was due to transaction costs or misunderstanding – were tested by comparing goods markets to induced-value markets under the same rules. If it was possible to trade to the optimal level in induced value markets, under the same rules, there should be no difference in goods markets.

The results showed drastic differences between induced-value markets and goods markets. The median prices of buyers and sellers in induced-value markets matched almost every time, leading to near perfect market efficiency. But goods markets sellers had much higher selling prices than buyers' buying prices. This effect was consistent over trials, indicating that this was not due to inexperience with the procedure or the market. Since the transaction cost that could have been due to the procedure was equal in the induced-value and goods markets, transaction costs were eliminated as an explanation for the endowment effect.

The third explanation was that people have habitual bargaining behaviours, such as overstating their minimum selling price or understating their maximum bargaining price, that may spill over from strategic interactions where these behaviours are useful, to the laboratory setting where they are sub-optimal.

An experiment was conducted to address this by having the clearing prices selected at random. Buyers who indicated a willingness-to-pay (WTP) higher than the randomly drawn price got the goods, and vice versa for those who indicated a lower WTP. Likewise, sellers who indicated a lower willingness-to-accept than the randomly drawn price sold the goods and vice versa. This incentive-compatible value elicitation method did not eliminate the endowment effect, but did rule out habitual bargaining behaviour as an alternative explanation.

Income effects were ruled out by giving one third of the participants mugs, one third chocolates, and one third neither a mug nor chocolate. They were then given the option of trading the mug for the chocolate or vice versa and those with neither were asked to merely choose between mug and chocolate. Thus, wealth effects were controlled for those groups who received mugs and chocolate. The results showed that 86% of those starting with mugs chose mugs, 10% of those starting with chocolates chose mugs, and 56% of those with nothing chose mugs. This ruled out income effects as an explanation for the endowment effect. Also, since all participants in the group had the same item, it could not be considered a "trophy", eliminating the final alternative explanation.

Thus, the five different explanations were eliminated in the following ways:

1 and 2: Induced-value market vs. consumption goods market.
3: Incentive-compatible value elicitation procedure.
4 and 5: Choice between endowed or alternative item.

By understanding the buyer-seller axis in this situation, you will begin to see that within the rational and expected (logic) approach to how a sale may be conducted you will observe that there is no true correlation, even there are attempts to mitigate some of the variables. The bottom line in this arena is simply to be aware and understand the variables and approaches being deployed upon you as a procurement agent. Furthermore, there is a compounding effect when we get large groups together, and this needs to be managed. The risk in this situation is that we need to change to a new way of working, but because we are averse to any perceived loss we end up maintaining the status quo of doing nothing, which is often the worst outcome of all!

Accordingly, to avoid the paralysis that may ensue, leaders of change need to ensure that this is not the end result. As change agents we need to consider what levers we can pull to move things forward positively, to overcome the organisation-wide issues such as the following:

- **Exploit unique events to reset the agenda.** For example, use a change in leadership, an acquisition, a profit warning, for example to "jump start" an organisation into action. These are moments when the whole company will embrace change by virtue of its necessity. Redefine the ways of working, policies, etc. as a means or rebasing the approach to a more considered procurement agenda that doesn't just measure bottom line savings.
- **Frame failure-to-transform in terms of losses.** Since individuals value losses more than gains, leaders should frame a change and transformation agenda in terms of what the organisation, and thus the individual, will lose: "If we don't embark upon this new programme, based upon a new approach, e.g. "back to basics" or "whole value chain", etc.
- **Create separate mental and physical spaces for transformation efforts.** This may be signalling the end of an opulent era with a new area of "fit for purpose" by holding a key conference in one of your warehouses and not the usual 5-star palace. Breaking free of what has preceded and setting a new tone is both respectful of those who may have suffered under an unfortunate demise, as well as signposting the change in real terms so that the deeds match the words.
- **Visibly embrace and engage in CEO support for the change, as it is and will be a lonely journey.** Leaders need to encourage and challenge others if they are to persevere against any opposition. Without affirming the need to change, doubts will emerge. Without pressure for bold outcomes, incrementalism will ensure the change and transformation dissipates into obscurity and abject failure. Lastly, employees need both public endorsement and private coaching to implement major change initiatives.

By understanding the behavioural force field you will succeed, but failure to recognise the magnitude of it will be counted long after you have gone!

8.4 Negativity Effect (Bias)

The negativity bias is also known as the negativity effect, and refers to the concept that, even when of equal intensity, things of a more negative nature (e.g. unpleasant thoughts, emotions, conversations, acts, etc.) will have a greater effect on a person's psychological state and processes than do neutral or positive things.

In other words, something very positive will generally have less of an impact on a person's behaviour and cognition than something negative that is equally emotional. This bias has been investigated from many different perspectives, such as attention span, learning, and memory, and decision-making and risk considerations.

Two psychologists, Paul Rozin and Edward Royzman proposed four elements of the negativity bias in order to explain its manifestation: negative potency, steeper negative gradients, negativity dominance, and negative differentiation.

- Negative potency refers to the notion that, while possibly of equal magnitude or emotionality, negative and positive items/events/etc. are not equally impactful.
- Positive and negative gradients – negative events are thought to be perceived as increasingly more negative than positive events are increasingly positive, the closer it gets to an event. For example, the negative experience of an impending dental visit is perceived as increasingly more negative the closer you get to the date, than the positive experience of a party, which is perceived as increasingly more positive the closer to the event but to a lesser magnitude.
- Negativity dominance describes the tendency for the combination of positive and negative items/events/etc. to skew towards an overall more negative feeling. i.e. if you sum the parts you end up with a negative result.
- Negative differentiation suggests that we think of things that are negative in a more elaborate and complex way than we do for positive events. This aspect is quite important for leaders and communicators, as the use of negative vocabulary is more richly descriptive of the affective experience than that of positive vocabulary – i.e. more impactful than any amount of praise or supportive comments we may give.

8.5 Group Serving Biases

In this instance the group constituents will have a (cognitive) tendency that means that they have a bias that contributes to an overvaluing of a person's group. This manifests itself in particular by the tendency to credit the group for its successes, but to blame external factors for its failures.

While this is over-simplistic, we can see how teams that are working on a project "blame" the rest of the organisation for not understanding and buying into the proposed new way of working, or not understanding the benefits of the change, etc. On a more serious note, when individuals are in a serious confrontation, the same actions on both sides are typically attributed to different causes, depending on who is making the attribution, so that reaching a common understanding can become impossible to achieve.

This was a central theme set out in Steven Pinker's book *The Better Angels of Our Nature: Why Violence Has Declined*[6], in which he argues that violence in the world has declined both in the long term and in the short term, and suggests explanations as to why this has occurred. He notes that, paradoxically, increased communication and external political factors focusing on harnessing our better motivations such as empathy and increases in reason, negates conflict.

Pinker himself examines four motives that "can orientate us away from "violence" (or as I would see it the serious disagreements that can be created between teams or groups) and towards cooperation and altruism." In this he identifies:

Empathy: which "prompts us to feel the pain of others and to align their interests with our own."
Self-Control: which "allows us to anticipate the consequences of acting on our impulses and to inhibit them accordingly."
The Moral Sense: which "sanctifies a set of norms and taboos that govern the interactions among people in a culture." These sometimes decrease violence but can also increase it "when the norms are tribal, authoritarian, or puritanical."
Reason: which "allows us to extract ourselves from our parochial vantage points."

The salient part of this introduction is that if we find ourselves in a situation where two groups or segments of a company or project end up in conflict, swift action and effective communication needs to be used to diffuse such situations, just as in the case of more violent conflict as outlined in Pinker's book – the principles are exactly the same.

There is also evidence to suggest that having respect between the groups, for their capabilities and achievements from a professional perspective, as well as a liking for what they do, can be mitigations to any potential conflict.

---

6. Pinker, S. (2012). *The Better Angels of Our Nature: Why Violence Has Declined.* Penguin Books; Reprint edition (September 25, 2012)

CHAPTER 9 | INSTITUTIONAL BIASES

9.1 Overview

In this chapter, I will deal with all those aspects that I believe are generally attributed to situations where there is a more of an institutionalised impact and/or attribution, which builds on self, group and societal biases in the previous chapters.

As before, this recognises of course that some of the biases are not confined to purely institutional situations alone. This moves away from the previous environments and moves into a wider organisational (or institutional) domain, thus completing the picture across all four dimensions. This approach I believe will help you to finalise your understanding of what you would otherwise see as a very complex multi-layered explanation of biases.

This is what I believe we need to consider for groups when we are looking at bias management, across institutions as a whole:

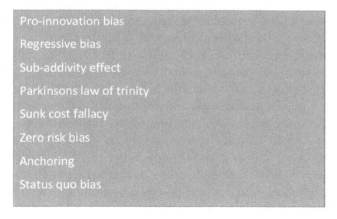

Pro-innovation bias

Regressive bias

Sub-addivity effect

Parkinsons law of trinity

Sunk cost fallacy

Zero risk bias

Anchoring

Status quo bias

Table 9.1. Institutional biases

Pro-innovation bias – this is the belief that an innovation should be adopted by the whole of society without the need for any alteration. The belief of the innovation's "champion" has such strong bias in favour of the innovation, that he/she may not see its limitations or weaknesses, and continues to promote it regardless or seemingly remains unaware of any potential or actual shortfalls.

By illustration, an example from General Motors in 1986, when then-Chairman, Roger Smith, said: "By the turn of the century, we will live in a paperless society." As we all know, this was and remains unrealistic, and shows his blind faith in what technology would do to revolutionise the world, without considering the reasonable limitations of his belief.

In terms of innovations that come about when considering a category of spend, this would be the category leader suggesting that all air travel and so forth will be replaced by video conferencing, leading to substantial savings. The reality is that, despite video conferencing being a viable supplementary meeting tool, we all know that human interaction and the building of trust networks through face-to-face interaction remains the primary method for doing business.

Regressive bias – this is an informal fallacy, and assumes that something has returned to normal because of corrective actions taken while it was abnormal. This fails to account for natural fluctuations. It is frequently a special kind of the *post hoc* fallacy.

Things like cricket scores, the earth's temperature and chronic back pain fluctuate naturally and usually regress towards the mean. The logical flaw is to make predictions that expect exceptional results to continue as if they were the norm/average. In this case though, people are most likely to take action when variance is at its peak. Then, after results become more normal, they believe that their action was the cause of the change when in fact it was not actually a consequence of anything other than a normal regression or re-balancing.

This issue could and has presented itself when dealing with natural commodities such as cocoa, palm oil, wheat, etc. (comparing of course the same grade and quality, etc.). – a typical fixed set of bonuses and objectives might suggest a saving against last year's contract that exceeds 10%, but actually due to a glut caused by favourable temperatures and growing conditions which produced a high yield, prices slump causing a favourable outcome when compared to a previous year.

Demonstrably, this was not a consequence of a good procurement, merely a regression to the norm when viewed over a longer period. The real skill would be to understand a multiple of factors and take more comprehensive actions that produced a layered hedging, even in years when prices rise due to adverse conditions, and thus perform better than market averages.

As the introduction to the above suggests, this is a fallacy when viewed more simplistically and when there is a need to isolate non-influenceable variables. For example, the frequency of accidents on a road fell after a speed camera was installed, therefore the speed camera has improved road safety.

In real terms this is like reporting an exceptional project that was in the pipeline that everybody in the department knew was coming, but was treated by marketing and communications as something exceptional. The downside I have experienced with this is the way it is seen and felt by the area of the business it relates to, and spotlight it puts on them – in certain companies this has a negative impact that jerks the organisation to randomly cutting budgets and damaging the relationship... an area that needs to handled sensitively every time.

Even, if the area of the business is happy with the publicity, remember there are emotions involved in this that should not be under estimated.

Sub-addivity effect is the tendency to judge probability of the whole to be less than the probabilities of the parts; a form of underplaying or watering down what is factually correct. This may happen when a party is trying to minimise a particular project impact, especially when departments are looking to play down an aspect to protect budgets and/or deflect attention to significant improvements that they should have been able to make themselves.

The following example was the way it was originally explained, from which you can see how we would want to be aware that this was happening in a business environment: The subjects in this particular experiment judged the probability of death from cancer in the United States at 18%, from heart attack at 22%, and the probability of death from "other natural causes" at 33%. Other participants judged the probability of death from a natural cause was 58%. Natural causes are made up of precisely cancer, heart attack, and "other natural causes", however, the sum of the last three probabilities was 73%, not 58%. According to Tversky and Koehler (1994), this kind of result is often observed.

In summary, this moves objective evidence (observation) into subjective estimates (judgment).

Parkinson's law (of trinity) is the principle that "work expands so as to fill the time available for its completion". It is also sometimes applied to the growth of the bureaucratic apparatus in an organisation.

This was first articulated by Cyril Northcote Parkinson as part of the first sentence of a humorous essay published in *The Economist* in 1955, since republished with other essays in the book *Parkinson's Law: The Pursuit of Progress* (London, John Murray, 1958). He derived the expression from his extensive experience in the British Civil Service.

A current form of the law is not the one Parkinson refers to by that name in the article, but a mathematical equation describing the rate at which bureaucracies expand over time. Much of the essay is dedicated to a summary of purportedly scientific observations supporting the law, such as the increase in the number of employees at the Colonial Office while Great Britain's overseas empire declined (he shows that it had its greatest number of staff when it was folded into the Foreign Office because of a lack of colonies to administer). He explains this as follows:

- "An official wants to multiply subordinates, not rivals".
- "Officials make work for each other." He notes that the number employed in a bureaucracy rose by 5–7% per year "irrespective of any variation in the amount of work (if any) to be done".

The first-referenced meaning of the law has remained dominant and sprouted several corollaries, the best known of which is the Stock-Sanford corollary to Parkinson's law:

- Work contracts to fit in the time we give it.
- Data expands to fill the space available for storage.
- The demand upon a resource tends to expand to match the supply of the resource (if the price is zero).

Over time these generalisations on the original principle have become very similar to the economic law of demand; the lower the price of a service or commodity, the greater the quantity demanded. This is also referred to as induced demand.

A detailed mathematical expression is proposed by Parkinson for the coefficient of inefficiency, featuring many possible influences. In 2008, an attempt was made to empirically verify the proposed model. Parkinson's conjecture that membership exceeding a number "between 19.9 and 22.4" makes a committee manifestly inefficient seems well justified by the evidence proposed. Less certain is the optimal number of members, which must lie between three (a logical minimum) and 20 (within a group of 20, individual discussions may occur, diluting the power of the leader.)

We all know in practical terms that the size of committees and teams is hugely important in driving cognitive diversity and control, as well as having sufficiency of sponsorship and executive support. Therefore, taking a more objective approach to governance and looking at what inputs are necessary to deliver a programme or project is often a good way to start, leaving functions to elect their best representative. This makes the construction and selection far more defensible and avoids the Parkinson's law issue.

9.2 Anchoring or Focalism, and Zero Risk Bias

Anchoring or focalism is a cognitive bias that describes the human tendency to rely too heavily on the first piece of information offered (the "anchor") when making decisions. During decision-making, anchoring occurs when individuals use an initial piece of information to make subsequent judgments. Therefore, once an anchor is set, other judgments are made by adjusting away from that anchor, and there is a bias toward interpreting other information around the anchor.

For example, the initial price offered for a bespoke piece of equipment sets the standard for the rest of the negotiations, so that prices lower than the initial price seem more reasonable even if they are still higher than what the equipment is really worth when you consider materials, labour and overheads (including reasonable profit), etc.

Similarly, the focusing effect (or focusing illusion) is a cognitive bias that occurs when people place too much importance on one aspect of an event, causing an error in accurately predicting the benefit of a future outcome.

People focus on notable differences, excluding those that are less conspicuous, when making predictions about happiness or convenience – for example, when comparing the quality of life in the north versus the south of a country and deducing one is better than the other, when, in fact, there is no difference between the two. The bias could lie in aspects such as weather, easy-going lifestyle, wealth, job prospects, disposable time, community, etc.

A rise in income only has a small and transient effect on happiness and well-being, but people consistently overestimate this effect. Kahneman et al[1] proposed that this is a result of a focusing illusion, with people focusing on conventional measures of achievement, rather than on everyday routine.

Anchoring and adjustment is a psychological heuristic that influences the way people intuitively assess probabilities. According to this heuristic, people start with an implicitly suggested reference point (the "anchor") and make adjustments to it to reach their estimate. A person begins with a first approximation (anchor) and then makes incremental adjustments based on additional information. These adjustments are usually insufficient, giving the initial anchor a great deal of influence over future assessments. Various studies have shown that anchoring is very difficult to avoid.

The anchoring and adjustment heuristic was first theorized by Amos Tversky and Daniel Kahneman. In one of their first studies, participants were asked to compute, within 5 seconds, the product of the numbers one through to eight. However, because participants did not have enough time to calculate the full answer, they had to make an estimate after their first few multiplications. When these first multiplications gave a small answer – because the sequence started with small numbers – the median estimate was 512; when the sequence started with the larger numbers, the median estimate was 2,250. (The correct answer was 40,320.)

In another study by Tversky and Kahneman, participants observed a roulette wheel that was predetermined to stop on either 10 or 65. Participants were then asked to guess the %age of the United Nations that were African nations. Participants whose wheel stopped on 10 guessed lower values (25% on average) than participants whose wheel stopped at 65 (45% on average). The pattern has held in other experiments for a wide variety of different subjects of estimation.

1. Tversky, A.; Kahneman, D., 1974. "Judgment under Uncertainty: Heuristics and Biases" in *Science 185* (4157): 1124–1131. doi:10.1126/science.185.4157.1124. PMID 17835457.

As a third example, in a study by Dan Ariely, an audience is first asked to write the last two digits of their social security number and consider whether they would pay this number of dollars for items whose value they did not know such as wine, chocolate and computer equipment. They were then asked to bid for these items, with the result that the audience members with higher two-digit numbers would submit bids that were between 60 % and 120 % higher than those with the lower social security numbers, which had become their anchor.

Whilst there is still no clear agreement as to how and why this anchoring effect occurs, scientifically the one thing we cannot avoid is that it happens consistently and is very powerful. Being aware that this may happen or indeed choosing to use this as a technique is clearly something to consider from negotiations to budget setting and much more.

Interestingly, experts (those with high knowledge, experience, or expertise in some field) have proven to be more resistant to the anchoring effect. However, while experience can sometimes reduce the effect, even experts are susceptible to anchoring. In short, we are all fallible. This is not a reflection of intelligence, either.

Northcraft and Neale[2] conducted a study to measure the difference in the estimated value of a house given by students and real-estate agents. In this experiment, both groups were shown a house and then given different listing prices. After making their offer, each group was then asked to discuss what factors influenced their decisions. In the follow-up interviews, the real-estate agents denied being influenced by the initial price, but the results showed that both groups were equally influenced by that anchor.

Specifically, in negotiations, anchoring refers to the concept of setting a boundary that outlines the basic constraints for a negotiation; subsequently, the anchoring effect is the phenomenon in which we set our estimation for the true value of the item at hand. In addition to the initial research conducted by Tversky and Kahneman, multiple other studies have shown that anchoring can greatly influence the estimated value of an object. For instance, although negotiators can generally appraise an offer based on multiple characteristics, studies have shown that they tend to focus on only one aspect.

In this way, a deliberate starting point can strongly affect the range of possible counter-offers. The process of offer and counter-offer results in a mutually-beneficial arrangement. However, multiple studies have shown that initial offers have a stronger influence on the outcome of negotiations than subsequent counteroffers.

2. Northcraft, Gregory, B and Neale, Margaret A. (1987). Experts, Amateurs, and Real Estate: An Anchoring and Adjustment Perspective on Property Pricing Decisions in *Organisational Behavior and Human Decision Processes. 39*, 84-97 (1987); Department of Management and Policy, University of Arizona

An example of the power of anchoring has been conducted during the Strategic Negotiation Process Workshops. During the workshop, a group of participants is divided into two sections: buyers and sellers. Each side receives identical information about the other party before going into a one-on-one negotiation. Following this exercise, both sides debrief about their experiences. The results show that the participants who anchor the negotiation had a significant effect on their success. The levels of success will vary from study to study and will be unique in each instance. However, the effect will always be positive.

Anchoring can have more subtle effects on negotiations as well. Janiszewski and Uy[3] investigated the effects of precision of an anchor. Participants read an initial price for a beach house, then gave the price they thought it was worth. They received either a general, seemingly nonspecific anchor (e.g., $800,000) or a more precise and specific anchor (e.g., $799,800). Participants with a general anchor adjusted their estimate more than those given a precise anchor ($751,867 vs $784,671). The authors propose that this effect comes from difference in scale; in other words, the anchor affects not only the starting value, but also the starting scale. When given a general anchor of $20, people will adjust in large increments ($19, $21, etc.), but when given a more specific anchor like $19.85, people will adjust on a lower scale ($19.75, $19.95, etc.). Thus, a more specific initial price will tend to result in a final price closer to the initial one.

This should be considered when you are preparing your negotiation plan and thinking about how you will approach the and maintain control in a negotiation.

Zero-risk bias is a tendency to prefer the complete elimination of a risk, even when alternative options produce a greater reduction in risk (overall). This effect on decision-making has been observed in surveys presenting hypothetical scenarios, and certain real-world policies have been said to be affected by this bias too.

In American Federal policy, the Delaney clause outlawing cancer-causing additives from foods (regardless of actual risk) and the desire for perfect clean-up of Superfund[4] sites have been alleged to be overly focused on complete elimination. Furthermore, the effort needed to implement zero-risk laws grew as technological advances enabled the detection of smaller quantities of hazardous substances in the ground. A pursuit of this type of policy is clearly seen as desirable in politics; conversely a healthy amount of well-managed risk is what allows commercial enterprises to be successful and profitable.

---

3. Janiszewski, C. and Uy, D. (2008). "Anchor Precision Influences the Amount of Adjustment" in *Psychological Science, 19* (February), 121-127.
4. Superfund sites: These are polluted locations requiring a long-term response to clean up hazardous material contaminations. CERCLA authorised the United States Environmental Protection Agency (EPA) to create a list of such locations, which are placed on the National Priorities List (NPL).

In reality, even when faced with a situation where it is impossible to achieve zero-risk, this may well still be demanded by some executives and politicians. To then set out a series of unknowns or potential risks is usually unwelcome and can need careful management. I have sought, on some occasions, to use the more extreme examples to highlight that there cannot be a zero-risk future as a means of trying to bring the conversation back to some form on near reality – remembering of course that the expectation of the sponsoring party may just be that they do not want to accept or agree to a scenario that contains the word risk!

Even changing language to consider potential eventualities that are beyond reasonable control and mitigation may be more reassuring to gain acceptance of an unpalatable truth. Finally, being aware of someone's zero-risk bias allows you to reframe the proposal or options in such a way as they may negate or diminish the anguish they clearly cause.

In addition, other biases might underlie the zero-risk bias, one of which is a tendency to think in terms of proportions rather than differences. A greater reduction in proportion of delay is valued more highly than a greater reduction in actual delay. The zero-risk bias could then be seen as the extreme end of a broad bias about quantities as applied to risk. Framing effects can enhance the bias, for example, by emphasizing a large proportion in a small set or can attempt to mitigate the bias by emphasising total quantities.

9.3 Sunk Cost Fallacy

In Daniel Kahneman's book *Thinking Fast and Slow*[5], he writes about how he and his colleague Amos Tversky, through their work in the 1970s and '80s, uncovered the imbalance between losses and gains in your mind. Kahneman explains that since all decisions involve uncertainty about the future, decision-making in the human brain has evolved an automatic and unconscious system for judging how to proceed when a potential for loss arises. Kahneman says organisations that placed more urgency on avoiding threats than they did on maximizing opportunities were more likely to pass on their genes. So, over time, the prospect of losses has become a more powerful motivator on your behaviour than the promise of gains.

Whenever possible, you try to avoid losses of any kind, and when comparing losses to gains you don't treat them equally. The results of his experiments and the results of many others who've replicated and expanded on them have teased out an inborn loss aversion ratio. When offered a chance to accept or reject a

5. Kahneman, D. (2011). *Thinking Fast and Slow*. Farrar, Straus and Giroux.

gamble, most people refuse to make a bet unless the possible payoff is around double the potential loss.

Behavioural economist Dan Ariely adds a fascinating twist to loss aversion in his book, *Predictably Irrational*[6]. He writes that when factoring the costs of any exchange, you tend to focus more on what you may lose in the bargain than on what you stand to gain. The "pain of paying" as he puts it arises whenever you must give up anything you own. The precise amount doesn't matter at first. You'll feel the pain no matter what price you must pay, and it will influence your decisions and behaviours.

Marketing and good salesmanship is often all about convincing you that what you want to buy is worth more than what you must pay for it. You see something as a good value when you predict the pain of loss will be offset by your joy of gain. If they did their job well, somewhere in your inverse perspective you feel as though you won't lose at all. Emotionally, you will come out ahead, unless you are buying something just to show others how much money you have as an outward visual display.

Imagine the scenario that you bought or paid for a different kind of sandwich to the one you usually buy, as it's on special offer and sounded good, but tasted awful. However, rather than waste it or throw it away you continue to eat it despite the displeasure and awful taste in your mouth. By continuing to eat that sandwich you have experienced sunk cost fallacy. This is a classic example of payments or investments which can never be recovered. An android with fully functioning logic circuits would never make a decision which took sunk costs into account, but you would. As an emotional human, your aversion to loss often leads you right into the sunk cost fallacy.

Furthermore, this loss lingers and grows in your mind, becoming larger in your history than it was when you first felt it. Whenever this clinging to the past becomes a factor in making decisions about your future, you run the risk of being derailed by the sunk cost fallacy.

This therefore supports the misconception that you always make rational decisions based on the future value of objects, investments and experiences. This is true in both our social and business lives. The unpalatable truth that your decisions are tainted by the emotional investments you accumulate, and the more you invest in something the harder it becomes to abandon it.

Putting it into everyday context for both adults and children: loyalty programmes and online games, even the most innocent ones for younger children, who invest time and effort in gaining points, level of status, accumulation of certain scale of build (as with Minecraft), etc. are all instances where you do not want to lose what you have. We are all stimulated to gain the next level, badge or status, even if there is cost or resource (your time) involved. In other words, once you are

6. Ariely, D. (2008). *Predictably Irrational*. HarperCollins.

into the programme or game you proceed to the next step, level, activity, etc. This becomes quite powerful and consuming. So once you've invested time, money or both you will not want to give them up or lose them.

Taking a sunken cost (or resource) perspective into a commercial business environment or public sector body, the issues are just the same, and manifest themselves in parallel ways. Probably the most classic global example is the story of Concorde, an aviation marvel, but a business disaster. As an adult, you have the gifts of reflection and regret. You can predict a future place where you must admit your efforts were in vain, your losses permanent, and when you accept the truth it is going to hurt. This then has potential consequences in most organisations where a degree of bad decision-making is seen as a weakness and could end a career or a position with an organisation which is something, we don't want to visualise or accept.

To see this happening in real life observe the behaviours displayed during e-auctions, where organisations go beyond economic positions simply to win a contract, haven sunken cost and resources into making the bid and not wishing to lose. For the buyer there is a great sense of achievement that the savings will be high, but then the harsh reality – a very short period into the contract the dawn of reality that the pricing is not viable and the supplier withdraws, damaging supply certainty, reputations and market pricing.

This is where we need to consider the ethics and governance of how we conduct business and assure our organisations of the right quality, assured supply, legal compliance and all the other things that we know sit alongside price.

Sunk cost fallacy appears in many instances in the world of Procurement and Supply Chain Management, especially in larger financial decisions, such as capital investments for new facilities, equipment and other one-off custom activities. One recent example was a site acquisition – made by a Managing Director (for a specific trading entity) – for a new facility, only to find that when we fully analysed all the aspects of access, fire escape, growth projections, maintenance costs, taxes, etc. the site was just too small.

The MD fought in vain to develop the site, due to the cost of acquisition already made, design costs for architects and engineers, etc. However, by being impartial to the original scheme, we were able to sell the land on and purchase a larger site and start again, thus avoiding a costly sunk cost fallacy. But they don't always turn out that way.

9.4 Status Quo Bias

Status quo bias is an emotional bias; a preference for the current state of affairs. The current baseline (or status quo) is taken as a reference point, and any change from that baseline is perceived as a loss. Status quo bias should be distinguished from a rational preference for the status quo ante, as when the current state of affairs is objectively superior to the available alternatives, or when imperfect information is a significant problem. Moreover, a large body of evidence shows that status quo bias frequently affects human decision-making.

Status quo bias interacts with other non-rational cognitive processes such as loss aversion, existence bias, endowment effect, etc. Experimental evidence for the detection of status quo bias is seen through the use of the reversal test[7]. A vast number of experimental and field examples exist, particularly in regard to pension plans, health choices, and ethical choices, that show evidence of the status quo bias.

During the late 1980s Kahneman, Thaler, and Knetsch created experiments that could produce the status quo bias consistently and reliably. Samuelson and Zeckhauser[8] reconfirmed this status quo bias equally consistently in their research too in the same period.

Status quo bias has been attributed to a combination of loss aversion and the endowment effect, two ideas relevant to Prospect Theory (something we will deal with in detail in a later chapter)[9]. An individual weighs up the potential losses of switching from the status quo more heavily than the potential gains; this is due to the Prospect Theory value function being steeper in the loss domain. As a result, the individual will prefer not to switch at all. In other words, we tend to oppose change unless the benefits (usually significantly) outweigh the risks.

This in procurement terms has been referred to as the "switching cost" (perhaps of moving from one supplier to another to gain better pricing). However, the status quo bias is maintained even in the absence of gain/loss in framing this. For example, when customers were asked to choose the colour of their new car, they tended towards one colour arbitrarily framed as the status quo, during experiments carried out to test this.[10] Loss aversion, therefore, cannot wholly explain the status quo bias, with other potential causes including regret avoidance[11], transaction costs and psychological commitment.

---

7. When a proposal to change a certain parameter is thought to have bad overall consequences, consider a change to the same parameter in the opposite direction. If this is also thought to have bad overall consequences, then the onus is on those who reach these conclusions to explain why our position cannot be improved through changes to this parameter. If they are unable to do so, then we have reason to suspect that they suffer from status quo bias. The rationale of the Reversal Test is: if a continuous parameter admits of a wide range of possible values, only a tiny subset of which can be local optima, then it is prima facie implausible that the actual value of that parameter should just happen to be at one of these rare local optima
8. Samuelson, W and Zeckhauser, R. (1988). "Status Quo Bias in Decision-making" in *Journal of Risk and Uncertainty 1:7-59*. Kluwer Academic Publishers, Boston USA.
9. Prospect Theory – see definition in chapter 11
10. Samuelson, William and Zeckhauser, Richard. (1998). "Status Quo bias in Decision-making" in *Journal of Risk and Uncertainty 1; 7-59*, page 55. Kluwer Academic Publishers, Boston.
11. Regret Avoidance is a situation where an investor would not accept the bad investment decision

A status quo bias can also be a rational route if there are cognitive or informational limitations. In other words, there is good reliable and sufficient data and access to core aspects of specification, current practice, market conditions, etc.

Equally, decision outcomes are rarely certain, nor is the absolute benefit or positive change that they may bring, because some errors are costlier than others and sticking with what worked in the past is a safe option, providing previous decisions are recognised as being good enough (and not problematic).

There is a tendency to overemphasize the avoidance of losses, which will favour those wishing to retain the status quo, resulting in a status quo bias. Even though choosing the status quo may entail forfeiting certain positive consequences, when these are represented as forfeited "gains", they are psychologically given less weight than the "losses" that would be incurred if the status quo were to be changed.

This area is clearly in the domain of change, and something I will look at in later chapters, as change is a key aspect of defining and implementing new ways of working, which is diametrically opposed to the notion of status quo and those who are biased towards it. Perhaps a diversion from science as the reason for maintaining the status quo may have more Machiavellian undertones (see quotes section at the end of this chapter), such as those in the position of the decision-maker stand to lose from change and therefore, by maintaining the status quo, will not be subject to a loss of power, authority, money, etc.

Equally, decision-makers may simply prefer to do nothing and/or to maintain their current course of action because it is easier, as it requires little or no effort. Status quo alternatives often require less mental effort to maintain. Another very salient factor is the perceived risk of simply making the wrong decision. Also, they may irrationally make the assumption that longevity and goodness are part of the status quo bias. People treat existence as a *prima facie* case for goodness, aesthetic value and longevity, which increases the preference for status quo. People simply assume, with little reason or deliberation, the goodness of existing states. I have witnessed multiple instances where executives have confided in me that keeping a "big name" consultancy, rather than pursuing a boutique consultancy with good credentials was better.

Longevity is a corollary of the existence bias: if existence is good, longer existence should be better. This thinking resembles quasi-evolutionary notions

---

made to avoid the unpleasant feelings. In general emotions have a negative effect on investment decisions. There may be times when the markets are at the peak and an investor might invest money without any rationale just by sentimental value, if the market goes down from there then the investor would have made a bad decision riding on emotions. People usually throw good money after bad in these situations.

of "survival of the fittest", and also the augmentation principle in attribution theory.[12]

I have covered loss aversion earlier in chapter 7, so I will not repeat this again, save to say this also plays into the space of status quo bias. Moreover, omission bias may account for some of the findings previously ascribed to status quo bias. Omission bias is diagnosed when a decision-maker prefers a harmful outcome that results from an omission, to a less harmful outcome that results from an action.

Public Sector organisations that are under the direction of a conservative membership or party will recognise that, in policy terms, the preference for the status quo represents a core component of conservative ideology. This is because conserving the constitutional impact on limiting government and control over individual rights and affairs is a major element of conservative ideology, and the bias in its favour plays a role in the outcomes. This can be said to be true in certain but not all conditions, in promoting political conservatism and promoting limited government.

A good example of status quo bias, up to the advent of electric vehicles, was in fleet vehicle policies that often remained the same, despite compelling arguments to change if the benefits in environmental and sustainability terms – these were not deemed significantly large enough to outweigh the pain of change.

I will close with a few quotes on the dangers of maintaining, participating in or perpetuating the status quo, which is probably a most pernicious state for those that seek to bring competitive advantage through a new order:

"Status quo, you know, is Latin for 'the mess we're in'".
– Ronald Reagan, 40th President of the United States of America.

I'm not interested in preserving the status quo; I want to overthrow it.
– Nicollo Machiavelli, Statesman and Philosopher

---

12. Attribution theory is concerned with how and why ordinary people explain events as they do. Heider (1958) believed that people are naive psychologists trying to make sense of the social world. People tend to see cause and effect relationships, even where there is none! Heider didn't so much develop a theory himself as emphasize certain themes that others took up. There were two main ideas that he put forward that became influential.
1. Internal Attribution: The process of assigning the cause of behaviour to some internal characteristic, rather than to outside forces. When we explain the behaviour of others we look for enduring internal attributions, such as personality traits. For example, we attribute the behaviour of a person to their personality, motives or beliefs.
2. External Attribution: The process of assigning the cause of behaviour to some situation or event outside a person's control rather than to some internal characteristic. When we try to explain our own behaviour, we tend to make external attributions, such as situational or environment features.

"The eurozone status quo is neither tolerable nor stable. Mainstream economists would call it an inferior equilibrium; I call it a nightmare - one that is inflicting tremendous pain and suffering that could be easily avoided if the misconceptions and taboos that sustain it were dispelled".
– George Soros, Hungarian hedge fund manager and philanthropist.

PART C
//
GAME THEORY AND NUDGING

CHAPTER 10 | GAME THEORY APPLIED TO NEGOTIATION IN PROCUREMENT AND SUPPLY CHAIN MANAGEMENT

The aim of this chapter is not to give you a comprehensive understanding of Game Theory and all the different disciplines and ways it can be applied, but simply provide an overview to orientate you in the area of Game Theory. As you will soon appreciate, the applications and approaches require considerable research and training to be able to fully utilise all the possibilities it may offer, and at the end of this section I will suggest some further more substantive reading to review.

10.1 What is Game Theory? Key principles and terminology

Game Theory is the formal study of conflict and cooperation. Game theoretic concepts apply whenever the actions of several agents are interdependent. These agents may be individuals, groups, organisations, or any combination of these. The concepts of Game Theory provide a language to formulate, structure, analyse, and understand strategic scenarios.

Game Theory was established as a field in its own right after the 1944 publication of the monumental volume *Theory of Games and Economic Behaviour*[1] by von Neumann and Morgenstern. This book provided much of the basic terminology and problem setup that is still in use today.

In 1950, John Nash demonstrated that finite games have always have an equilibrium point[2], at which all players choose actions which are best for them given their opponents' choices. This central concept of non-cooperative Game Theory has been a focal point of analysis since then. In the 1950s and 1960s, Game Theory was broadened theoretically and applied to problems of war and politics. Since the 1970s, it has driven a revolution in economic theory.

1. Neumann, J and Morgenstern, O. (1944). *The Theory of Games and Economic Behaviour.* Princeton University Press
2. Nash, J. (1950). "Equilibrium points in n-person games" in *Proceedings of the National Academy of Sciences 36(1)*: pages 48-49. And (1951) "Non-Cooperative Games" in *The Annals of Mathematics 54(2)*: pages 286-295

Additionally, it has found applications in sociology and psychology. Game Theory received special attention in 1994, as the Nobel prize in Economics was awarded to John Nash, John Harsanyi, and Reinhard Selten.

By the end of the 1990s, a high-profile application of Game Theory has been the design of auctions. Prominent game theorists have been involved in the design of auctions for allocating rights, to the use of bands of the electromagnetic spectrum, to the mobile telecommunications industry. Most of these auctions were designed with the goal of allocating these resources more efficiently than traditional governmental practices, and additionally raised billions of dollars in the United States and Europe. I will illustrate this further in section 10.3. In considering the theory and the strategies to be adopted it is first necessary to understand the terminology used to gain an appreciation of the approach and principles being applied.

Key Terminology

Backward induction: is a technique to solve a game of perfect information. It first considers the moves that are the last in the game, and determines the best move for the player in each case. Then, taking these as given future actions, it proceeds backwards in time, again determining the best move for the respective player, until the beginning of the game is reached.

Common knowledge: A fact is common knowledge if all players know it, and know that they all know it, and so on. The structure of the game is often assumed to be common knowledge among the players.

Dominating strategy: A strategy dominates another strategy of a player if it always gives a better payoff to that player, regardless of what the other players are doing. It weakly dominates the other strategy if it is always at least as good.

Extensive game (or extensive form game): describes with a tree how a game is played. It depicts the order in which players make moves, and the information each player has at each decision point.

Game: is a formal description of a strategic situation.

Game Theory: is the formal study of decision-making where several players must make choices that potentially affect the interests of the other players.

Mixed strategy: is an active randomisation, with given probabilities, that determines the player's decision. As a special case, a mixed strategy can be the deterministic choice of one of the given pure strategies.

Nash equilibrium[3]: also called strategic equilibrium, is a list of strategies, one

---

3. A Nash equilibrium - the definition in the simple setting of a finite player and action game in normal form. There are I players, indexed by i = 1, ... , I. Player i chooses from N; (pure) strategies; we write S; for this set of strategies, and s; for a typical member of S;. A strategy profile,

for each player, which has the property that no player can unilaterally change his strategy and get a better payoff.

Payoff: is a number, also called utility, that reflects the desirability of an outcome to a player, for whatever reason. When the outcome is random, payoffs are usually weighted with their probabilities. The expected payoff incorporates the player's attitude towards risk.

Perfect information: a game has perfect information when at any point in time only one player makes a move, and knows all the actions that have been made until then.

Player: is an agent who makes decisions in a game.

Rationality: A player is said to be rational if he seeks to play in a manner which maximises his own payoff. It is often assumed that the rationality of all players is common knowledge.

Strategic form: A game in strategic form, also called normal form, is a compact representation of a game in which players simultaneously choose their strategies. The resulting payoffs are presented in a table with a cell for each strategy combination.

Strategy: In a game in strategic form, a strategy is one of the given possible actions of a player. In an extensive game, a strategy is a complete plan of choices, one for each decision point of the player.

Zero-sum game: A game is said to be zero-sum if for any outcome, the sum of the payoffs to all players is zero. In a two-player zero-sum game, one player's gain is the other player's loss, so their interests are diametrically opposed.

Now that you know the different terms and references being used, you will be able to familiarise yourself with the approach and examples that follow in this book, and the cross-referenced papers that inform this theory and/or approach.

In addition to the terminology, there are different types of games and game strategies that can be used or deployed. The object of the approach (or study/ analysis) in Game Theory is the game itself, which is a formal model of an

---

written s = (s 1 , ... , s I), is a vector of strategies for the individual players - we write S for TI[= 1 S ;, the set of all strategy profiles. For a strategy profile s = (s 1 , ••• , s I)E S and a strategy s;E S; for player i, we write sIs; for the strategy profile (s 1 , ... , s;_ 1 , s;+ 1 , ... , si) or s with the part of i changed from s; to s;. For each player i and strategy profiles, u;(s) denotes i's expected utility or payoff if players employ strategy profile s. Definition. A Nash equilibrium (in pure strategies) is a strategy profile s such that for each i and s;ES;, u;(s)? u;(sls;). In words, no single player, by changing his own part of s, can obtain higher utility if the others stick to their parts. This basic definition is often extended to independently mixed strategy profiles, as follows. Given S;, write Li for the set of mixed strategies for player i; that is, all probability distributions over si. Write: E for n[=1:Ei,a=(0'1, ... ,0'I),·ala;, and so on, as before. Extend the utility functions ui from domain S to domain: E by letting ui(a) be player i's expected utility: u i (0') = I ... I u i (s 1 '..• 's I) 0' 1 (s d ... 0' I (s I). s, S1 Then define a Nash equilibrium in mixed strategies just as above, with a in place of s and ai in place of si. Equivalently, player i puts positive weight on pure strategy si only if si is among the pure strategies that give him the greatest expected utility.

interactive situation. It typically involves several players; a game with only one player is usually called a *decision problem*. The formal definition lays out the players, their preferences, their information, the strategic actions available to them, and how these influence the outcome.

Games can be described formally at various levels of detail. A coalitional (or cooperative) game is a high-level description, specifying only what payoffs each potential group, or coalition, can obtain by the cooperation of its members. What is not made explicit is the process by which the coalition forms. As an example, the players may be several parties in parliament. Each party has a different strength, based upon the number of seats occupied by party members. The game describes which coalitions of parties can form a majority, but does not delineate, for example, the negotiation process through which an agreement to vote en bloc is achieved.

Cooperative Game Theory investigates such coalitional games with respect to the relative amounts of power held by various players, or how a successful coalition should divide its proceeds. This is most naturally applied to situations arising in political science or international relations, where concepts like power are most important. For example, Nash proposed a solution for the division of gains from agreement in a bargaining problem which depends solely on the relative strengths of the two parties' bargaining position.

The amount of power a side has is determined by the usually inefficient outcome that results when negotiations break down. Nash's model (see footnote 3 for the mathematical expression as first derived in a simple form) fits within the cooperative framework in that it does not delineate a specific timeline of offers and counteroffers, but rather focuses solely on the outcome of the bargaining process.

In contrast, Non-cooperative Game Theory is concerned with the analysis of strategic choices. The paradigm of Non-cooperative Game Theory is that the details of the ordering and timing of players' choices are crucial to determining the outcome of a game. In contrast to Nash's cooperative model, a non-cooperative model of bargaining would propose a specific process in which it is prespecified who gets to make an offer at a given time.

The term "non-cooperative" means this branch of Game Theory explicitly models the process of players making choices out of their own interest. Cooperation can, and often does, arise in non-cooperative models of games, when players find it in their own best interests.

Branches of Game Theory also differ in their assumptions. A central assumption in many variants of Game Theory is that the players are rational. A rational player is one who always chooses an action which gives the outcome he most prefers, given what he expects his opponents to do. The goal of game-theoretic analysis in these branches, then, is to predict how the game will be played by rational players, or, relatedly, to give advice on how best to play the game against opponents who are rational. This rationality assumption can be relaxed, and the resulting models have been more recently applied to the analysis of observed behaviour[4]. This kind of Game Theory can be viewed as more "descriptive" than the prescriptive approach taken here.

This non-prescriptive approach focuses principally on non-cooperative Game Theory with rational players. In addition to providing an important baseline case in economic theory, this case is designed so that it gives good advice to the decision-maker, even when – or perhaps especially when – one's opponents also employ it.

The strategic form (also called normal form) is the basic type of game studied in non-cooperative Game Theory. A game in strategic form lists each player's strategies, and the outcomes that result from each possible combination of choices. An outcome is represented by a separate payoff for each player, which is a number (also called utility) that measures how much the player likes the outcome.

The extensive form, also called a game tree (see example in figure 10.1 below), is more detailed than the strategic form of a game. It is a complete description of how the game is played over time. This includes the order in which players take actions, the information that players have at the time they must take those actions, and the times at which any uncertainty in the situation is resolved.

A game in extensive form may be analysed directly, or can be converted into an equivalent strategic form. Examples in the following sections will illustrate in detail the interpretation and analysis of games in strategic and extensive form.

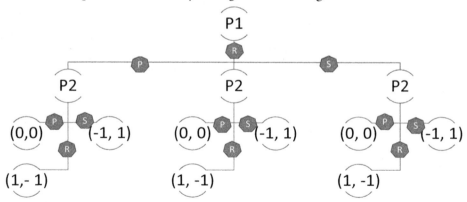

FIGURE 4.5: Rock, Paper, scissors with perfect information: Player 1 moves first and holds up a symbol for either rock, paper or scissors. This is illustrated by the three edges leaving the root node (P1), which is assigned to player 1. Player 2 then holds up a symbol for either rock, paper or scissors. Payoffs are assigned to Player 1 and 2 at terminal nodes. The index of the payoff vector corresponds to the players.

Figure 10.1. Game tree – Extract from Lecture notes[5]

4. Kagel and Roth (eds). (1997). *Handbook of Experimental Economics.* Princeton University Press.
5. Griffin, Christopher. (2010-2012). *Game Theory: Penn State Math 486 Lecture Notes*, Version 1.1.1, published 2010-2012. With Major Contributions By: James Fan, George Kesidis and Other Contributions By: Arlan Stutler (Licensed under a Creative Commons Attribution-Non-Commercial-Share Alike 3.0 United States License)

10.2 Strategies for Negotiation

There are four primary sub-disciplines within Game Theory:

- Classical Game Theory
- Dynamic Game Theory
- Combinatorial Game Theory
- Evolutionary Game Theory

As you will see below, I am cross referencing the work of Griffin[6] to focus on classical Game Theory as the primary discipline for the purposes of negotiation.

As you will see below in Figure 10.2, the four sub-disciplines and their principal attributes are set out in diagrammatic form.

Figure 10.2. Four sub-discipline characteristics as identified by Griffin[6]

6. Griffin, Christopher – diagrams 4.1 and 4.3

10.3 Negotiation models and practice

Consider the following game of *Matching Coins* between two players, A and B. Both A and B simultaneously place a coin on the table. Let D be A's strategy of playing heads (placing heads up), and G be B's strategy of playing tails. Similarly, let "d" be B's strategy of playing heads, and "g" that of playing tails. If the coins match, then A wins B's coin (and keeps his own); if not, B wins A's coin (and keeps his own). The game can be conveniently represented by a strategy matrix, as shown below in the table:

Player B			
		d	g
Player A	D	+1;-1	-1;+1
	G	-1;+1	+1;-1

Table 1

Here is how to read the matrix. The top-left column with +1;-1 tells us that when both A plays D and B "d", A wins one penny and B loses one; the box immediately below shows that when A plays G and B "d", A loses his penny and B wins one. The rest of the matrix is read in a corresponding way.

Matching coins is a *zero-sum game* in that whatever one player wins must be lost by another player. Since there are only 2 players, one's wins are the other's losses: the game is one of pure competition.

Note that in matching coins each player knows:

1.   The payoffs of each player and the strategies available to each player
2.   The fact that each player knows that all the players know this.

A game in which such knowledge is available is a game of *complete knowledge*. Therefore, unless otherwise stated, we consider only games of *complete knowledge.*

The central notion for studying games is that of *equilibrium,* namely, a combination of strategies such that each player uses a best strategy, namely one most likely to maximise his or her payoff, given that the other players are playing with their optimal strategies too. As to what counts as the best strategy, depends on the type of equilibrium the player pursues. Solving a game consists in exhibiting its *equilibrium or equilibriums,* if it has more than one.

The simplest type of equilibrium is *dominance equilibrium*. Consider the following, as shown in table 2 overleaf, which is a strategy matrix where S1 and S2 are A's strategies and s1 and s2 are B's strategies.

Player B		s1	s2
		s1	s2
Player A	S1	1,1	-2,2
	S2	2,2	0,3

Table 2

A brief analysis of the payoffs shows that A should adopt strategy S2 *no matter what strategy B adopts*, as in each box S2 has a greater payoff than S1.

When, in a game, both players have a dominant strategy, then the game has a *dominance strategy equilibrium*. In the game we are considering, S2 and s2 provide such equilibrium. We shall then say that (S2; s2) is the dominant equilibrium of the game. Notice that an equilibrium need not be fair, as in the game 1,1 or 2,2 are fair outcomes, while dominant strategy equilibrium outcome 0,3 is not.

In the game in table 3, neither of B's strategies dominates the other. However, if we look at A's strategies, we see that S1>S2.

Player B		s1	s2
		s1	s2
Player A	S1	4;4	2;-2
	S2	3;-3	-4;4

Table 3

Now both players know that S1>S2, and therefore both will reason as follows: As S1>S2, player A will always choose S1 no matter what. Hence, the S2 row can be deleted. But now, s1>s2, and therefore the column for s2 can be eliminated. This leaves only one strategy per player, namely (S1; s1), which is the solution to the game. The solution is reached by *dominance iteration*, namely by the sequential elimination of dominated strategies. Games that are solvable by the elimination of dominated strategies are *dominance solvable*. It is a nice feature of dominance solutions in that they are *unique*.

Even when dominance iteration does not lead to equilibrium, it is important to apply it whenever possible in order to simplify the game.

It is possible to simplify games by also eliminating *weakly* dominated strategies, as set out in table 4 below.

Player B				
		s1	s2	s3
Player A	S1	2;6	1;3	1;6
	S2	0;6	0;3	1;4
	S3	0;6	1;3	0;7

Table 4

S1 weakly dominates both S2 and S3, which can therefore be eliminated. Then, s2 is eliminated because it is dominated by s1 and s3. So, the game is greatly simplified and turns out to have two equilibriums, (S1, s1) and (S1, s3). (Note that weak dominance solutions need not be unique).

Matching coins is a *zero-sum* game: the interests of the players are diametrically opposite.

Strategically, the more interesting games are mixed-motives games, which are much closer to real life situations and as such are neither zero-sum nor coordination. The most famous mixed-motive game is *Prisoner's Dilemma*[7]. Consider the following scenario: two criminals are arrested and the prosecutor has not enough evidence to convict either of a serious crime unless one or both confess; however, the two criminals do not know this. Hence, he tells one of prisoners: "If you confess and the other guy does not, I'll grant you immunity and you walk free. If the other confesses and you don't, I shall make sure that you get a heavy sentence. If neither of you confesses I shall settle for misdemeanour charges, with the result that you will pay a small fine and walk free. If both of you confess, I shall charge both with a crime, but also argue for shorter sentences than you would have ordinarily received, if the other

---

7. Prisoner's Dilemma is a standard example of a game analysed in Game Theory that shows why two completely "rational" individuals might not cooperate, even if it appears that it is in their best interests to do so. It was originally framed by Merrill Flood and Melvin Dresher working at RAND Corporation in 1950. Albert W. Tucker formalised the game with prison sentence rewards and named it, "prisoner's dilemma": This was referred to in the publication by Poundstone, 1992.

prisoner confesses and you do not." Keeping in mind that the game is one of complete knowledge, what should a prisoner do?

Here is the strategy matrix, with S representing "keeping silent" and T "talk", +10 the utility of walking free, -10 that of a heavy sentence, -6 for the crime as charged, but with shorter sentence, and +6 for misdemeanour charges:

Player (prisoner) B			
		S(ilent)	T(alk)
Player (prisoner)A	S(ilent)	+6;+6	-10;+10
	T(alk)	+10;-10	-6;-6

Table 5

The game is neither a coordination nor a zero-sum game, but it is dominance solvable: T dominates S; consequently, (T,T) provide a dominance equilibrium. No matter what the other does, it's better to talk: if you confess and the other does not, you walk free (+10); if you confess and the other does as well, you get a -6 payoff. *At all cost* you want to avoid keeping silent when the other confesses. Self-interest prevents both from following (S, S) (both keep silent), which would provide a better outcome for the two together. This is why this game is called "*Prisoner's Dilemma*": *purely self-interested private rationality leads to common failure.* One can think of *Prisoner's Dilemma* in terms of cooperation (cooperating with the other by keeping silent) and defection (going at it alone by confessing). Notice two things:

1. If the players are self-regarding (only trying to maximise their own payoffs) communication does not solve the problem: even if I know that you will not confess, it is still in my self-interest to confess.
2. Even finite iteration of the game need not change its outcome. For example, suppose both players know that the game will be played 10 times. Then A knows that in the *tenth* round he/she should confess, independently of what happened in the ninth round. Hence, in the eighth round he/she should confess because what happens in the ninth does not affect what happens in the tenth, and so on. The same applies to B.

Fortunately, most people do not behave as classical Game Theory suggests; in fact, there's ample experimental evidence that very often we tend to cooperate unless we perceive that we are being taken advantage of. Hence, since most people are conditional co-operators, it often makes sense to cooperate, at least initially, unless the stakes are so high that cooperating against a defector leads to immediate big losses. Note that in *Prisoner's Dilemma* it *may* be reasonable for the self-interested players to set up an enforcer that compels them to choose cooperation: in some cases, limiting your options is perfectly rational as it maximizes the possible payoffs.

When *Prisoner's Dilemma* is played an indefinite number of times between two players, the structure of the reiterated game is different from that of each *Prisoner's Dilemma* round. We shall come back to that later.

The *Prisoner's Dilemma* can provide a rough strategic description of many real life situations. For example:

A one-off tariff confrontation between two countries (hence the delicacy of Brexit negotiations and subsequent/related trade deals) has the same logic: if A raises its tariffs and B doesn't, A will improve its trading balance, and if A doesn't raise tariffs and B does, A will do worse than if both raise tariffs. So, raising tariffs dominates over not raising them. Hence, both countries will raise tariffs, with a decrease in business for both.

Nash equilibriums are effectively the same as everyday conventions such as shaking hands, driving on the right or left depending on which country you are in, etc. There are, of course, informal examples such as dress code in an office – where some offices require a full suit and tie approach versus a more casual jeans and shirt attire, etc. Essentially, when we look at negotiations or trade agreements, this entails that if the conditions of the game do not change, a Nash equilibrium is stable. However, note that a dominance equilibrium is a Nash equilibrium, but *not* vice versa, as a Nash equilibrium need not be fair and need not result in the best possible payoff for either player.

Nash equilibriums are important for two reasons:

- The first has to do with dynamical systems, of which more later. Suppose we leave players out and consider only strategies competing against one another. Typically, they will outcompete each other until they reach a Nash equilibrium, at which point all of them will be optimal in the sense of being best responses to each other, at least as long as the environmental conditions do not change.
- The second reason involves the assumption of the rationality of the players, which is a more traditional ground for the theory. If the game is of complete knowledge, the players intend to maximize their payoffs, they are rational and try to predict the moves of their opponents, and all this is common knowledge among them, they can avoid much strife by settling for a Nash equilibrium. In summary, this is the reason why: imagine a book that told every player which strategy to follow to maximise a

player's payoff, given that all the others also maximize theirs. If the book is to be fully authoritative, then it must settle for some Nash equilibrium, because otherwise at least one of the players would improve his payoff by changing strategy as the other players keep the same strategies. Of course, if the game has more than one Nash equilibrium there may be coordination problems; moreover, if different players maximise their payoffs at different Nash equilibriums, they'll find it difficult to settle on one. What's needed in this case is some sort of coordinator that decides what equilibrium will be adopted.

As we saw above, games may have two or more Nash equilibriums that do not even produce the same payoffs. A famous example comes from *Battle of the Sexes*, which goes as follows: Joe and Jill want to go on holiday, where Joe can choose to go to the sea (S) or to the mountains (M), as likewise for Jill, who can choose the sea (s) or the mountains (m) too. In this scenario Joe prefers the sea to the mountains and Jill the mountains to the sea. However, they prefer going on holiday together rather than going alone. This then produces a result that can be seen in Table 6 below:

Jill			
		s	m
Joe	S	4;1	0;0
	M	0;0	1;4

Table 6

This game has two Nash equilibriums, (S,s) and (M,m), that do not produce the same payoffs, and therefore are not interchangeable, as obviously Joe prefers the former and Jill the latter.

Note that pre-commitment is advantageous in this game: if Joe has already a non-refundable train ticket for the sea, he has an advantage over Jill, another case in which limiting one's options may be rational. However, Jill might decide to retaliate if she thinks Joe's pre-commitment amounts to cheating.

The most important theorem on equilibriums in classical Game Theory is the *Nash Existence Theorem*:

Every finite sum game has at least one Nash equilibrium in mixed strategies. Such equilibriums (if the game has more than one) are not interchangeable, unless in two-player zero-sum games.

There are formal techniques for determining the expected payoffs of strategies and finding the Nash equilibriums in games, but to do so would require setting out endless scenarios and significantly more complex attributes, which is not the intended purpose of this chapter in the book. Equally, this is not intended to be a mathematical exercise, but a behavioural one, and so I will attempt to summarise this in a final section.

10.4 Sumarising Game Theory

In summary, to put these theories into practical use requires careful judgment about where and how they apply. These considerations include:

- How much impact a given category has on the buyer organisation's financial performance: revenues, margins, and risk exposure.
- What the degree of leverage the buyer has in the supply marketplace, such as obtaining better commercial terms from a monopoly, oligopoly or open market situation. e.g. categories with low leverage, applying Game Theory techniques greatly helps where natural spend aggregation is not a very effective option.
- Is the supplier or service provider historically difficult to deal with?

Hopefully it is clear that one size doesn't fit all, so being clear on where and how you intend to apply Game Theory and the reward versus effort needs to be vert clear upfront. Determine clearly what you can and can't leverage.

The approach that seeks to gain as much market and supplier/service provider intelligence is still necessary, the approach and use of it will differ if you intend to apply Game Theory. Also, be prepared to change the game after each round: more often than not, smart suppliers can see through the pattern of your negotiation and manipulate their pricing structures accordingly. It's important to change the negotiation script at each stage.

For example, for some categories with high labour content, if the first round is all about margin structures, the next round could be about deconstructing the cost of operations in a specific project, plant or site and subsequently changing the parameters and scope of the project itself. This may be obvious, but before initiating a game, buyers must also be well aware of their total costs, risks and trade-offs.

Optimise on a few factors, and not all at the same time: when sourcing organisations arrive at a negotiation table trying to optimize on all fronts, they risk being able to create a mutual supplier win-win. For each category it's important to extract value over a sustained period of time, rather than putting in all boundary conditions all at once. This leads to poor supplier relationships and is difficult to sustain leverage over time. If the first wave was Unit Price reduction, the following rounds could include Payment Terms or Minimum Order quantities. For Game Theory to play out evenly in a balanced two-sided manner, it's important to have some occasional hooks – in the Prisoner's Dilemma context, adequate incentives that compel one of them to confess.

It may be your intention to conduct an e-auction if so; timing and structuring and lotting strategy will still be necessary as part of an overall game plan. However, if you intend to adopt a Supplier Relationship Management approach post-award, be very careful you understand and manage the dynamics and communication well to ensure the relationship is not damaged in the process.

In consideration of the right parameters, and that you need to deliver value not just cost out, it is essential you consider the supplier's/service provider's position as it is important they feel the process has been fair too.

I have created a few diagrams to orientate the situation visually in negotiation, which can be seen below, noting that you are trying to seek an agreement that is fair. Of course, the worst scenario is no agreement, as there are no winners, only losers if you fail to purchase and the supplier fails to sell:

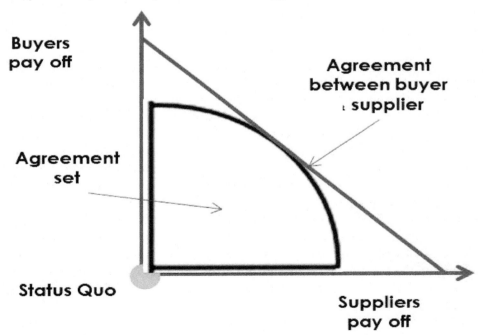

Figure 10.3. Optimal point for agreement between supplier and buyer (Loseby)

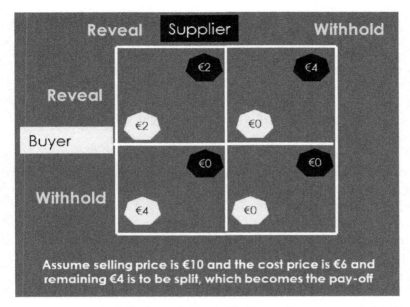

Figure 10.4. Modelled on the payoffs for each party on a simple commodity (Loseby)

So now some simple considerations, which are not pure Game Theory, but need recognition nonetheless, as Game Theory is exactly that – "a theory". Even Nash, before he tragically died, gave no hint as to how to calculate equilibrium in multiplayer and other complex scenarios, so:

- Consider Objectivity versus Emotions.
- Improving our chances of success in negotiation, most of which will come from behaviours.
- Other improvements come from planning, "finance" (Whole Life Costing, ABC, etc.)
- Environmental factors: how you manage the physical situation of a meeting (waiting, greeting, heating, etc.)?
- Foundations of the approach are "mathematical" via Nash equilibriums and Nash Bargaining Solution
- At the beginning of the negotiation, there is said to be the status quo with payoffs to buyer and seller, if an agreement is reached. No agreement results in status quo, so both have a risk of loss if no agreement.
- Risk in the negotiation context is determined by 3 factors:
  - Information, commitment and time.
- Bringing particular behaviours like aggression, disrespect, unfavourable personal remarks, or even remarks you think may be "clever": just don't

do it! Conversely, in one-time negotiations it may be appropriate, when there is little more at stake than pure cost.

- Surprises should be carefully considered and managed and the potential effects clearly mapped.
- Exercise patience and persistence, but not to the point of procrastination or pointlessness.
- Remove anxiety as it is scientifically proven to have a negative effect.
- Good negotiations often result from collaborative approaches rather than competitive approaches.
- Build rapport even before meetings, as this will enhance the possibility for collaboration and a better outcome.
- Reframe anger, and disappoint in another context such as regret or sadness.
- Don't be too eager to close things down once you have agreement. Remember relationships last long beyond a transaction or a contract.
- Balance consideration and scepticism as a buyer – you may only need to ensure that the other party feels a sense of equilibrium in order to satisfy the fairness rule.
- Don't let the euphoria of a deal suck you into agreeing something you later regret or simply can't deliver.
- Sometimes things are just what they are and don't deserve over-analysis.
- Actions and words have consequences, so ensure you know what they are.

CHAPTER 11 | PROSPECT THEORY

11.1 Prospect Theory: An Analysis of Decision under Risk

The whole concept of Prospect Theory[1] came from a paper written by Daniel Kahneman and Amos Tversky in 1979, which was further revised in 1992. The principal concept describes the way people choose between probabilistic alternatives that involve risk, where the probabilities of outcomes are unknown.

The theory states that people make decisions based on the potential value of losses and gains, rather than on the final outcome, and that people evaluate these losses and gains using certain heuristics. The model is descriptive: it tries to model real-life choices, rather than optimal decisions, as normative models do. In the original formulation, the term prospect referred to a lottery.

The theory describes the decision processes in two stages:

During an initial phase termed *editing*, outcomes of a decision are ordered according to a certain heuristic. In particular, people decide which outcomes they consider equivalent, set a reference point and then consider lesser outcomes as losses and greater ones as gains. The editing phase aims to alleviate any framing effects. It also aims to resolve isolation effects stemming from individuals' propensity to often isolate consecutive probabilities instead of treating them together. The editing process can be viewed as composed of coding, combination, segregation, cancellation, simplification and detection of dominance.

In the subsequent *evaluation phase*, people behave as if they would compute a value (or utility, as referenced in economic terms), based on the potential outcomes and their respective probabilities, and then choose the alternative that has the highest value.

The value function that passes through the reference point is s-shaped and asymmetrical (refer to Fig 1. overleaf). The value function is steeper for losses than for gains, indicating that losses outweigh gains.

It is important at this point to fall back on the term 'prospect' as this poses an interesting and relevant expression for how people view things, especially when there is discontent about or a total rejection of a current state of affairs or way of working. Looking at the term 'prospect' and relating it to more familiar gambling terminology, it starts to reveal to us that people are prepared – at times when they are dissatisfied – to gamble or prospect their options,

1. Tversky, A. and Kahneman, D. (1979). "Prospect Theory: An analysis of decision under risk" in *Econometrica*, Volume 47, No 2. pages 263-292.

The formula that Kahneman and Tversky assume for the evaluation phase is (in its simplest form) given by:

$$V = \sum_{i=1}^{n} \pi(p_i)v(x_i)$$

where V is the overall or expected utility of the outcomes to the individual making the decision, $x_1, x_2, \ldots, x_n$ are the potential outcomes and $p_1, p_2, \ldots, p_n$ their respective probabilities and v is a function that assigns a value to an outcome. The value function that passes through the reference point is s-shaped and asymmetrical. Losses hurt more than gains feel good (loss aversion). This differs from expected utility theory, in which a rational agent is indifferent to the reference point. In expected utility theory, the individual does not care how the outcome of losses and gains are framed. The function π is a probability weighting function and captures the idea that people tend to overreact to small probability events, but underreact to large probabilities. Let $(x, p; y, q)$ denote a prospect with outcome x with probability p and outcome y with probability q and nothing with probability $1 - p - q$. If $(x, p; y, q)$ is a regular prospect (i.e., either $p + q < 1$, or $x \geq 0 \geq y$, or $x \leq 0 \leq y$), then:

$$V(x, p; y, q) = \pi(p)v(x) + \pi(q)v(y)$$

However if $p + q = 1$ and either $x > y > 0$ or $x < y < 0$, then:

$$V(x, p; y, q) = v(y) + \pi(p) \left[v(x) - v(y) \right]$$

It can be deduced from the first equation that $v(y) + v(-y) > v(x) + v(-x)$ and $v(-y) > v(x) + v(-x)$. The value function is thus defined on deviations from the reference point, generally concave for gains and commonly convex for losses and steeper for losses than for gains. If (x, p) is equivalent to (y, pq) then (x, pq) is not preferred to (y, pqr), but from the first equation it follows that $\pi(p)v(x) + \pi(pq)v(y) = \pi(pq)v(y)$, which leads to $\pi(pr)v(x) \leq \pi(pqr)v(y)$, therefore:

$$\frac{\pi(pq)}{\pi(p)} \leq \frac{\pi(pqr)}{\pi(pr)}$$

This means that for a fixed ratio of probabilities the decision weights are closer to unity when probabilities are low than when they are high. In prospect theory, π is never linear. In the case that $x > y > 0$, $p > p'$ and $p + q = p' + q' < 1$, prospect $(x, p'; y, q')$ dominates prospect $(x, p'; y, q')$, which means that $\pi(p)v(x) + \pi(q)v(y) > \pi(p')v(x) + \pi(q')v(y)$, therefore:

$$\frac{\pi(p) - \pi(p')}{\pi(q') - \pi(q)} \leq \frac{v(y)}{v(x)}$$

As $y \to x$, $\pi(p) - \pi(p') \to \pi(q') - \pi(q)$, but since $p - p' = q' - q$, it would imply that π must be linear, however dominated alternatives are brought to the evaluation phase since they are eliminated in the editing phase. Although direct violations of dominance never happen in prospect theory, it is possible that a prospect A dominates B, B dominates C but C dominates A.

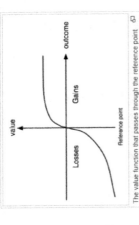

The value function that passes through the reference point is s-shaped and asymmetrical. The value function is steeper for losses than gains indicating that losses outweigh gains.

Figure 11.1. The formula that Kahneman and Tversky assume for the evaluation phase

especially when they feel there are no other credible options to turn to. This is analogous to the saying, "Never corner a rat as its only option to get out is to bite you". In life's applications, the lesson is never to present someone with a *fait accompli,* as it may just provoke them to prospect giving you a response you don't expect!

When we start to consider the prospect of certainty, probability and possibility, we begin to realise that different people will have different preferences and that we should look to understand these at the outset. Additionally, recognising that all sorts of other biases and heuristics come into play, such as anchoring, loss aversion (a central theme in chapter 8), value maximising, framing, etc. show that Prospect Theory is integral to daily business activity. Interestingly, there have been no research papers on procurement activity directly, but yet there are some related to aspects of buying insurance, air fares, tickets, etc., something I will return to later in this chapter. However, first, we must look at the principles as set out, particularly as they relate to losses and gains.

The Prospect Theory states that people are risk aversive in positive situations, and risk takers in negative situations when the probability of outcome is high. The same rule also applies vice versa as we can see in the Prospect Theory's fourfold table below.

	GAINS	LOSSES
HIGH PROBABILITY	95% chance to win 10 000 €. Fear of disappointment Risk averse	95% chance to lose 10 000 €. Hope to avoid loss Risk seeking
LOW PROBABILITY	5% chance to win 10 000 €. Hope of large gain Risk seeking	5% chance to lose 10 000 € Fear of large loss Risk averse

Table 11.1. Losses and gains

The effect of risk aversive behaviour is 1.5 to 2.5, factored across the general population. So, when we are considering a new product or service, it has to be offered on the basis of being generally cheaper or a better product in relation to the current one, at a ratio that is twice as good, for the person to take the chance and replace the current product or service.

Looking at this from the perspective of the incoming sales manager and the approach they may take and/or consider, it might reflect a scenario in which – if the products features and functionality as well as the cost is lower than current supply – then the probability of a sale, as described by Kahneman and Tversky, would look like the table below:

Probability %	Decision weight
0	0
1	5,5
2	8,1
3	13,2
5	18,6
10	26,1
20	42,1
50	60,1
80	71,2
90	79,3
95	87,1
99	91,2
100	100

Table 11.2. Probability weighting to convert a sale

The sales manager benefits from the situation where the buyer has a need and the gain is not probable, but substantial. Therefore, any improvement to the current situation is felt more greatly than the reality. This is the case, for example, in a situation where the organisation/buyer currently don't have a product or service for their need. A more challenging situation occurs when the organisation already has an equivalent product or service, and the new one is only slightly better than the current one. In this situation the buyer will behave "risk aversively" and have a more dominant position in negotiation.

Continuing the theme from a sales perspective, Prospect Theory, as described from table 11.2 above, can be applied in many ways. As an example, consider consumers' willingness to test a new market entrant for taxi services, instead of using traditional taxi service in a provincial town. Let's assume that decision-making is based on the quality of the ride and the price paid for it. The quality of the ride is a subjective factor that consumers feel uncertain about, and therefore we could assume that consumers will behave according to Prospect Theory.

When you are driving in a provincial town as opposed to a capital area, the most likely distances are few kilometres – an average taxi ride is about 17 kilometres in the country, so the calculation is based on a 15 kilometre average distance. When we count the price for a ride with two passengers at the new entrant's average price, we can represent the information as shown in table 11.3 below – presenting the passengers decision weight prices depending on the quality (80-100%):

Quality of ride (probability %)	80	90	95	98	99	100
Decision weight	60,1	71,2	79,3	87,1	91,2	100
Distance (km)	15	15	15	15	15	15
Price of taxi (min-max)	29,15 €	29,15 €	29,15 €	29,15 €	29,15 €	29,15 €
Price of Uber ride (min-max)	21,50 €	21,50 €	21,50 €	21,50 €	21,50 €	21,50 €
Price of Uber ride in decision weights	35,77 €	30,20 €	27,11 €	24,68 €	23,57 €	21,50 €

Table 11.3. Passenger's decision weight prices depending on quality (80-100%)

According to the calculation, the new taxi (market) entrant would be a more tempting option for a 15 kilometre ride if the quality or customer experience is at least 90% of the regular taxi service. The customer experience of the quality is influenced by the availability of rides, delivery assurance, quality of the car and driver's service knowledge. From the new entrant taxi's point of view, it is essential to set the quality right compared to the competition, and follow up how the service delivery succeeds. This way it is possible to ensure market penetration.

Conversely, if taxis were not price regulated in a market (irrespective of geography) in the country, taxi companies could use the model to calculate the right pricing to block new entrants. Additionally, the existing taxi companies could investigate what kind of customer experience or quality the new entrant needs to provide to challenge (with the current pricing structure) and enter the market successfully.

The model can be used to calculate price sensitivity to different products and services when the product or service features are similar to competitors. It could also be used to evaluate how much more the new product should improve the customer's life in order for them to make the switch from one vendor to another, if the price between vendors is coherent.

The interplay of overweighting of small probabilities and concavity-convexity of the value function leads to the so-called fourfold pattern of risk attitudes: risk-averse behaviour when gains have moderate probabilities, or losses have small probabilities; risk-seeking behaviour when losses have moderate probabilities, or gains have small probabilities.

Some behaviours observed in economics, like the Disposition effect[2] or the reversing of risk aversion/risk-seeking in case of gains or losses (termed the reflection effect)[3], can also be explained by referring to Prospect Theory.

An important implication of Prospect Theory is that the way economic agents subjectively frame an outcome or transaction in their mind affects the value they expect or receive. Narrow framing is a derivative result which has been documented in experimental settings by Tversky and Kahneman, whereby people evaluate new gambles in isolation, ignoring other relevant risks.

11.2 The use of Libertarian Paternalism in Procurement

Libertarian Paternalism is the idea that it is both possible and legitimate for private and public institutions to affect behaviour while also respecting freedom of choice, as well as the implementation of that idea. The term was coined by behavioural economist Richard Thaler and legal scholar Cass Sunstein in a number of papers.[4/5/6/7]

2. The Disposition Effect is an anomaly discovered in behavioural finance and relates to the tendency of investors to sell shares whose price has increased, while keeping assets that have dropped in value. Barberis, N. and Xiong, W. (2009). "What Drives the Disposition Effect? An Analysis of a Long-Standing Preference-Based Explanation" in *The Journal of Finance*, Vol LXIV, No 2.
3. The Reflection Effect in experimental economics and psychology involve gambles whose outcomes are opposite in sign, though of the same size, and they can be a problem in identifying people's 'rational' preferences. Compare two choices, one between a certain gain of £20 or a one-third chance of £60 and the other between a certain loss of £20 and a one-third chance of losing £60. Most people choose the certain gain in the first choice but the one-third chance of loss in the second. The effect is predicted by Prospect Theory as a consequence of the S shape of the value function.
4. Thaler, Richard and Sunstein, C.R. (2003). "Libertarian Paternalism" in *The American Economic Review* 93: 175–79.
5. Sunstein, Cass and Thaler, Richard. (2003). "Libertarian Paternalism is Not an Oxymoron" in *University of Chicago Law Review* 70(4): 1159–202.
6. Thaler, R.H. and Sunstein, C.R. (2009). *Nudge: Improving Decisions About Health, Wealth and Happiness 2nd edition*. New York: Penguin Books.
7. Thaler, R. H. (2009). "Opting In vs. Opting Out" in *The New York Times* 26 September.

The intended reference to Paternalism is in the context that "it tries to influence choices in a way that will make choosers better off, as judged by themselves"; note and consider, the concept 'paternalism' specifically requires a restriction of choice. It is libertarian in the sense that it aims to ensure that "people should be free to opt out of specified arrangements if they choose to do so". The possibility to opt-out is said to "preserve freedom of choice". Some may argue that this is in itself a contradiction, but is said to reflect more closely the political era under leaders such as Margaret Thatcher, Ronald Reagan, and so forth.

In the context it was proposed, it is said to refer to policies and policy-making that is/was designed to help people who behave irrationally and so are not advancing their own interests, while interfering only minimally with people who behave rationally. Such policies are also asymmetric in the sense that they should be acceptable both to those who believe that people behave rationally, and to those who believe that people often behave irrationally.

This is equally relevant when you come to look at policies within any organisation too. Advancing knowledge and approach to embrace the use of Behavioural Science, Purchasing and Supply Chain Management could and should be in a prime position to optimise competitive advantage by such interventions. In short: value maximisation through the lens of cost, quality, service, environmental, sustainability, etc.

My personal experience has allowed me to consider how this might be reflected in a company fleet policy, where there was an overarching need to reduce cost of service, but balance this with the emotional aspects of what most people consider to be a sign of status, benefit, right, entitlement, etc. – all of which are emotional factors.

By exercising an approach that is parallel to Libertarian Paternalism, it is possible to look at ways in which the appeal of an environmentally-sustainable organisation can be enhanced. This can be achieved through policy and advocacy in the market, as part of the choice architecture to bring into play – for example, electric and hybrid vehicles, challenging the sacred cows of CO_2 emissions over diesel-powered vehicles. The net result of this meant we were able to deliver a policy that was significantly more environmentally responsible without challenging the emotional triggers, and take significant cost out due to lower whole life cycle costs of such vehicles – a true win-win with no loss of functionality too.

There are clearly many applications to this in terms of policy-shaping for the good, that provide better outcomes as well as removing unnecessary cost to organisations to achieve the same functionality or benefit.

In application, I want to stimulate thoughts that this can be applied more widely, and in a more creative way than perhaps previously envisaged by challenging the traditional narrow-focused approach, and embracing the use of the supply chain as business partners to organisations. So, consider the following:

Countries that have an "opt-out" system for voluntary organ donation (anyone who did not explicitly refuse to donate their organs in the case of accident, is considered a donor) experience dramatically higher levels of organ donation consent, than countries with an opt-in system. Austria, with an opt-out system, has a consent rate of 99.98%, while Germany, with a very similar culture and economic situation, has an opt-in system, and a consent rate of only 12% (based on 2016 statistics).

Taxi drivers in London have seen an increase in tips in excess of the traditional 10%, after passengers were offered the facility to pay using credit cards on a device installed in the cab, the screen of which presented them with three default tip options ranging from 10% to 20%. This was more robustly measured in New York, where commuters were presented with options from 15% to 30% and as a result tips grew to 22% on average.

There are some similarities here with "nudging" – something I will address in a later chapter – but the move from an automatic opt-in position to one of opt-in by discretion and choice post-event is clearly a good one, and can be applied to a whole range of things we may have put in the "custom and practice" basket. They can also be challenged in an effective way organisationally through policy change. Clearly this requires collaboration at a senior level, something I have personally been party to, along with many peers in the procurement profession.

11.3 What does this have to do with Political, Economic, Social, Technology, Legal and Environment (PESTLE)?

We might ask, "Where does PESTLE fit with Prospect Theory and in particular loss aversion?" The link lies in policy-making at a political and/or country/economic block level – and ultimately at a global level. Further, the rapid and accelerating change in technology (moving from servers and software to SaaS)[8] solutions and finally legal changes, especially where they cross over in Modern Day Slavery, General Date Protection Regulations (GDPR), all have a profound effect on competitive advantage, innovation and resource allocation in the wider enterprise.

As always, we can either use these changes that are not within our organisational control or see them as opportunities to maximise our value by the way we use then to drive competitive advantage.

---

8. Software as a Service – removes the need for owning, implementing and operating your own hardware, as well as the requisite software, and moving to what is effectively a rental model that can be scaled across many businesses, with multiple cost-saving benefits.

From personal experience, when considering changes in insurance levels and the criteria being applied to companies within the fleet sector, the "do nothing" option amounted to an increase in costs, both of the policy and in day-to-day operational costs. So that was not an option for me! The alternative was to look at what was driving the increased premiums and life cycle costs, and soon it became clear that simply by changing the behaviours of the fleet drivers and parameters that drove the premiums from the insurance companies, we were able to reduce costs. Additionally, and perhaps more importantly, this provided advanced driver training, tutorials and a reward and recognition scheme.

The very notion that prospect can be seen as a gamble with outcomes seems more than fair when you consider that entities need to cut cost and create differentials from the competition.

Recent case studies (in the last 5-7 years) look at how Executives would respond to an economic downturn, with different groups being instructed differently to test the loss aversion principles in Prospect Theory. This is appended below:

For this research, Corporate Visions[9] contracted Dr Zakary Tormala – an expert in persuasion and social influence and a social psychologist at the Stanford Graduate School of Business – to test whether loss aversion affects the judgments and decisions of corporate executives. The aim was to test the principle using well-established research paradigms spanning business and personal decision-making contexts.

In all, 113 executives participated in the online experiment. The participants came from a vast array of industries (e.g., oil, software, finance, aerospace, etc.) and occupied a diverse set of high-level roles in their respective companies (e.g. president, VP, CEO, CFO, CMO, etc.).

At the outset of the experiment, participants were informed that the researchers were trying to learn more about executive decision-making, and that participants would be presented with several different hypothetical scenarios. Unbeknownst to the participants, they were randomly assigned to one of two conditions – a gain frame condition or a loss frame condition – which they were placed in before the first scenario and remained in for the entirety of the experiment.

In each case, participants were instructed to imagine being in a specific scenario and then were asked a question that varied depending on their condition assignment.

Scenario 1: Business Decision-Making

In the first scenario, all participants received the following instructions:
"The following question asks you to choose between two courses of action

---

9. *Corporate Visions: 2017, Losses and Gains: Does Loss Aversion Influence Executive Decision-Making?* Contributions from Dr. Zakary Tormala, Tim Riesterer, Erik Peterson and Conrad Smith.

when facing an economic downturn. Please read the question and choose one course of action: A large car manufacturer has recently been hit with a number of economic difficulties and it appears as if three plants need to be closed and 6,000 employees laid off. The vice president of production has been exploring alternative ways to avoid this crisis. She has developed two plans."

Following this overview, participants received information about the two options. The options were mathematically identical across the gain and loss frame conditions. Importantly, though, they differed in whether they were framed in terms of gains or losses. In the gain frame condition, the options were described in terms of how many plants and jobs would be saved:

Plan A: This plan will save one of the three plants and 2,000 jobs.
or
Plan B: This plan has one-third probability of saving all three plants and all 6,000 jobs, but has two-thirds probability of saving no plants and no jobs.

In the loss frame condition, the options were described in terms of how many plants and jobs would be lost:

Plan A: This plan will result in the loss of two of the three plants and 4,000 jobs.
or
Plan B: This plan has two-thirds probability of resulting in the loss of all three plants and all 6,000 jobs, but has one-third probability of losing no plants and no jobs.

In both conditions, the choices were mathematically equivalent. But, the wording was changed to see if we could affect the persuade-ability of executives to consider the riskier alternative (in both conditions, Plan B).

In fact, there was a statistically significant difference in participants' choices across the two conditions, as illustrated in figure 11.4 (opposite). In the gain frame condition, 74% of participants chose Plan A and 26% chose Plan B. In the loss frame condition, 55% of participants chose Plan A, while 45% chose Plan B. The jump from 26% to 45% is significant. Essentially, there was a 70+ % increase in the number of executives willing to take the risky bet when it was framed in terms of a loss versus a gain.

This is a classic example of the concept of loss aversion, and powerful proof that executives can be emotionally swayed by the positioning of a choice despite having the exact same "math equations" to choose from.

In sales and marketing terms, asking a prospect or customer to make a change and do something different than what they're doing today is often perceived as the "risky" choice – especially when compared to the incumbent solution or status quo. The above findings show that you will significantly improve your chances of persuading them to take a risk by positioning the alternative as a loss condition.

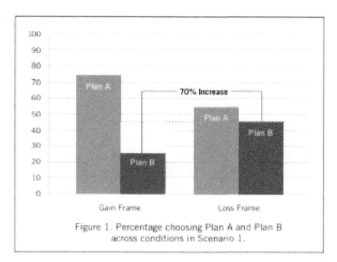

Figure 1. Percentage choosing Plan A and Plan B across conditions in Scenario 1.

Figure 11.2. The gain frame condition

In the second scenario, the study moved away from business decision-making into a more personal context. Specifically, participants were asked about wine.

In the gain frame condition, participants were instructed to imagine there was one bottle of their favourite bottle of wine – a rare vintage – in a local wine shop, and they were asked how much they would be willing to pay for it. In the loss frame condition, participants imagined there was one bottle of their favourite wine, also rare, in their wine cellar, and they indicated for how much they would be willing to sell that bottle.

In each case, participants typed their answer into an open-ended box on the computer screen. In this context, loss aversion predicts that the price participant's list would be higher in the loss frame (selling) condition than in the gain frame (buying) condition. This would suggest that participants weigh losses more heavily than otherwise equivalent gains.

As illustrated in figure 11.5 (overleaf), there was a statistically significant difference across conditions, as participants listed a substantially higher price in the loss frame condition ($1,950.71) than in the gain frame condition ($173.38). In essence, participants demanded significantly more money to sell (or be compensated for losing) their favourite bottle of wine than they would be willing to pay to buy their favourite bottle of wine.

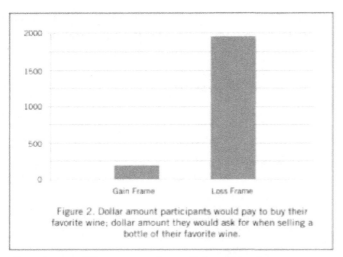

2000
1500
1000
500
0
Gain Frame
Loss Frame
Figure 2. Dollar amount participants would pay to buy their favorite wine; dollar amount they would ask for when selling a bottle of their favorite wine.

Figure 11.3. The cost and condition framing

This study provides evidence that loss aversion influences business and personal decisions in a sample of executives. In the business context, participants were more attracted to a risky proposal when the safer alternative was framed as a loss.

Similar to most of your selling situations, your offering is viewed as the risky option because it requires prospects to change and do something different. In order to increase your odds that the prospect or customer will choose your riskier option, you must frame the status quo or competitive option as a potential loss.

In the personal scenarios, loss aversion assumed the form of endowment effects and mere ownership biases, as participants required more money to sell (i.e. lose) the items than they were willing to pay to buy them.

The results suggest that executive decision-makers are not as rational as might be imagined by marketers and salespeople, and that their decision-making can be swayed by simple changes in word choice that can make a seemingly risky selling scenario (like leaving their current situation) seem more attractive.

CHAPTER 12 | NUDGING (INCLUDING ETHICS AND GOVERNANCE)

12.1 What is Nudging?

Nudging came to public attention as part of Behavioural Economics in the 2009 book by economist, Richard Thaler and legal scholar Cass Sunstein[1], which described an approach to changing behaviour based on manipulating *"the choice architecture[2] that alters people's behaviour in a predictable way without forbidding any options or significantly changing their economic incentives".[3]*

In practice, this means that policymakers in the public sector, and increasingly those in the private sector too, present information in such a way as to take advantage of predictable patterns of behaviour to encourage people to make a particular choice without coercing them.

By way of example, here are a few everyday nudges that you can observe:

*   As you approach a pedestrian-crossing, you may well see the letters "LOOK LEFT" or "LOOK RIGHT" painted on the ground, to make you aware of which way the traffic will be coming from so that you can focus your view in the right direction to avoid being knocked down.
*   As you leave the ports straight off the ferry from UK to Europe and vice versa, the road signs will remind you which side of the road to drive on.
*   The urinal fly nudge is a well-known mind hack that originated at Schipol airport in Amsterdam, but can now be seen in urinals all over the globe. By having images of flies etched near the drains of the bathroom urinals, spillages were reduced by 80%! (see Fig 12.1 overleaf). This is a great example of a nudge that is rarely consciously processed, yet taps into a quirk in most male's behaviour – we men like to aim at things!

---

1. Thaler, R. and Sunstein, C.R. (2008). *Nudge: Improving decisions about health, wealth and happiness.* Penguin.
2. Choice architecture is the design of different ways in which choices can be presented to consumers, and the impact of that presentation on consumer decision-making. For example, the number of choices presented, the manner in which attributes are described, and the presence of a "default" can all influence consumer choice. As a result, advocates of Libertarian Paternalism and asymmetric paternalism have endorsed the deliberate design of choice architecture to nudge consumers toward personally and socially desirable behaviours like saving for retirement, choosing healthier foods, or registering as an organ donor.
3. Economic incentives: something, often money or a prize, offered to make someone behave in a particular way: e.g. the state has an economic incentive program that provides an additional incentive to companies that already are located and employ workers here and are considering expansion.

Figure 12.1. The Fly Nudge

Having orientated you hopefully into the right space, I will move onto a few other nudges that will help develop the concept for you, but are more complex in their design – we can use these examples to prepare us for how we apply this to business-related issues more effectively as we proceed through the chapter. I will set out a few more complex scenarios:

Scenario 1: Over-the-counter non-prescription medicines

In September 1998, the UK changed the packaging regulations for Paracetamol (the active ingredient in Tylenol, sold in the U.S.A), to require blister packs for packages of 16 pills when sold over the counter in places like convenience stores, and for packages of 32 pills when sold in pharmacies.

The result: a study by Oxford University researchers showed that over the subsequent 11 or so years, suicide deaths from Paracetamol-related overdoses declined by 43%, and a similar decline was found in accidental deaths from medication poisoning. In addition, there was a 61% reduction in liver transplants attributed to toxicities. Also, the regulation dictated that only one pack per customer could be sold. This was critical to the overall choice architecture as suicide attempts are almost always impulsive rather than planned events.

In addition, and parallel to this in the USA, the Food and Drug Administration required blister packaging for iron pills which can cause death (by poisoning) in young children; the number of iron-ingestion calls to poison control centres in the country dropped by about 33% and the number of deaths dropped to almost zero.

Scenario 2: Driving in France

As I am fortunate enough to own a property in this wonderful country I will describe a journey one night on my way across the country to our house.

A spooky, black human silhouette suddenly appeared out of nowhere on the roadside of a picturesque country road in southern France. It was the size of an adult, but it had no face; instead, a lightning bolt seemed to split its head in two.

I was cruising down this road with no traffic, no lampposts and no speed traps, just ancient trees towering on both sides. There seemed nothing else unusual, so I dismissed the figure as a local farmer's folly. But then there was another. And then two more – an adult and what looked like a child. Then it dawned on me. The cut-outs represented people who had died on this road in car accidents. The message came across: I slowed down.

This was in start contrast – and perhaps far more effective – than the more obvious practice of using signs to display speed restrictions or remind drivers to take regular breaks. Recently, too, there have been more subtle methods introduced, such as average speed cameras.

The nudging has been proven to work – in 2005 average speed cameras were installed on a 32-mile stretch of the A77 motorway near Glasgow in Scotland,. Since then, the number of road casualties has fallen by 37% on that stretch of road.

Scenario 3: Carbon Dioxide Pollution

Worldwide, airlines produced 781 million tons of CO_2 in 2015. To put it into perspective, if the industry were a country it would be the world's seventh largest emitter of CO_2. In 2016 Virgin Atlantic Airlines (VAA) decided that they wanted to reduce their CO_2 footprint which required them to reduce fuel consumption.

They began using data from 2014, with the following measurement metrics: 40, 000 flights, 335 Captains and 3 flight phases; take off, mid-air and landing.

By focusing on pilots' pre-flight, in-flight and post-flight behaviours and throwing in a few small incentives, the project led to some huge fuel savings and an unexpected jump in work satisfaction for many of the pilots.

The project saved 22,000 tonnes of CO_2 (through a saving of 6,828 metric tons of fuel) and £3.3-million as a result.

The pilots were split into four groups:

- An 'information' group where pilots received a monthly feedback report on their flying behaviours.
- A 'targets' group where pilots were given the same feedback, but also individual-specific targets to reach.

- An 'incentives' group where pilots got both the information and targets, as well as the promise of a £10 donation to a chosen charity for each target they met in a given month.
- A 'control' group where pilots were told they were being tracked but received no feedback.

The results were mixed but still impressive. One of the surprise factors from the study project was the drastic impact on the control group, who received neither feedback nor incentives for adopting more sustainable flying techniques, but by simply knowing their behaviour was being monitored, introduced substantial changes in their flying techniques.

Captains within the pro-social (incentives aimed at the carbon reduction aspect and other environmental factors) incentives group not only reduced their carbon footprint but reported higher job satisfaction – attributed to the fact they were helping their chosen charities every time they reached a target.

An important aspect that also needs to be recognised is that the pilots did not personally benefit in their actions; however they developed an emotional connection to the project because they knew their actions could have a postive impact on the charity of their choice in the incentives group.

The recognition that highly-skilled pilots can make material changes in how they pilot the aircraft, such as how much fuel to take on, speed, altitude, route, taxing on fewer engines, etc. also points to the trust and respect the company and study group have for the skill of their pilots.

Of primary relevance to me was the link between the pilots and the measurements/incentives, and the fact it was not aimed company-wide or group-wide. It is an individual action. This is something that helped me design a parallel choice architecture in another sector (automotive) and category of spend (energy).

12.2 Nudging applied to Decision-making

The concept that you may want to nudge someone or a defined group or population in a particular direction is appealing, especially when in commercial terms the sooner you get a "go" decision, the sooner you move to implementation and deliver benefits. However, there needs to be reasonable consideration and planning in this approach, based on sound basis of facts and information. This also implies that it has to be without a detrimental level of assumptions and must be ethically-derived, something we will tackle shortly in this chapter.

I find it is often the case in procurement that the leader and team members who follow a structured approach, such as category management, are likely to be well-informed of the category (spend, market knowledge, suppliers, etc.). Given this situation, the motivation is to help inform the decision-makers to the right course of action as soon as possible for the benefit of the organisation as a whole. For me this is justification enough to enable nudging to precipitate the right decision in an optimal timeframe.

The nudging can take place at multiple levels; across a cross-functional team, stakeholders and decision-makers on a one-to-one basis or small group basis. Moreover, this can then be consolidated at a formal level in stakeholder meetings, with budget holders or at an Executive level depending on the type of decision sought.

Nuding can be implement using a range of practical techniques, as described in the scenarios in the first section of this chapter i.e. positively framing information, incentivisation (plain and simple), etc. and planning the whole approach to choice architecture. This is very much like a well-orchestrated symphony involving many players with different instruments collaborating to deliver the same tune.

12.3 Ethics and Governance of Good Nudges

There has been much debate about how and where a code of conduct for the use of nudges may come from. In fact I learnt recently that India has introduced one and I suspect there may be others out there. The reason is that there are unethical nudges taking place out there every day – I have observed many being deployed in supermarkets around the globe, something I personally find abhorrent. These often appear in the form of a 'buy 2 for X price', when the lower price is often to be found in the same product placed above eye level, with a lower price per litre/kg, pro rata. There are other examples, but this is the easiest to relate to. For me this conjures up the image of my grandparents in the supermarket believing and trusting that they had been given a good bargain, only to find their trust and vulnerability had been exploited. Perhaps it's just me...

Accordingly, the need for clarification and/or a code of conduct is very apparent to those of us who have studied and used this approach in a professional manner, but witness others operating in a less ethical way. Interestingly the co-author of *Nudge*, Sunstein, has subsequently published a paper[4] with no less than 106 clarifications and commentary on the approach he and Thaler had clearly originally intended, to try and put things beyond all reasonable doubt.

---

4. Sunstein, C.S. (2014). *The Ethics of Nudging.* (preliminary draft)

The paper is broken down into the following sections, and offers an insight into the areas of both consideration and focus for the choice architect:

- Abstract
- I – Introduction
- II - The Diversity of Nudges and the Dangers of Abstraction
- III. "As Judged by Themselves"
- IV. Seven Objections
- A. Paternalism
- B. Autonomy
- C. Coercion
- D. Dignity
- E. Manipulation
- F. Learning
- G. Biased officials
- VI. What Do People Think?
- A. Transparency About Nudging
- B. Politics matters
- C. Nudging System 1
- V. Conclusion

To summarise and extract some of the more important points, I think it necessary to set the context of what an "ethical nudge" should be bounded by:

- Interventions that steer people in particular directions, but also allow them to go their own way. As a reminder, a nudge is intended as a warning. Therefore, a Global Positioning System (GPS) nudges; a default rule nudges. To qualify as a nudge, an intervention must not impose significant material incentives. For clarity, a nudge is not a subsidy, a fine or a jail sentence. To qualify as a nudge, the action/intervention must fully preserve freedom of choice, and not impose significant material costs on choosers.
- When people make decisions, they must do so against a background consisting of choice architecture. For example, a cafe has a design, and that design or its layout will affect what people choose to do, just in the same way as websites do.
- People's attention is or could be classified as a scarce resource. Hence when applying nudges which are complex, people need to apply themselves to those decisions in a more considered way, e.g. mortgages, loans, etc.
- Spontaneous prompts nudge no more or less than intentional designs, and invisible hands can nudge every bit as much as the most visible ones.

However, it is fair to say that these invisible hands may be less dangerous than unethical intentions.

- Designed in such a way as to help choosers, by increasing their welfare or promoting their autonomy, is ethical. However, some nudges, equally ethical, are designed to help third parties, for example, by reducing environmental harm.
- Anything by design that has the potential to raise serious ethical questions should be avoided.
- Possible concerns about nudging and choice architecture point to four foundational commitments:
- welfare
- autonomy
- dignity
- self-government.
- Using certain assumptions that are known to invoke a self-conscious choice architecture is especially dangerous, because it is explicitly directed at achieving certain goals. Therefore, acting in a malevolent way as a choice architect is unacceptable. Experience by many of the leading proponents of nudging such as Thaler and Sunstein show that the most serious harm tends to come from mandates and bans, from coercion, and not from nudges which maintain freedom of choice.
- Some nudges are able, by way of their choice architecture, to alter default rules which establish what happens if people do nothing at all. Others include simplification (for example, of applications for job training or financial aid); disclosure of factual information (for example, calorie labels, designed to promote healthier choices, or of the use of conflict minerals known to finance conflicts in other countries, such as The Democratic Republic of the Congo); warnings, graphic or otherwise (e.g. cigarette packages); reminders (for example, of bills that are about to become due); increases in ease and convenience (for example, of healthy goods); uses of social norms (for example, disclosure of how your energy consumption compares to that of your neighbours); nonmonetary rewards, such as public recognition; active choosing (as in the open question: "what retirement plan do you want?"); and pre-commitment strategies (through which people agree, in advance, to a particular course of conduct, such as a smoking cessation programme).
- Justification on the grounds that it helps counteract a behavioural bias, but (and this is an important but), such a bias is not a necessary justification for a nudge. Disclosure of information can be helpful even in the absence of any bias. A GPS is useful even for people who do not suffer from present bias, probability neglect, or unrealistic optimism. A default rule simplifies

life and might therefore be desirable, whether or not a behavioural bias is involved.

- Best practice in choice architecture often calls for active choosing. Sometimes it is best to prompt choice by asking people what they want, without imposing any requirement that they do so. Accordingly, a prompt is emphatically a nudge designed to get people to express their will, and it might be unaccompanied by any effort to steer people in a preferred direction, except in the direction of choosing.
- Choice architecture should be transparent and subject to public scrutiny, certainly if public officials are responsible for it.
- Ethical concerns principally relate to: autonomy, dignity (sometimes described as "respect for persons"), manipulation, and learning. Obviously, this might be true if their goal is illicit, but some people believe that some kind of violation (for example, an insult to autonomy) can occur even without an illicit goal.
- Recognise the aspect of, bounded rationality as typically most people lack the full suite of information to make an effective choice or decision. Moreover, most people tend to be unrealistically optimistic and show *present bias*[5], focusing on the short-term and downplaying the future. People do not deal well with probability, in part because they use heuristics, or mental shortcuts, that sometimes lead them in unfortunate directions.

I have provided here a collection (in no particular order) of potential objections that could apply to the practice of nudging, so that they can be considered when applying a design to a choice architecture:

- They are paternalistic.
- Intrude on people's autonomy.
- Seen as coercive, even if they preserve freedom of choice
- Insult people's dignity (the "nanny state" captures this objection).
- Forms of manipulation. (automatic enrolment into schemes)
- Do not promote learning or understanding

Political values greatly matter to people's assessment of nudges and may provoke both positive and negative affinity because of this. Some nudges make challenge their substantive policy preferences. The result is partisan nudge bias[6]. Accordingly, are more problematic when applied to policy objectives they

---

5. Present bias refers to the tendency of people to give stronger weight to payoffs that are closer to the present time when considering trade-offs between two future moments (O'Donoghue, and, Rabin, 1999).

6. Partisan Nudge Bias: Todd Rogers, Harvard Kennedy School, September 2015: Presenting

oppose, etc. and of course the reverse is true in gaining empathy. In conclusion this is what was offered by Sunstein in the same paper:

- Nudges and choice architecture cannot be avoided, and so it is pointless to object to them or to attempt to wish them away. However, intentional changes in choice architecture, deliberately made by choice architects, can indeed run into ethical concerns – most obviously where the underlying goals are illicit. Indeed, a concern about illicit goals underlies many of the most plausible objections to some nudges.

- Where the goals are legitimate, an evaluation of ethical concerns needs to be made with close reference to the context. Disclosure of accurate information, reminders, and factual warnings are generally unobjectionable. If nothing is hidden or covert, nudges are less likely to run afoul of ethical constraints.

- Default rules frequently make life more manageable, and it does not make much sense to reject such rules generally. At the same time, it must be acknowledged that active choosing might turn out to be preferable to default rules, at least where learning is important and where one size does not fit all.

- It is possible to consider some nudges as manipulative in part, questioning autonomy and dignity. Even when nudges target System 1 judgements (as previously outlined), it might well strain the concept of manipulation to categorise them as nudges. To counter this by being transparent is critical to be considered effective. Equally, there should be no constraint on the rationale (not hidden), and no limitation of freedom of choice either.

The practice and governance around how designers and choice architects work in this area requires a high level of skill, consideration and clear ethical principles to adhere to. I can visualise in years to come that this will be included in ethical standards and codes of conduct for all professional bodies, wherever they sit or practice in Purchasing and Supply Chain Management spectrum.

---

participants of varying political persuasions with short descriptions of various behavioural policy nudges (e.g., designating enrolment in a programme as a default). To explain how such policy tools could be applied, we illustrated them using either an example of a liberal policy priority (e.g., encouraging low-income individuals to enrol in food stamps programs for which they were legally eligible) or a conservative policy priority (e.g., encouraging the wealthy to take advantage of capital gains tax breaks they were legally eligible for). The participants were then asked to rate how ethical, manipulative and coercive they found the nudge to be, as a general policy approach. In almost every case, respondents on the left of the political spectrum supported nudges when they were illustrated with a liberal agenda but opposed them when they were illustrated with a conservative one; meanwhile, respondents on the political right exhibited the opposite pattern.

12.4 Nudge applied to Policy-making and Case Studies

The most famous instances of, or institutions for applying nudges is the Behavioural Insights Team (BIT), established in the UK in 2010 and then replicated in many other countries after this. The Behavioural Insights Team is more popularly known as the Nudge Unit, referencing the book, *Nudge*. One example of a nudge unit experiment is testing different reminder letters to people who hadn't paid their taxes. According to the BIT, "One nudge was a sentence telling recipients that a majority of people in their community had already paid their taxes. Another said that most people who owe a similar amount of tax had paid. Both messages bolstered tax collection, and combining them had an even stronger effect."

Nudge experiments have been done in the U.S.A, Denmark, Sweden, India amongst many others. In the U.S.A, examples include voter mobilisation campaigns, which have tried asking not only "Are you going to vote?" but also "What route are you taking to the polling station? At what time are you planning to go? What bus will get you there?" Doing this makes it twice as likely that the individual will actually vote. That's a big result for a little nudge.

Rohan Silva, an adviser to David Cameron, then-British prime minister, is quoted as saying, "Governments have a set of nudges in everything they do, even if they don't do anything. You can either be deliberate about it or not." This is an important statement in relation to the concept that every ethics environment has unwritten rules that govern ethical decision-making. These rules nudge – and sometimes push or elbow – officials and their subordinates into making decisions that can harm both the community and themselves. Central to an unhealthy ethics environment is the refusal to deliberately and openly discuss these rules and decide if other rules may be more appropriate.

At a board meeting, whenever the board moves on to a new agenda item, the chair should ask not only if anyone has a motion, but also if anyone has or knows of a potential conflict situation. Here is language that can be used at public meetings: "Does anyone here have a special relationship with anyone involved in this matter? Or would a decision on this matter benefit or harm you, your family, or your business or business associates? If you are not sure, ask for more information or for ethics advice. The matter can be tabled if your questions cannot be answered immediately."

Questions like this are asked at some public meetings; however, it is recognised that this may not be sufficient and that the same questions should be asked at closed agency and department meetings too.

Another example, initiated in 2013 by a student named Ben at the University of Bristol, resulted in thousands of school pupils in England receiving a letter.

The recipients of the letter had just gained good marks in their GCSE exams (normally taken at age 16), but they attended schools where only a few pupils progressed to university at age 18, and those that did were likely to go to their nearest university rather than consider alternatives. That suggested the schools were poor at nurturing aspiration. In his letter, Ben explained that employers cared about the reputation of the university a job applicant had attended. He pointed out that top universities can be a better – and financially more feasible – option for poorer pupils, because they give more financial aid. He added that he had not known these facts when he was the same age as the recipients of his letter.

The letters had the effect that was hoped for. A study published in March 2017[7] found that after leaving school, the students who received both Ben's letter and another similar one some months later, were more likely to be at a prestigious university than those who received just one of the letters, and more likely again than those who received none.

The study covered over 11,000 students in 300 schools. The 'cost of acquisiton', for lack of a better term here, for each extra student that attended a better university, was just £45 ($58), much less than universities' own attempts to broaden their intake. And the approach was less heavy-handed than imposing quotas for poorer pupils. The Department for Education is considering rolling out the scheme more fully.

One of the most-effective nudges is to set the desired outcome as the default. For example, enrolling all workers in a company pension scheme, and requiring them to opt out if they do not wish to be members greatly increases savings rates compared with opt-in as the default position.

The power of making things easy was also demonstrated by an experiment in the U.S.A in 2012, in which the application forms used by poor Americans to apply to university were pre-filled with data from tax returns. That raised the likelihood that they would go to university by a quarter. Nudges that involve making the desired choice more attractive, or at least more obvious, range from making the wording on letters about late payment of taxes more emphatic to placing healthy food at eye level in canteens.

Other organisations such as the United Nations (UN), the Organisation for Economic Co-operation and Development (OECD), and soon to follow the World Bank in the areas of aid and development have recently started using nudges to tackle corruption. The World Bank has been involved in several trials, for example one in Nigeria, to improve record-keeping in health clinics, making it less likely that money will be stolen, due to the choice architecture and language being used. It has found that giving health

---

7. Sanders, M., Chande, R. and Selley, E. (2017). *Encouraging People into University Research report*, March 2017. Behavioural Insights Team, Government Social Research.

workers who keep good records certificates that they can display in their clinics makes a worthwhile difference. Another promising area involves motivating people to refuse bribes. Anti-corruption policies generally rely on punishment. But behavioural insights suggest harnessing social norms, for example by publicly celebrating those who stay on the right side of the law, is far more effective.

The list is extensive and the parallels in policy-making across the private sector are no exception. From car policies, pension policies and savings schemes, to training and development, these are all fertile areas for procurement to be pro-active and lead the way to deliver increased competitive advantage.

12.5 Nudge: Beware of the Marketers and Sellers (an inside story!)

Taking a look at nudging from the other side of the table, so to speak, presents a view that I have aggregated with other articles to shed some light on how the procurement community is viewed, as follows:

In short, the articles proclaim that sales need to use the latest insights from psychology (Behavioural Science) to nudge the buyer towards a decision.

An interesting lens from a sales perspective, is one that sets out how to tackle those "purchasing and contracting" types in nine easy steps[8]. This has been the case for many years, and indeed there are also poachers turned gamekeepers out there, corralling buyers into conferences to disclose to them all what the "enemy" has to unleash on the unsuspecting buyer/ purchaser. The important thing is to be aware of it.

A series of articles that specifically refer to nudging in the procurement and contracting community caught my attention. I have aggregated and blended the articles to produce a light read that serves to make the procurement community aware of the potential nudging presents as an approach:

- **Speed of decision-making:** we, as purchasers, go too slowly. The problem is that the information provided is simply not sufficient, and while it's not the problem of the sales proposal, the buyer's interpretation is that this is where the problem lies.
- **Information is not objectively reviewed because we are not rational as buyers:** people are prone to misread the information, be unduly influenced by others, or be swayed by impulse and emotion. It can be compensated

---

8. Collis, R. (2013). "9 new ways to nudge your customer to buy" in *Customer Think*. http://customerthink.com/9_new_ways_to_nudge_your_customer_to_buy/. Accessed 23 May 2013.

though through a number of remedies, which the seller can adjust to his or her message to nudge the buyer more effectively towards a decision.

- **The power to nudge:** the 9 step approach to nudge the buyer to make a decision; set out on the premise of a number of the leading books in the field of cognitive research, but taking some short-cuts in their explanations and simplifying some of the concepts to help the seller apply it fast! The objective being on the part of the seller to help nudge the buyer, by adjusting how your information is communicated and the choices presented to the them. So, sellers need to have their messages or pitch to hand and follow steps 1 to 9:

1. **Simplify the choice:** The buyer simply doesn't have the time to pay attention to all the detail. The role of the salesperson is to help simplify the decision for the buyer.

2. **Fuel the buyers' optimism:** There is a likelihood that the buyer sees him or herself as above average in comparison to others in their peer set, so the seller must appeal to the buyer's positive self-concept. At the same time the seller can carefully help the buyer to more objectively benchmark themselves with others. The buyer may have an optimistic expectation regarding outcomes, or results achieved. The downside here is that the buyer may be overlooking some of the risks involved. At its simplest, the seller must help the buyer to envisage their future success while managing any risks involved.

3. **Preserve an element of the status quo:** The tendency is to stick with what we know, versus taking a chance on what we don't know. That is until the tension for change becomes so great that the binds with status quo are separated. In the meantime, it can result in a resistance to change and leave people settling too long for unsatisfactory situations. The seller needs to understand how the various stakeholders are invested in the status quo and the risks associated with change.

4. **Ensure your message fits with existing beliefs:** For the seller, drawing attention to beliefs is first step in change. The role of the seller is to help the buyer to hold a mirror up to their needs and their beliefs. Sellers need to understand the strength and rigidity of buyer attitudes and beliefs and tailor their message accordingly. For the seller some tension among the buyer's existing attitudes and perceptions may be important to creating the demand for their solution. However, if the tension is too great, then the seller's message is likely to flounder.

5. **Connect with the Buyer's Emotions:** Sellers must connect with the buyer's emotions. There are as many as 48 different emotions ranging from pride to fear. They add context and depth to how even the most hard-nosed, rational decision criteria are applied. Also, does the message connect with

the audience's emotions? The buyer's interpretation of information, people or events related to the sale may be determined by pre-programmed emotional responses (often subconscious). For example, an immediate like or dislike of a salesperson, or a gut instinct that something either does, or does not feel right. Such emotions may be helpful or unhelpful, they may be rational, or not. Regardless, they are of interest to the seller.

6. **Help the buyer to avoid risk:** The implication, as sellers know, is that people will pay to avoid the risk of loss. However, their calculation of the likelihood or the extent of the loss tends not to be very scientific. It can be easily swayed by emotion and other factors.

7. **Provide the Buyer with a powerful peer comparison:** Social comparison can play an important role in our decisions. Telling the buyer about what their peers are doing and how they are using your solution is probably the most effective way of telling them about your product. Some customers and markets are influenced by a tendency to conform, what is otherwise called 'herd mentality'. However, to leverage this effect it is important to know just what herd your customer belongs, or aspires to belong to.

8. **Ensure your message is a familiar one:** Familiarity isn't necessarily fussy about the source, and therefore can become blurred. Sellers must strive to ensure that all those involved in the buying decision have some level of familiarity with their company and its solution. They must also deepen their appreciation of marketing's role in building marketplace familiarity for their brand.

9. **Focus your benefits on the short-term:** Buyers are often biased in favour of the immediate value, putting short-term gain ahead of long-term consequences. Quarterly corporate performance targets often reinforce similar short-termist behaviours. Present benefits promised sufficiently close to hand, or short-term.

While this is a summary of various articles and selling approaches, it nevertheless reinforces the fact that the process of selling can and will deploy the use of Behavioural Science upon the procurement community. Hopefully this serves as food for thought, but remember the practice of Behavioural Science has been in place in retail, sales, business development for well over a decade to date!

PART D
//
CHANGE MANAGEMENT
AND ALLIED SUBJECTS

CHAPTER 13 | FRICTIONLESS

Firstly, the aim of *frictionless* is to make solutions in business, technology, enterprise-wide activity, design, transactions, decision-making, governance and compliance as intuitive and easy as possible. This extends to removing barriers, simplifying choices, reducing the number of steps/stages to a decision, use of clearer/simpler language or any action that enables and simplifies anything pre-existing.

13.1 Concept and Approaches to easier Decision-making in Purchasing and Supply Chain Management

First of all, it is probably worth clarifying in what context we wish to apply *frictionless,* and what it is about. Examples of this could be extended to the following:

- Creating an efficient B2B portal
- Customer Experience programme
- Requisition process
- P2P process or system/approach

Frictionless in the context of strategic and/or business decision-making is principally initiated as part of a designed approach to seek and gain approvals and agreements to key decisions within an organisation. Frictionless in this context can be further defined as:

The removal of obstacles, dissension, conflict (between parties, groups), misalignment and unnecessary complexity with the aim of creating the optimal route or steps to a defined decision point.

A quote from Albert Camus, "Life is the sum of all your choices" provokes the thought that none of our decisions is in isolation, and/or the notion that a decision is defined by rational alone is misconceived.

Decision-making is the fusion of many non-rationally derived inputs including sociology, psychology, Behavioural Science and political science to name but a few. Decision is and will become more complex in shorter time spans and dimensions, and on a scale we have yet to discover. As I stated earlier, we need to remember the bounded rationality that constrains our outcomes. We are always at the mercy of live variables – people – so we need to measure our approach and cognition in everything and anything that is dynamic.

In researching this area more deeply it intrigued me that after the Bay of Pigs[1] fiasco, it was in fact then-President of the USA, John F. Kennedy who instigated the discipline of retrospective reviews, that served him well in the neutralisation of the Cuban Missile Crisis[2] in October 1962. His approach ordered a review, post-Bay of Pigs to institute 4 changes for critical decision-making:

1. Each participant to a critical decision should function as a "sceptical generalist", focusing on the problem as a whole rather than approaching it from his or her department's standpoint.
2. To stimulate freewheeling discussions, the group should use informal settings, with no formal agenda and protocol, so as to avoid the status-laden meetings in the White House.
3. The team should be broken up into sub-groups that would work on alternatives and then reconvene.
4. The team should sometimes meet without Kennedy present, so as to avoid people simply following his views.

As you read through this chapter you will begin to see the significance of these 4 simple steps in debiasing and avoiding GroupThink and many of the other attributes that prevent good decision-making. JFK's approach as above resulted in the option not to go to war with Russia in the Cuban missile crisis, but to implement a naval blockade.

The principal reason why we would want to consider this is because making and receiving better quality first-time decisions means we improve the level of trust and engagement within an organisation and deliver outcomes in the optimum time period. This conserves valuable resources and enables delivery of added value and competitive advantage to the organisation in an optimum timeframe.

In terms of considerations in this area and concept, frictionless will principally relate to the process or activity centred around decision-making. Some of the

---

1. The Bay of Pigs Invasion was a failed military invasion of Cuba undertaken by the Central Intelligence Agency (CIA)-sponsored paramilitary group Brigade 2506 on 17 April 1961. A counter-revolutionary military (made up of Cuban exiles who travelled to the United States after Castro's takeover), trained and funded by the CIA, Brigade 2506 fronted the armed wing of the Democratic Revolutionary Front (DRF) and intended to overthrow the increasingly communist government of Fidel Castro. Launched from Guatemala and Nicaragua, the invading force was defeated within three days by the Cuban Revolutionary Armed Forces, under the direct command of Castro.
2. Also known as the October Crisis, the Caribbean Crisis, or the Missile Scare, was a 13-day (October 16–28, 1962) confrontation between the United States and the Soviet Union concerning American ballistic missile deployment in Italy and Turkey with consequent Soviet ballistic missile deployment in Cuba. The confrontation is often considered the closest the Cold War came to escalating into a full-scale nuclear war.

principal drivers for why we don't have a frictionless experience may be because of the following:

- Too much complexity in what we are attempting to decide or transact
- Missed expectations
- Conflicting information
- Does not clearly support the organisations strategy/objectives
- State of disorder
- Task overload
- Competing priorities
- Simply not priority for the decision-maker
- Hidden biases
- Competing projects/programmes for investment/resource
- Hidden agendas
- Contrary to self-interest
- Change in external factors

The list is quite extensive already, so a pragmatic approach is generally a good axiom to apply in business. However, we as practitioners must do all we can to shape, influence and control the factors that we can, recognising those that we can't and the impact they may have on any given decision, transaction or action.

There are many things that can prevent a decision from being made, so we have to improve the probability of success (in getting to a decision) as well as recognising when not to – when this may be a form of sunk cost fallacy, in that we must recognise, even when we have already expended large amounts of time, energy and emotion, we must stop, yes stop; as to continue to pursue something at all costs will be detrimental to our relationship, value to the organisation, trust, etc.

The Cynefin Framework
An approach that we may wish to consider, given all the competing factors detailed above, is the Cynefin Framework[3] (pronounced: KUN-iv-in). This is a conceptual framework used to help managers, policy-makers and others reach decisions. Developed in the early 2000s within IBM, it has been described as a "sense-making device". Cynefin is a Welsh word for habitat.

Cynefin offers five decision-making contexts or "domains", and these are: 'obvious' (originally referred to as simple), 'complicated', 'complex' and 'chaotic'. There is also another aspect referred to as 'disorder'. Adopting the principles of

---

3. Kurtz, C.F. and Snowden, D.J. (2003). "Cynefin Framework. The new dynamics of strategy: sense-making in a complex and complicated world" in *IBM Systems Journal*, Vol 42. No3. Pages 462-483

this framework can help managers to identify how they perceive situations, and to make sense of their own and other people's behaviour.[4]

Appended below is the current version of Cynefin framework.

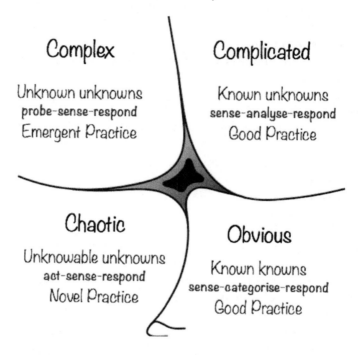

Figure 13.1. Cynefin Framework (David Snowden, https://commons. wikimedia.org/w/index.php?curid=33783436)

In order to use this framework, the following summarises the 5 domains that apply to the framework:

1. Obvious (originally simple): Known knowns (legal structures, specifications, procedures, etc.
2. Complicated: Known unknowns (AI-impact of, Brexit, etc.)
3. Complex: Unknown unknowns (a complex living entity such as a palm oil plantation and surrounding areas, subject to weather, deforestation, etc., with loss of species)

---

4. Kurtz, C.F and Snowden, D.J. (2003) "The new dynamics of Strategy: Sense-Making in a complex and complicated world" in *IBM Systems Journal*, Vol 42, No 3 2003, pages 462-483. The framework sorts the issues facing leaders into five contexts defined by the nature of the relationship between cause and effect. Four of these – Obvious (originally simple), Complicated, Complex, and Chaotic – require leaders to diagnose situations and to act in contextually appropriate ways. The fifth—disorder—applies when it is unclear which of the other four contexts is predominant.

4. Chaotic: (too confusing events to wait for valid knowledge based information)
5. Disorder: (a domain where the framework simply recognises the aspects you simply can't categorise)

Moving through the domains there is a clockwise shift from chaotic to complex and complicated to obvious. Equally, there is a "build-up of biases", complacency or lack of maintenance that can cause catastrophic failure.

This technique has been successfully used in product development, Supply Chain Management, policy-making and many other areas of applicability. However, it must be recognised that it is only a framework and an additional tool in the support of key decision-making activity.

In real-life business situations, decisions often fail because the best alternatives are not clear at the outset, or key factors are not considered as part of the process. To stop this happening, you need to bring problem-solving and decision-making strategies together to clarify your understanding.

A logical and ordered process can help you to do this by making sure that you address all of the critical elements needed for a successful outcome. This will need to be customised for each and every activity.

Working through the Cynefin Framework process will systematically reduce the likelihood of overlooking important factors. Speed of decision-making and the communication of those decisions as they effectively stream and filter through the organisation is equally critical to the final outcome. Some users of the framework argue that having a single process owner for decision-making is a way of reducing the cycle time to decisions, and this efficiency brings time savings and value/benefits to an organisation too. Enabling shared visions, promoting a culture of problem-solving and parallel decision-making are all seen as supportive to this approach.

A process that combines problem-solving and decision-making strategies when making complex decisions in challenging situations can be equally appropriate. Setting this out in a clear and transparent process and allowing all parties to socialise and understand the approach will give them ownership, rather than a sense of being dictated to.

Working through this process systematically will reduce the likelihood of overlooking important factors. An approach that considers the following will enable this:

1. Clarity of attendees and their contribution, functionally or budgetary, etc.
2. Clear and concise approach and any forms of rules or decision-making approaches.
3. Create a constructive environment.

4. Investigate the situation in detail beforehand, so that the current situation and facts/issues are available.
5. Generate ALL alternatives, don't be quick to close options down.
6. Explore your options and variants of options, including combinations.
7. Selection criteria for narrowing the options and gaining consensus.
8. Challenge your plan, where are the flaws in what you have developed?
9. Get non-participants to review your objective and proposal in an unbiased way.
10. Communicate your decision, and agree ownership.

There are many techniques available in addition to Cynefin, such as:

The Charette Procedure (sometimes spelled 'Charrette')[5]. This involves organising people into several small groups, each of which brainstorms ideas one after the other until everyone involved has had a chance to contribute fully. You then take the ideas generated by a group and move them to the next group, for them to be augmented, refined, and finally prioritised.

The Charette Procedure allows for maximum participation in idea generation, without compromising the quality or effectiveness of the brainstorming. The benefits of the process include: Effective use of time, improved buy-in, sense of fairness and inclusion, avoiding GroupThink, etc.

The Stepladder Technique[6] is a simple tool that manages how members enter the decision-making group. This approach encourages all members to contribute on an individual level BEFORE being influenced by anyone else hiding within the group or being overpowered by stronger more dominant members.

Typically, this is a 5-step process is as follows:

Step 1: Before getting together as a group, present the task or problem to all members. Give everyone sufficient time to think about what needs to be done and to form their own opinions on how to best accomplish the task or solve the problem.

Step 2: Form a core group of two members. Have them discuss the problem.

Step 3: Add a third group member to the core group. The third member presents ideas to the first two members BEFORE hearing the ideas that have already been discussed. After all, three members have laid out their solutions and ideas, they discuss their options together.

5. The Charette Procedure is an intense period of design or planning activity. 'Charrette' is French for "cart" or "chariot." Its use in the sense of design and planning arose in the 19th century at the École des Beaux-Arts in Paris, where it was not unusual at the end of a term for teams of student architects to work right up until a deadline, when a charrette would be wheeled among them to collect up their scale models and other work for review.
6. Developed by Steven Rogelberg, Janet Barnes-Farrell and Charles Lowe in 1992.

Step 4: Repeat the same process by adding a fourth member, and so on, to the group. Allow time for discussion after each additional member has presented his or her ideas.

Step 5: Reach a final decision only after all members have been brought in and presented their ideas.

We have mentioned before the use of pre-mortems too, which are effective in most situations where there is a complex or key decision to be made. Clearly there are many other tools available too. Remember you don't need a sledge hammer to crack a nut – the techniques listed above require time and resource investment that should be used for significant decision stages or programmes or where a critical decision is highly likely to fail.

Cycling back to the 4 step approach adopted by Kennedy in 1962 is always a great place to start, but putting additional layers into this, such as the Cynefin framework will clearly enhance the quality.

As a further posit to the decision-making arena, David Snowden – a management consultant and researcher in the field of knowledge management – once relayed an occasion when the designers at IBM had created a game based on a fictional planet that was based on the culture of a client organisation. When Executives landed on the alien planet, they were asked to address problems and opportunities facing the inhabitants. The issues they encountered were disguised but designed to mirror real situations, many of which were controversial or sensitive. Because the environment seemed so foreign and remote, however, the players found it much easier to come up with fresh ideas than they otherwise would have done. A metaphorical game that increased managers' willingness to participate and be more creative and productive!

13.2 How can Frictionless help?

There is no doubt that technology can enable easier, simpler and more intuitive actions, decisions and work flows, but it can of course also do the opposite. The simple rule of frictionless is that it needs to be at least twice as quick, easy or intuitive than what currently exists. The whole concept of frictionless is the path to an activity or decision is unimpeded. A simple analogy is that of a road: a straight Roman road with no speed restrictions, junctions, roundabouts, traffic lights, speed bumps, road calming, crossings or the like will give a clear route and path forward at speed with minimum stress and distraction. Sounds easy, but it's not.

All too often procurement and contract rules, set by the function, are maligned and criticised, even by those working in the profession as being the reason they are impeded. So, we have to look at an approach which offers the best possible experience; which is frictionless. We often use the term "Amazon experience", as a benchmark for ease of use, transaction etc.. Hence, this is what we are looking for in a frictionless process. It is quite acceptable to start with a process that may be complex and cumbersome, but we should consider that to be only the prototype of what we are looking for. From there we must consider how we can ensure we get adoption by making it:

- Intuitive
- Simple
- Quick efficient
- No hidden steps or stages in the process
- Transparent
- Flowing

The reasons this is important are many, but starting with the first principle, it helps us make more System 1 judgements and removes or excludes, as far as reasonably possible, all System 2 judgements. We are looking to remove the "effort" from the decision-making process and getting people to a decision point or points in as few and simple steps as possible.

Recognising in the real world there are limitations to this, as in nudging, too much complexity, lack of clarity, will negatively impact the outcome. To illustrate the importance of an effective nudge, think of a time when you were travelling to a new destination, facility or attraction. A well-signposted or a poorly-signposted route in and around the destination, facility or attraction makes a huge difference between a pleasurable experience and a thoroughly miserable one.

Reflecting on a decision-making process that has parallel features like turnstiles, signs, stairs, corridors that might well look the same but isn't, and so the list goes on in a metaphorical sense, these must be avoided. This is equally true of someone giving directions to places that they have worked in, for many, years to a new employee. They will miss out vital information as well as use past memory to recall things that have changed, so the directions become poor or ineffective. This is another critical juncture where people then lose trust – the parallel again being if you are that person seeking a decision and give poor directions your trust will similarly be impacted.

A recent successful trail by the BIT team in the UK changed an outdated 50-100 page pension "wake-up" pack for a single page "pension passport"[7] that

7. Glazebrook, K., Larkin, C and Costa, E. (2017). "Improving engagement with pension decisions: The results from three randomised controlled trials". A report prepared by the Behavioural Insights Team for the Government's Pension Wise Service, October 2017. http://38r8om2xjhhl25mw24492dir.wpengine.netdna-cdn.com/wp-content/uploads/2017/10/Pension-wise-trials.pdf

delivered significantly higher level of engagement for precisely the reasons I have mentioned, namely too much complexity, etc. as a blocker to engagement – far from frictionless.

13.3 Frictionless by Design

The aims of frictionless design should consider most if not all of the following "*Ten commandments of Frictionless*":

1. Clarity of direction = inspires trust.
2. Simplicity of information "module" = System 1 judgement.
3. Transparent = no hidden agenda.
4. Aligns with current objectives or strategy = salience to the organisation.
5. Business language that is common to the organisation = Effective communication.
6. Complexity is broken down into assailable modules = hyperbolic discounting.
7. Positively worded = framed.
8. Proposition benchmarked and referenced = anchoring, weights and contrasts experience and new evidence and avoids status quo bias.
9. Range estimates (where appropriate and needed = removes optimism bias.
10. Parallel sector references (where needed) = removes not invented here bias, zero-sum risk bias, etc.

Most of the research to date has been focused on customer experience, but this can easily be exchanged to look at internal customers, stakeholders, budget holders, decision-makers, etc. and, of course should be.

Imagine the adoption rate for all the indirect (goods and services that do not get sold directly to the end customer) areas of expenditure, such as stationery, print, IT hardware, teas, coffees, sandwiches for meetings, etc. was all through a portal that recognised the individual. This would thereby pre-populate each individual's location, cost code(s), billing points, delivery points, delivery instructions, etc. – whilst this is a tactical/operational level of frictionless decision-making, we can move it to the strategic level.

At the strategic level the same principles (ten commandments of frictionless) still apply, it simply means we are applying them to a different context and audience.

At the outset there are 4 key stages to consider:

1. Define the Strategic or key objective(s) as they exist today to ensure alignment of the solution.
   a) What is or are the outcomes you are looking to achieve
   b) What are the boundary conditions in terms of current strategy, objectives, KPIs etc.
   c) What is your customer and/or client base advocating as a strategy and outline plan?

2. Define the Options and/or Approaches and weight them.
   a) Select a singular or number of models that will enable you to link the desired outcome and the linkages between them and your market, strategy, etc.
   b) What external (non-influenceable) and internal (influenceable) factors are there?
   c) What has and hasn't worked previously?
   d) What have other sectors done to deliver success in similar areas?
   e) Are there any parallels to what you are considering?

3. Develop a Design and Approach for challenge in a safe environment
   a) Create a flow diagram
   b) Identify the trigger mechanisms
   c) What changes in behaviour are you looking for and how you will measure the changes?
   d) Consider what you want and don't want, as well as need to avoid, etc.

4. Launch the Proposal or options for consideration and be ready to modify and implement (or scale up)
   a) Target individual decision-makers on a one-to-one basis to ensure that you can tailor the core approach to each key stakeholder and keep the visual design and format the same for each, as this needs to be a familiar version when presented in a formal context for sign off.
   b) Reflect any language or key references collected in the one-to-one journeys (this will build trust and acceptance).
   c) Agree how you will cascade the outcome and don't be too ready to put your name on it too!

Putting this into an organisational context, such as changing a company car policy, a scenario seen as possibly one of the most emotionally charged tasks to undertake, the outcome was relatively simple – save £X million and recognise our values as a business.

To some this may not seem very helpful. However, recognising the steps above the approach was as follows:

Step 1:
- We need to save (hypothetically) £2-million annually
- We are in the public transport sector
- Move from diesel to electric
- We have a grey fleet (non-beneficial user, such as a pool car or van)
- More legislation and shift to reducing CO_2 emissions and NOx and particulates.

Step 2:
- Link legislation to personal fleet choice (walk the talk).
- Other sectors in grey fleets have already made the shift to all electric vehicles.
- We have charging facilities in the bus depots.
- We can benchmark ourselves and take a lead too.

Step 3:
- Model the changes in CO_2 to existing fleet choice.
- Define what cannot be continued on the list as too high CO_2/NOx, etc.
- What if the ALL grey fleet moved to electric.
- Model the total cost of ownership not just the one-off costs.
- Will senior execs and others really vote for such a change in phase 1 – answer NO, so don't advocate this!
- Confirm which option(s) deliver on financials and reputational aspects.
- Apply 3 dimensions: Economic, Sustainability, Reputation.

Step 4:
- Get sponsor onboard and under their name not procurement's.
- Detailed review of costs with CFO and get agreement.
- Test with difficult stakeholders with position of framing positively support from sponsor and CFO.
- Get Exec agreement in full and move to formally present, with small modification to trial and phased roll-out and grants for electric grey fleet.

I realise this is a huge simplification, but it proves that this can be done, if I check back on my notes, 10 slides (plus 6 appendices slides) delivered to my Executive Committee for sign off. The approach will improve the chances of success in getting positive outcomes to bigger decisions, but also gains trust and confidence on other tactical and operational dimensions which are just as critical.

In the context of tactical and operational areas we can observe the use of digitalisation techniques to improve both the front end and back end of processes such as Purchase to Pay (P2P), Source to Pay (S2P), Private Trading Networks (PTNs), etc. Simple measures such as reducing the number of clicks, screens, sign-on and visits to move from need to fulfilment is key, as is having a smooth hand-off from the digital aspect to query and/or help-desk resolution.

Approaches that reduce approvals for small spend prompts the right questions like "Is this within your authority to approve?", "Do you have sufficient budget to proceed?"; these can ensure that the conscious element of judgements one makes are there to be seen, and operating at the right points without stopping the transaction.

Remember sometimes processes and decisions are a bit like water flowing in a water channel – it's designed to flow, but if blocked will find an alternative route, perhaps one more destructive than just stopping the flow!

CHAPTER 14 | CULTURAL PRACTICES AND THE SOCIAL SCIENCES

14.1 An Overview of Cultural Dynamics and Differences

As more and more teams and/or suppliers become matrix-managed functions, the need to understand and work more effectively across the globe becomes more and more critical. Recognising when a term used on one continent means or translates to a different meaning can occur in so many ways, and can be something very simple. But if we know this is possible, then we have a chance to manage that dimension.

This continues to be true when we consider behaviours and social norms that are not only accepted but expected in one part of the world, and viewed very differently by another part of the world. Recognising that our heuristics are part hard-wired and part-accumulated over time from our childhood, it is not surprising that we might be tempted to pass judgement all too quickly.

Experience shows that some things can be accepted, tolerated or even become amusing (in certain circumstances), while others are seen as either rude, aggressive or disrespectful. Perhaps the most serious of circumstances is when, for example, a disrespectful event has occurred, but without any form of malicious intent at all. So, all in all cultural dynamics can be a bit of a cultural Molotov Cocktail[1] at times if we're not careful. The challenge is not only to develop an awareness, but find ways in which we can effectively engage and utilise this cognitive diversity in its simplest form to our competitive advantage.

Attitudes and in turn behaviours can be some of the most profound differences across cultures, and when we consider how we need to engage in the emerging economies such as China, Russia, Turkey, Bangladesh, India and Pakistan, where hierarchy and deference to this hierarchy are deeply engrained in the national psyche, means the Western-style management approach of cascading authority doesn't work.

---

1. The name "Molotov cocktail" was coined by the Finns during the Winter War. The name was an insulting reference to Soviet foreign minister Vyacheslav Molotov, who was one of the architects of the Molotov-Ribbentrop Pact signed in late August 1939. It is a generic name used for a variety of bottle-based improvised incendiary weapons. Due to the relative ease of production, Molotov cocktails have been used by street criminals, protesters, rioters, gangsters, urban guerrillas, terrorists, irregular soldiers, or even regular soldiers short on equivalent military-issue weapons. They are primarily intended to set targets ablaze rather than obliterate them.

In my experiences of working in China, it is usual for the workforce to follow instructions and not proffer ideas or solutions, because that is seen as the management's prerogative. A measure of managements effectiveness in general (irrespective of geography) is their ability to respond and deal with these issues as presented and come up with effective solutions. However, the recognition of hierarchy alone is simply not enough or indeed the whole story when viewed across the different cultures, depending on the axis of where each party sits in the relationship.

Cultural differences are of course sometimes difficult to simply observe and measure, as well as recognising people who clearly don't conform to the ascribed norm for that culture/country. Therefore, any measure can only be a reference point and should be considered an anchor or a frame that then becomes a bias!

Also remember that first impressions count for a great deal, and need to be handled in a way that deserves your fullest attention. It is so easy to overlook this when a new team member joins as part of the function, especially an internal transfer, and as a leader you continue as if it's business as usual. Also remember that different cultures have comparable values and ways of working to whatever culture or background you are from, so try to recognise these too.

There are a number of ways cultural diversity has been expressed over the recent decades, perhaps the most comprehensive, but not without criticism is Geert Hofstede's Power Distance Index[2], an overview and some sample indices of which are below for reference. Also, a more recent study by Gurnek Bains[3] which appeared in *Harvard Business Review* has been appended to provide a comparison.

Looking firstly at Hofstede, it can be seen that there are 6 dimensions in the 2010 model, which are as follows:

1. **Power Distance Index (PDI):** The power distance index is defined as "the extent to which the less powerful members of organisations and institutions (like the family) accept and expect that power is distributed

---

2. Hofstede's cultural dimensions theory is a framework for cross-cultural communication, developed by Geert Hofstede. It describes the effects of a society's culture on the values of its members, and how these values relate to behaviour, using a structure derived from factor analysis. Hofstede developed his original model as a result of using factor analysis to examine the results of a worldwide survey of employee values by IBM between 1967 and 1973. It has been refined since. The original theory proposed four dimensions along which cultural values could be analysed: individualism-collectivism; uncertainty avoidance; power distance (strength of social hierarchy) and masculinity-femininity (task orientation versus person-orientation). Independent research in Hong Kong led Hofstede to add a fifth dimension, long-term orientation, to cover aspects of values not discussed in the original paradigm. In 2010, Hofstede added a sixth dimension, indulgence versus self-restraint. http://www.clearlycultural.com/geert-hofstede-cultural-dimensions/power-distance-index/

3. Bains, Gurnek. (2015). "Leadership across cultures" in *Harvard Business Review*, May 2015, pp 30-31. Reprint F1505Z

unequally." In this dimension, inequality and power is perceived from the followers, or the lower level. A higher degree of Index indicates that the hierarchy is clearly established and executed in society, without doubt or reason. A lower degree of the Index signifies that people question authority and attempt to distribute power.

2. **Individualism vs. collectivism (IDV)**: This index explores the "degree to which people in a society are integrated into groups." Individualistic societies have loose ties that often only relates an individual to his/her immediate family. They emphasise the "I" versus the "we." Its counterpart, collectivism, describes a society in which tightly-integrated relationships tie extended families and others into in-groups. These in-groups are laced with undoubted loyalty and support each other when a conflict arises with another in-group.

3. **Uncertainty avoidance index (UAI)**: The uncertainty avoidance index is defined as "a society's tolerance for ambiguity," in which people embrace or avert an event of something unexpected, unknown, or away from the status quo. Societies that score a high degree in this index opt for stiff codes of behaviour, guidelines, laws, and generally rely on absolute Truth, or the belief that one lone Truth dictates everything and people know what it is. A lower degree in this index shows more acceptance of differing thoughts/ideas. Society tends to impose fewer regulations, ambiguity is more accustomed to, and the environment is more free-flowing.

4. **Masculinity vs. femininity (MAS)**: In this dimension, masculinity is defined as "a preference in society for achievement, heroism, assertiveness and material rewards for success." Its counterpart represents "a preference for cooperation, modesty, caring for the weak and quality of life." Women in the respective societies tend to display different values. In feminine societies, they share modest and caring views equally with men. In more masculine societies, women are more emphatic and competitive, but notably less emphatic than the men. In other words, they still recognize a gap between male and female values. This dimension is frequently viewed as taboo in highly masculine societies.

5. **Long-term orientation vs. short-term orientation (LTO)**: This dimension associates the connection of the past with the current and future actions/challenges. A lower degree of this index (short-term) indicates that traditions are honoured and kept, while steadfastness is valued. Societies with a high degree in this index (long-term) views adaptation and circumstantial, pragmatic problem-solving as a necessity. A poor country that is short-term oriented usually has little to no economic development, while long-term oriented countries continue to develop to a point.

6. **Indulgence vs. restraint (IND)**: This dimension is essentially a measure of happiness; whether or not simple joys are fulfilled. Indulgence is defined as "a society that allows relatively free gratification of basic and natural human desires related to enjoying life and having fun." Its counterpart is defined as "a society that controls gratification of needs and regulates it by means of strict social norms." Indulgent societies believe themselves to be in control of their own life and emotions; restrained societies believe other factors dictate their life and emotions.

Below are some examples and results of how this can be expressed:

1-20	21-40	41-60	61-80	81-100	101-120

COUNTRY	PDI	IDV	MAS	UAI	LTO
China	**80**	20	66	40	118
Iraq	**80**	38	52	68	
United Arab Emirates	**80**	38	52	68	
India	**77**	48	56	40	61
Nigeria	**77**	20	46	54	16
Singapore	**74**	20	48	8	48
Brazil	**69**	38	49	76	65
France	**68**	71	43	86	
Hong Kong	**68**	25	57	29	96
Poland	**68**	60	64	93	
Ethiopia	**64**	27	41	52	25
Chile	**63**	23	28	86	
Portugal	**63**	27	31	104	
Pakistan	**55**	14	50	70	
Japan	**54**	46	95	92	80
Italy	**50**	76	70	75	
South Africa	**49**	65	63	49	
United States	**40**	91	62	46	29
Netherlands	**38**	80	14	53	44
Australia	**36**	90	61	51	31
Germany	**35**	67	66	65	31
United Kingdom	**35**	89	66	35	25
Switzerland	**34**	68	70	58	
Denmark	**18**	74	16	23	
Israel	**13**	54	47	81	

Figure 14.1. Sample of Hofstede's Power Distance Index

As we begin to understand where we fit in on the index, it becomes easier to see how close or far away we are from other cultures. As a consequence we can adapt our approaches to appropriately recognise what our ways of working should be.

Even within countries and cultures there will be differences. For example, between the North and South of England; between Scotland, Wales and England; and even perhaps between Paris and the rest of France. In Brazil one may observe differences between Rio de Janeiro (the Cariocas) and Sao Paulo (Paulistas); and that of the East and West coasts of the USA.

Another model by Bains examined the corporate and leadership aspects in organisations, with greater recognition of the Emotional Intelligence (EQ) skills of individuals. Bains and his team summarised the findings as follows:

	UNITED STATES	MIDDLE EAST	INDIA	LATIN AMERICA
ADVICE FOR LEADERS ON THE WORLD STAGE	• Recognize that others may not share your action orientation • Don't let your positivity come across as naïve optimism • Build your capacity to listen	• Adopt a less hierarchical, more inclusive leadership style • Display comfort with ambiguity • Don't be proud or defensive in response to feedback	• Resist interpreting your role too narrowly • Think "team first" • Develop ideas inclusively • Be less process-bound	• Don't feel rejected when others behave formally • Adopt a less directive style • Be ready to give and receive honest feedback
ADVICE FOR PEOPLE WORKING WITH THOSE LEADERS	• Get to the point, be brief, and focus on tangibles • Recognize that Americans value efficiency and action • Be straightforward and open	• Invest in building trust and long-term relationships • Be sensitive to the tension between tradition and modernity	• Discourage individualism • Give feedback sensitively and be patient with resistance • Encourage initiative and questioning	• Build warm relationships • Ensure that structures and processes are tight • Deliver tough feedback in a sensitive and positive manner

	SUB-SAHARAN AFRICA	EUROPE	CHINA
	• Build deep relationships and close teamwork • Recognize the value of structure and organization • Work to win hearts and minds	• Be more action-oriented • Be more flexible in response to change or uncertainty • Operate in a less structured and rigid manner	• Stay positive when facing setbacks • Be less cautious in airing views and taking action • Balance analysis with conceptual exploration
	• Break down barriers by being less formal; use humor • Recognize the value of clarity • Invest time in developing people and teams	• Respect people's desire for inclusion • Focus on alignment and buy-in • Devote more time to execution • Honor roles and decision rights	• Play into the drive to improve • Use insiders to help build relationships • Appreciate the importance of harmony and balance

Figure 14.2. Regional EQ skills summary

In further work, they also described the following derived from the research:
- Sub-Saharan African leaders score relatively low on commercial thinking but highest on intellectual flexibility.
- Only 3% of Latin American leaders are strong on strategic thinking.
- European leaders score the highest on their ability to win hearts and minds, while Sub-Saharan African leaders the lowest.
- Latin American leaders demonstrate extraordinary drive and ambition.
- Emotional openness and authenticity appear to be a challenge for leaders everywhere, but least so in Europe.

- Forming close bonds does not appear to be a priority for most leaders.
- The most engaging and likeable leaders are from Latin America, then China.
- Collaboration is a strength among Latin American leaders.

While this can be subject to personal insight, it is nevertheless very true in my own personal experience and is useful in informing cultural frameworks generally, wherever they may come from originally.

Language can cause social disconnection too, if only because of poor or clumsy translation from another tongue into English; something perhaps as English speakers we take for granted too often.

For example, on a recent visit to Moscow, the translation of the word 'integrity' proved confusing and amusing as there is no direct translation for the word into Russian – this left me slightly perplexed. However, this type of situation cannot and must not be seen as a cultural difference. Rather the sentiment, the meaning of 'integrity' has been "lost in translation". As I set out earlier, the area of active listening can have a parallel in the context of the written communications, on occasion, if wording is ambiguous or unclear. Hence, we must seek to clarify things before we make a series of false assumptions and deductions.

Another view of the dimensions under consideration was published by Erin Meyer[4] in her book, which I have appended below with her kind permission:

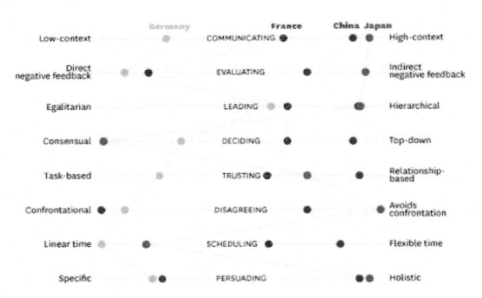

Figure 14.3. Leadership dimensions

---

4. Meyer, Erin. (2014). *The Culture Map: Breaking Through the Invisible Boundaries of Global Business.* Public Affairs, a member of the Perseus Group.

14.2 The Social Sciences as Applied to Purchasing and Supply Chain Management

The application of the Social Sciences to areas of business is not a new concept, nor should it be for Purchasing and Supply Chain Management. Perhaps one of the most powerful attributes of an effective leader is one who makes and emotional connection with all those they rely upon to deliver and collaborate within a function.

Added to this is all those upon whom the leader depends, inside and outside of the organisation, to support them and encourage them, to stimulate the process of innovation – all are an integral part of this activity. Some people have loosely referred to this as having the 'right chemistry' in place between teams and people. However, we need to be much clearer as to what that "chemistry" is and what it can and can't do.

At the most basic level, a company or business leader can establish a structured process of learning about its employees, team members and emotional motivators, and establish programmes to help leverage their skills and other attributes to the organisation's benefit. Clearly this can be scaled up at some later date.

At the other end of the spectrum, organisations can invest in deep research and big data analytics or engage consultancies with specific expertise. Companies in many sectors private and public can and have used a detailed understanding of emotional connections and preferences to improve performance across the team, and retain their most valuable employees.

However, we must not restrict this to the internal dimension as many organisations rely upon external provision and delivery of services. Hence the rise of behavioural assessments, which are covered in more detail in the case study at the end of this book.

The most sophisticated organisations are making this relevance and understanding of emotional connections and preferences a part of a broader strategy that involves every function in the value chain, from product development, operations, procurement. marketing to sales and (customer) service.

A significant number of emotional motivators drive employee behaviour in a positive way. I have set out a few of them in the table overleaf:

I am inspired by a desire to:	Organisations can leverage these emotional motivators by helping employees to:
Belong to an organisation that has high ethical standards	Project a unique social identity; be seen as special and actively doing things that make a social contribution
Have confidence in the future strategy	Perceive the future as better than the past; have a positive mental picture of what's to come
Enjoy a sense of well-being	Feel that life measures up to expectations and that balance has been achieved; seek a stress-free state without conflicts or threats
Feel a sense of freedom within a framework	Act with a degree of independence, without unnecessary obligations or restrictions
Feel a sense of belonging	Have an affiliation with people they relate to or aspire to be like; feel part of a group
Protect the environment	Sustain the belief that the environment is sacred; take action to improve their surroundings
Be the person I want to be	Fulfil a desire for ongoing self-improvement; live up to their ideal self-image
Feel secure	Believe that what they have today will be there tomorrow; to pursue goals and dreams within a professional context.

Table 14.4. Emotional motivators – what they mean or how they are expressed

The value of a relational contract, as distinct from a performance or commercial contract, is quite different, and the need to treat this in a distinctly different way is key. This in turn will require the acquisition or use of new academic or professional skills as necessary, if we are to unlock the untapped value that is there. Simply using people from the same backgrounds, education, experience, sectors or industry will not leverage the value of diversity available and needed. This in itself will challenge leadership to understand and adapt approaches that may at first be uncomfortable and challenging in themselves, and require an agility and flexibility to be able to manage and motivate the self-change this will present. However, the untapped value from diverse cultures or indeed social groups will be a dual axiom of being tested and rewarded for leadership. A neoclassical approach will simply not suffice for the future, and as leaders we need to adapt to a new order of the economy.

Another area where we seem to drawn to the same old incentives model, and indeed KPIs that we drive performance by, is simply the one of savings or at best cost avoidance and savings. It is within our gift to revisit this and the other mechanisms of reward and incentivisation – they do not all have to be monetary. Essentially, we are or should be driven by a common endeavour to derive a collective benefit, which cannot all be measured in terms of money. Clearly, as a function we are required to deliver savings and cost avoidance, just like sales need to deliver new customers, operations need to make sure service levels and customer satisfaction is to a desired level, and so forth, but these are end products not enablers.

Looking specifically at the social and relational attributes as enablers, it is clear we can incentivise through less conventional approaches or simply resorting to the use of money as the only means of incentive. Remembering our old friend reciprocity, we can then begin to look at other actions we can take:

- Creating a vision as to how we can collectively share in something.
- How can we create an environment that is safe and fun?
- How can we be socially inclusive, while respecting cultural differences; where's the common ground?
- What do other people value?
  - Maybe a specialist conference that is non-functional relative.
  - Book.
  - Special mention in a newsletter.
  - E-mail from the CEO to a team member.
  - Free time to study for an upcoming exam.
  - Mentor.
  - A text that simply says "thanks" after losing a week or weekend away from home.
  - Tolerance for those things we need to do in our lives:
    - Be at home for the boiler service.
    - Home early for your child or partner's birthday.

The list could be endless. However, the key takeaway here is doing something to motivate others without relying on monetary incentives, which have been proven to be only partially effective. The goodwill and disposition towards delivering the results is unquestionable. The cascade of these principles into every programme, cross-functional team, supplier/service provider we engage with, opens up the possibilities wider still. The difficulty in part is the unlearning and relearning to do things differently.

14.3 Cultural Layers and Models, and Practical Steps for Purchasing and Supply Chain Management

A simple realisation that a relationship will outlast any contract or transaction needs a firm place in your value system from the outset. Often the reason we have cross-cultural relationships is to trade, something we have done for centuries. So, some foundational ground rules based on what we already know:

- Is mutual satisfaction the real purpose of the meeting?
- The goal of business negotiation may be a substantive outcome (Americans) or a long-lasting relationship (Japanese). Determine which it is.
- There are as many kinds of business etiquette as there are nations in the world. Protocol factors that should be considered are dress codes, number of people to attend, status, function, etc.
- What degree of formality, meeting and greeting, gift giving, entertainment, etc.?
- Verbal and non-verbal communication is a key factor of persuasion. The way we express our needs and feelings using body language and tone of voice can determine the way the other side perceives us, and in fact positively or negatively contributes to our credibility.
- A direct or indirect approach to exchanging information. Is the meaning of what is said exactly in the words themselves? Does "...it's impossible" really mean impossible or just difficult to realise?
- Always use OPEN questions to identify the other side's needs, otherwise assumptions may result in you never finding common interests.
- In terms of risk, the most common dilemma is related to personal relations between counterparts, i.e. do we trust them? Will they trust us? Certain cultures are more risk averse than others, e.g. Japan.
- If a culture is risk averse there will be less innovative and creative alternatives available to pursue, unless there is a strong trust-based relationship between the counterparts.
- In some cultures, time is money and something to be used wisely.
- Punctuality and agenda may be an important aspect of negotiation. In countries such as China or Japan, being late would be taken as an insult.
- The main goal when negotiating with an oriental counterpart is to establish a firm relationship, which takes time. Don't expect one big meeting will secure the relationship or an agreement to trade.
- Another dimension of time relevant to negotiation is the focus on past,

present or future. Sometimes the past or the distant future may be seen as part of the present, especially in Latin American countries.

- Define a consensual process. In Japanese companies the practice of *nemawashi (speaking to every stakeholder prior to the meeting)*, is important.
- It's crucial to identify who is the leader and who has the authority to make a decision.
- In most cultures, only written agreements confirm that an agreement has been formally reached. It seems to be the best way to secure everyone's interests in case of any unexpected circumstances. In China, where a contract is likely to be in the form of general principles, in the case of dispute they prefer to focus on the relationship than the contract to solve the problem.
- Remembering our own biases and being able to recognise and deduce the other parties is still key in this context.
- Formal or informal approaches and communication are good for some cultures, and not others and need to be respected. Initially formal is the right approach in China, and as the relationship builds this can move to informal. Whereas the USA see a more informal approach as advantageous from the beginning.
- Hofstede framework: understand the Power Distance Index.
- Don't apply stereotypes! Seek to understand, recognising you may have a frame of reference, but don't let your biases fool you!
- Remember the other side will be approaching this potentially the same as you.
- Find the other side's values and beliefs independently of values and beliefs characteristic of the culture or group being represented by your counterpart.
- Adjust to the situation and environment, we can also try to persuade the other side to use elements of our own culture too.
- In some situations, it is also possible to use a combination of both cultures, for example, regarding joint venture businesses. Another possible solution is to adopt a third culture – by defining common ground through focusing on common professional attributes or bodies may be a way of initiating the new culture and business relations.
- Be a pragmatist and not a moralist.
- Ensure that there is no possibility of "losing face" and what that exactly means to them.
- When they position an anchor, is it a realistic one or is it at the extreme end of the spectrum sent to test you?
- How do they perceive "silence" during a negotiation?

- Observe their tendency to discuss each item in a detailed way, or will they simply focus on broader spectrum and functionality?
- Do they get emotional easily? And what is the significance of this?
- How does their society perceive women, lawyers, unions, and "money is everything"?
- Do they respect patents and designs not just by contract but in deed?
- Use visual aids as much as possible (always a personal favourite). Flip charts and writing numbers and expressing things visually, as well as showing samples and photographs can communicate so much and avoid the traps of unintentional misunderstandings.
- Avoid technical jargon and any references that refer to things in your own culture that may be familiar to you, but not the other party, e.g. sports, politics, local/national news, etc.
- Ask the other party to review and play back what you have said and any written documents, photographs, samples, etc., and confirm that they have the same understanding as you.
- Adjust your own level of English to match that of the other party.

There are some very helpful guidelines we can apply from the work of J.W. Salacuse[5], especially in terms of how cultural dimensions have an influence over negotiations – for example, when looking at the goal of getting to contract, the axis between forming a relationship and how they are interdependent. Further how different cultures will look at a scenario as a win-lose and others a win-win from exactly the same situation. This supports the previous references to ensuring what and how you communicate, and how it is received in different cultures or environments as this may not be the same as your own assumption or expectation.

In summing this section up, I would suggest the following key takeaways:

- Be patient – Negotiations or seeking agreements will take longer than a typical negotiation between identical cultures, languages and values.
- Be considerate – recognise their position and culture.
- Ensure you truly have a common understanding.
- Build rapport and a relational contract.
- Avoid "off the cuff" comments.
- Be flexible.
- Be informed and make an effort to "build a bridge" – they are constructed from two sides not one!

5. Salacuse, Jeswald W. (1998). Ten Ways that Culture Affects Negotiating Style: Some Survey Results. First published in July 1998 in *Negotiation Journal*, Harvard Law School, pp 221-240, DOI: 10.1111/j.1571-9979.1998.tb00162.x

14.4 Managing Diverse Teams – Globally

Having spent many years working and living overseas (from the UK), as well as managing teams on many continents, I have had many successes and failures in managing diverse teams, up close and at a distance. The focus cannot be two dimensional as the points of contact and the number of variables is effectively the matrix you are seeking to motivate and maximise the potential of.

To do this requires an understanding not only of the cultures and social dimensions you are working with, but also the nature of the programme and its impact, both positive and negative in terms of the wider organisation from the initial direct team. A simple multiplication of the number of relationship permutations should help identify the complexity in one dimension, which is then augmented by the complexity of the programme or activity you are undertaking.

A good place to start is by mapping out the number of people involved; the direction of flows (information, decision, communication, etc.); number of current suppliers, spend, quality of goods, stock levels, etc. as this will allow you to quickly build up a picture at a physical level. In addition to this we can then begin to map the PDI (refer to table 14.1).

From here we can start to look at where and how we can represent this in a star diagram, which will visually show us on a country by country basis what the physical and cultural, social and behavioural factors look like. I have taken a hypothetical example of pharmaceutical vaccines to illustrate the primary factors. Please see the table overleaf:

COUNTRY	PDI	SPEND	SUPPLY CHAIN COMPLEXITY	BEHAVIOURS	MANUFACTURING BASE	CONSUMER BASE	LEAD EQ SCORE	CHANGE READY (1 = LOW)-5	RISK (PESTLE)
INDIA	77	£50m	HIGH	H/T-D (MID)		X	LOW	1	HIGH
GERMANY	35	£75m	MEDIUM	C/H (MID)		X	LOW	5	LOW
UK	35	£50m	LOW	T-D/E (LOW)	X	X	MID	3	MID
USA	40	£250m	LOW	T-D/E (MID)	X	X	HIGH	3	MID
AUSTRALIA	36	£25m	HIGH	E/T-D (MID)		X	LOW	5	LOW
NETHERLANDS	38	£40m	MEDIUM	E/C (MID)		X	HIGH	4	LOW
BRAZIL	69	£120m	HIGH	T-D/H (LOW)		X	MID	2	HIGH

Table 14.5. Base table for setting out the key observations in managing across diverse teams globally.

In this final section I want to focus on the practical aspects of managing effectively across cultures and geographies. Moreover, this is typically less about the organisation, and more about you and the people involved in the project or programme.

First recognise your own starting position on the PDI index, known factors and how key stakeholders/ players will enable you to map the primary dynamics. Then from a very simple matrix you can begin to build a picture and understand the gaps and/or synergies.

From here you will be able to construct not only a list of do's, don'ts, but also what sequence and order for your approach and how you may need to adopt your own style and/or biases in any given context. Finally keeping it simple will help too. In offering up my own list of thoughts and considerations you will see the list does not need to be exhaustive.

	DOs	DON'TS	Consider carefully
1	Listen carefully and playback and ensure you are aligned.	Assume the response to something will be in the same terms as you get in your native culture.	There will always be a range of responses from overtly positive to positive.
2	Tailor your response to the situation, not your automatic response as a "System 1 judgement".	Assume somebody knows what your response will be or your position will be on something in your native culture.	What is known and should be known and therefore fully explain yourself.
3	If there are blockers in any culture you need to deal with them quickly if you are a leader.	Allow excessive "gaps" in approaches to remain you need to find a solution and make a decision that is clear on this.	How you must adjust your behaviour if you need to change the order of things or ways of working?

4	For critical meetings and discussions "rehearse" then before the actual event to ensure it is clear how you will approach this and better still seek someone you trust you validate your approach.	Assume, that people know how you operate, you will need to explain your approach in a considered way.	How and what basis you build relationships within teams as this will be necessary.
5	Initially face-to-face is better as you will be able to judge people's reactions to what you are saying and doing and correct any issues quickly.	If there are multiple languages are involved don't use complicated language or contexts. Keep it simple, clear, explicit and precise.	Think carefully about the use of technical or potential jargon.
6	Make friendly observations only after you have established a good working relationship and not before.	Use or make jokes or references that are only valid in your own culture. They don't work!	Presentations need to thought through to see what can be expressed visually or in tabular format, etc.
7	In more formal situations, operate like a news reader; tell the audience the headlines of what's coming, give the detail and then summarise what you have said.	Don't assume because you have presented it that there is no need to follow up in writing. You must summarise the main points always.	Consider carefully the style with which you might summarise a presentation and the level of formality and action orientated approach needed as well as how explicit, etc.

8	Plan what you are going to do, what outcomes and deliverables you are looking for and test them before the event.	Don't rely on a version or a model you used before in a different scenario, it won't be good enough.	A plan needs to consider all the new dimension as well as those that may not apply. Fresh thinking is always a good option.
9	Collaborate, but within the confines of the culture.	Don't be autocratic, some cultures will simply reject this.	Consider carefully the unseen players that will be working in the background.
10	Do understand non-verbal communication and other signs.	Don't rely upon e-mail.	Carefully research the approaches, even if time is your enemy, buy some time to do this.

Table 14.6. Practical considerations for managing cross-culturally

Recognise that there will be a range within which to behave and interact with a new team, depending on whether you are the leader or within a peer group or team, etc. Equally, people will give latitude to new members in the early days, but you can't trade on that forever, as you will need to adapt and show willingness to be flexible too. Management styles and behaviours have been built up over many years, so don't expect dramatic changes in a short space of time, even if you are the boss.

Recognise that some of the gaps will never be fully bridged, but do try and find a workable solution, as to work without this will place too much stress on you, the team, the organisation and ultimately whatever you work upon. This will ultimately mean, in most situations, that there will be unlearning and relearning required. This is a process that I personally needed to undertake on a supply chain re-organisation programme in South America, that involved new facilities, facility closures, new MRP and ERP systems and much more. Doing this programme with 9 different nationalities and multiple cultures, some of which were conflicting, meant that a change to my current ways of working were necessary to ensure a successful outcome.

In the situation where you have a multicultural team there is the risk of confusion and inefficiency, and as a team leader, you need to understand these and turn them to an advantage to succeed. Use all the tools and approaches you can to explore, gaps, strengths and weaknesses to determine what the plan and approach needs to be. The shift in approach cannot simply be in one dimension, it will need approaches on as many dimensions and levels as are needed to suit the complexity of the situation, the environment and the people involved.

Other research has leveraged the work of Hofstede to create further categorisations and models for helping define the respect distances and proximity to cultural dimensions, which I have set out below:

The GLOBE (Global Leadership and Organisational Behaviour Effectiveness Research)[6] Project took Hofstede's original 1980 research findings into exploring the differences of cultures. This was led by Robert J. House of the Wharton School of the University of Pennsylvania, and directly involved 62 of the world's cultures. The project assembled data from 17,300 middle managers in 951 organisations to identify nine cultural competences and group them into ten convenient societal clusters.[7]

The GLOBE researchers used acquired data to put nations into cultural clusters that are grouped based upon cultural similarities due to shared geography and climate conditions, which all influence perceptions and behaviour. For example, it created 10 clusters, most of which I would propose were logical in the grouping. However, one cluster; Latin Europe appeared not to be and included Israel, Italy, Spain, Portugal, France and Switzerland (FR speaking).

The GLOBE project went on to define nine cultural competences, which are defined as follows:

- **Performance orientation:** refers to the extent to which an organisation or society encourages and rewards group members for performance improvement and excellence.
- **Assertiveness orientation:** is the degree to which individuals in organisations or societies are assertive, confrontational, and aggressive in social relationships.
- **Future orientation:** is the degree to which individuals in organisations or societies engage in future-oriented behaviours such as planning, investing in the future, and delaying gratification.
- **Humane orientation:** is the degree to which individuals in organisations

6. House R.J. et al. (Eds). (2004). *Culture, Leadership, and Organisations: The GLOBE Study of 62 Societies.* Thousand Oaks, CA: Sage. House, R. J., M. Javidan, and P. Dorfman. (2001). The GLOBE Projec in *Applied Psychology: An International Review.* Vol. 50, issue 4, pp. 489-505. House, R.J., M. Javidan, P. Dorfman, and de Luque, M. Sully. (2006). *A Failure of Scholarship: Response to George Graen's Critique of GLOBE,* Academy of Management Perspectives.
7. Javidan, M. and Dastmalchian, A. (2009). "Managerial implications of the GLOBE project: A study of 62 societies" in *Asia Pacific Journal of Human Resources,* 47: 41–58. doi:10.1177/1038411108099289

or societies encourage and reward individuals for being fair, altruistic, friendly, generous, caring, and kind to others.

- **Collectivism I:** Institutional collectivism, which reflects the degree to which organisational and societal institutional practices encourage and reward collective distribution of resources and collective action.
- **Collectivism II:** In-group collectivism, which reflects the degree to which individuals express pride, loyalty and cohesiveness in their organisations or families.
- **Gender egalitarianism:** is the extent to which an organisation or a society minimizes gender role differences and gender discrimination.
- **Power distance:** is defined as the degree to which members of an organisation or society expect and agree that power should be unequally shared.
- **Uncertainty avoidance:** is defined as the extent to which members of an organisation or society strive to avoid uncertainty by reliance on social norms, rituals, and bureaucratic practices to alleviate the unpredictability of future events.

After an extensive review of the research the GLOBE project team strategically grouped over 21 primary leadership dimensions into six encompassing dimensions of global leadership. Furthermore, they made the recommendation about how the dimensions of culture and leadership could distinguish in terms of those influences from one country to another, through the culturally endorsed implicit leadership structure (Change Leadership Team), which is set out below:

- **Charismatic/value based:** characterised by demonstrating integrity, decisiveness, and performance oriented by appearing visionary, inspirational and self-sacrificing, but can also be toxic and allow for autocratic commanding.
- **Team-orientated:** characterised by diplomatic, administratively competent, team collaboration and integration. A Toxic leader would be malevolent alienating the team, but driving cohesion.
- **Self-protective:** characterised by self-centred, face saving, procedural behaviour capable of inducing conflict when necessary while being conscious of status.
- **Participative:** characterised by (non-autocratic) participative behaviour that is supportive of those who are being led.
- **Human orientation:** characterised by modesty and compassion for others in an altruistic fashion.
- **Autonomous:** being able to function without constant consultation.

It is entirely up to the team leader to decide which approach suits them best and what approaches and methods give the most satisfactory method of working. By experience this needs to a blended approach, with the pragmatism and simplicity in real world situations when time is never on your side.

CHAPTER 15 | CHANGE MANAGEMENT ESSENTIALS

15.1 The Change Process and Phases

Before I start talking about change processes, the salient factor to observe here is our inbuilt resistance to change (prevalence of status quo bias) – most notably, therefore, change is all about people, not processes. So, having got that straight we can consider, just like any other project or programme, what structured approach or approaches are available and indeed appropriate for effective change management.

When considering change management, the initial focus for most companies is about changing or creating new structures, or altering or implementing new Enterprise Resource Planning (ERP) systems to creating new policies and procedures. Often these fall short on intended deliverables, which is at the heart of all change management programmes (even when they are referenced as a new system implementation).

Principally, the focus should be on the people who are directly and indirectly affected by the change to their ways of working – the "hearts and minds" element. This is essential not only to implement the new order, system or whatever the focus of the programme is, but also to sustain, optimise and drive benefit from the very change.

According to change management author and expert John Kotter[1], nearly 70% of all major change programmes will fail to deliver the intended outcomes or benefits; we need to understand, therefore, what the key failure attributes are.

These can be summarised as follows:

- The (reason for the) change is unclear.
- The benefit for those impacted isn't apparent – no WIIFM (What's in It For Me) factor.
- Senior managers and leaders don't 'walk the talk' or convincingly support the change.
- Only recognise the technical dimension to a change and ignore the people aspect.
- The change doesn't recognise the internal and external dimensions fully.
- Leaders and key members exhibit negative behaviour during pressured periods of the change.

---

1. Kotter, John P. (1996). *Leading Change*. Harvard Business School Press.

- Overreaction to events.
- Poor communication prior to, during and post-change phases, as well as underestimating the quantum and tailoring of communication at each stage.
- The approach is too complex or not broken down to allow people to assimilate the change at each stage.
- The change has not been derived from or is inclusive of a bottom-up approach.
- The pace of change demanded is out of sync with the organisation or culture it is being applied to.
- Those designing the change are bounded by their own (limited) rationality and produce a sub-optimal design and approach.
- We fail to recognise the "hard-wired" resistance to change from our DNA.
- We ignore the impact of loss aversion.
- Status quo bias is more engrained and widespread and is not sufficiently recognised or planned for.
- We haven't sufficiently or objectively recognised the "start point" or current state of affairs (optimism bias has told us things are more change-ready than they actually are, resistance to change is lower, etc.)
- There is change fatigue in the organisation.
- System 1 thinking overrides our System 2 thinking to such an extent that we can't challenge our belief systems and preference for constant effort versus greater effort needed for change.
- The perpetrators of change see people as targets, groups or functions but not as individuals, all of whom have their own values, system of beliefs, heuristics and much more that is different to our functional competences. Effectively, this is our own unique operating system, albeit typically operating within a manageable spectrum on a function by function grouping, but certainly not to be relied upon.

Looking at the processes that have been developed over the period during which change management has been recognised as an approach, the starting point for this is the work of Kurt Lewin[2], which is as recent as 1947.

---

2. Lewin, K. (1947i). "Frontiers in group dynamics: Concept, method and reality in social science; equilibrium and social change" in *Human Relations* 1(1): 5–41. Lewin, K. (1947ii). "Group decision and social change" in Newcomb, T.M. and Hartley, E.L. (eds). (1947) *Readings in Social Psychology*. New York: Henry Holt, 330–344. Lewin, K. (1948). *Resolving Social Conflicts: Selected Papers on Group Dynamics* (ed. Lewin, G). New York: Harper and Row. Lewin, K. (1949). "Cassirer's philosophy of science and the Social Sciences" in Schilpp, P.A. (ed.) (1949). *The Philosophy of Ernst Cassirer*. Evanston, IL: Library of Living Philosophers. Lewin, K. (1951). *Field Theory in Social Science: Selected Theoretical Papers* (ed. Cartwright D). New York: Harper and Row.

The simplicity of the model is as follows, referenced as 'Changing As Three Steps' (CATS):

LEWIN'S CHANGE MODEL
Lewin's Three Stage Change Process – Practical Steps

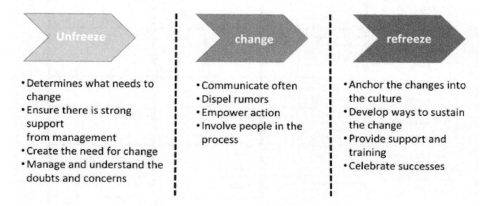

Figure 15.1. Changing As Three Steps (CATS)

This is regarded as the 'classic' approach to, or classic 'paradigm' for managing change. The study of change management has subsequently followed on from Lewin, by many other scholars, academics and theorists, however, they recognise that all theories of change are 'reducible to Lewin's CATS', as referenced by Hendry[3]. The many derivatives, as illustrated in table 15.2 overleaf, all show a series of steps and approaches by their creators.

---

3. Hendry, C. (1996). "Understanding and creating whole organisational change through learning theory" in *Human Relations* 49(5): 621–641.

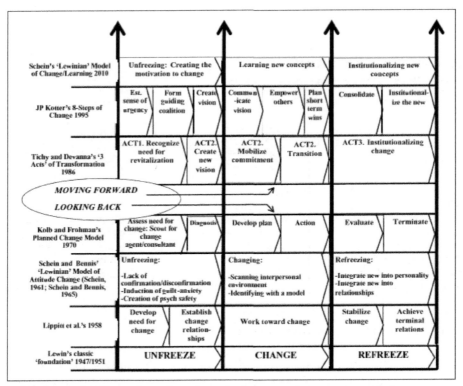

Schein's 'Lewinian' Model of Change/Learning 2010	Unfreezing: Creating the motivation to change			Learning new concepts			Institutionalizing new concepts	
JP Kotter's 8-Steps of Change 1995	Est. sense of urgency	Form guiding coalition	Create vision	Commun-icate vision	Empower others	Plan short term wins	Consolidate	Institutional-ize the new
Tichy and Devanna's '3 Acts' of Transformation 1986	ACT1. Recognize need for revitalization		ACT2. Create new vision	ACT2. Mobilize commitment		ACT2. Transition	ACT3. Institutionalizing change	
MOVING FORWARD								
LOOKING BACK								
Kolb and Frohman's Planned Change Model 1970	Assess need for change: Scout for change agent/consultant	Diagnosis		Develop plan		Action	Evaluate	Terminate
Schein and Bennis' 'Lewinian' Model of Attitude Change (Schein, 1961; Schein and Bennis, 1965)	Unfreezing: -Lack of confirmation/disconfirmation -Induction of guilt-anxiety -Creation of psych safety			Changing: -Scanning interpersonal environment -Identifying with a model			Refreezing: -Integrate new into personality -Integrate new into relationships	
Lippitt et al.'s 1958	Develop need for change	Establish change relation-ships		Work toward change			Stabilize change	Achieve terminal relations
Lewin's classic 'foundation' 1947/1951	UNFREEZE			CHANGE			REFREEZE	

Table 15.2. CATS as the prime foundation to subsequent works[4]

This is aside from the 8-Step model developed by change management guru John Kotter, which I have chosen to show separately as I believe it has a more pragmatic sense to its design and approach – this is shown in table 15.3.

Kotter intentionally takes a different approach that is more action-orientated, and as such I feel is more befitting of the commercial environment. Kotter has also provided additional commentary and observations, as well as research, which I will reflect on in this chapter.

Of importance too, according to Kotter, is the order in which each of the 8 steps are carried out, and from personal experience, structured to allow you to move to the next step in a progressive and logical manner – almost a 'gateway' structure, in which each step is to be cleared and verified before proceeding to the next gate or step in the process.

---

4. Cummings, S., Bridgman, T., and Brown, K.G. (2016). "Unfreezing change as three steps: Rethinking Kurt Lewin's legacy for change management" in *Human Relations*. The Tavistock Institute: 2016, Vol. 69(1) 33-60: DOI: 10.1177/0018726715577707

EIGHT STEPS TO TRANSFORMING YOUR ORGANIZATION

1 Establishing a Sense of Urgency
- Examining market and competitive realities
- Identifying and discussing crises, potential crises, or major opportunities

2 Forming a Powerful Guiding Coalition
- Assembling a group with enough power to lead the change effort
- Encouraging the group to work together as a team

3 Creating a Vision
- Creating a vision to help direct the change effort
- Developing strategies for achieving that vision

4 Communicating the Vision
- Using every vehicle possible to communicate the new vision and strategies
- Teaching new behaviors by the example of the guiding coalition

5 Empowering Others to Act on the Vision
- Getting rid of obstacles to change
- Changing systems or structures that seriously undermine the vision
- Encouraging risk taking and nontraditional ideas, activities, and actions

6 Planning for and Creating Short-Term Wins
- Planning for visible performance improvements
- Creating those improvements
- Recognizing and rewarding employees involved in the improvements

7 Consolidating Improvements and Producing Still More Change
- Using increased credibility to change systems, structures, and policies that don't fit the vision
- Hiring, promoting, and developing employees who can implement the vision
- Reinvigorating the process with new projects, themes, and change agents

8 Institutionalizing New Approaches
- Articulating the connections between the new behaviors and corporate success
- Developing the means to ensure leadership development and succession

Table 15.3. Kotter's 8-Stage process for leading change

As far as models go, I wouldn't consider many other than those I have referenced, as ultimately you have to make the approach that is relevant for your organisation – the models are principles, and still require appropriate implementation.

15.2 Behavioural Interventions and Prerequisites

I will refrain in this section from looking at or commenting on the planning and management aspects of a change and/or transformation initiatives or programmes, and focus on the behavioural interventions and prerequisites. This picks up on the central theme that this is fundamentally about people, people and people.

We should begin by looking in the mirror to assess what it is about ourselves that needs to be in our conscious mind when we consider change, and to what extent we need to change and flex to adapt to the organisation and the intended new state of order post-change. Behaviourally this is where it all begins, with the leader of the change. It should also be recognised that active, not passive sponsorship from the CEO and the whole of the C-suite needs to be behind the change, even when the pressure is on mid-stream during change or at critical points.

Creating visual images and ensuring clarity of vision are prerequisites to being able to get people onboard with planned change – these were part of my first recognition and indeed assimilation of what I had personally felt, as part of a major change programme, and which I later came to recognise as the Kubler-Ross Curve.[5]

The change curve was originally created by Elisabeth Kübler-Ross in 1969 to illustrate how people dealt with the tragic news that they have a terminal illness. This very same model is used by change managers by or for communicating to individuals BEFORE they go through any form of organisational change to help manage the expectations of their normal emotional states.

Originally the curve served to illustrate and articulate communication to people and where they might be in terms of their journey through change. I have set out some of the common expressions used at the various phases, from the neutral state prior to the change being announced, and the downward "negative" emotion to a bottom plateau, all the way back to a new and desired more effective way of working, or state of mind.

5. Kübler-Ross, Elizabeth. (1969). *On Death and Dying*. London: Routledge.

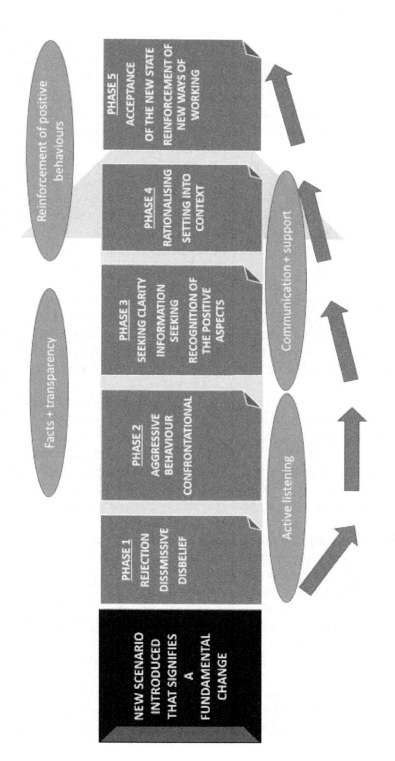

Figure 15.2. The Block Curve of Mental States from pre- to post-change (Loseby, 2018)

As change agents we must diagnose the phases, recognising that each individual will be at different points on the curve at any one time. The risk, as with many programmes, is the failure to refine things to the individual level, where for convenience or expediency the focus remains on group functions and as a consequence the signals that could derail the change programme are missed. Accordingly, a change agent must recognise that as an individual dealing with change, the length of time it takes to successfully go through this curve very much depends on that person; some can go through quickly, while others take significantly longer.

The challenge is to help bring people through their own change curve by understanding which phase they are in and also what support tools they need to transition through and embrace the proposed change.

The general phases of the Change Curve as articulated by Kübler-Ross are as follows:

- **Denial** – The first stage: Once information has been received as to the ideals of change, the natural reaction is to deny that there is a need for change, and that it is happening. In a change sense, typical reactions stage include, "It won't work here", "We have tried it before", "Why is this happening to me?" In this phase, maximising face-to-face communication is critical and you must address the What's in it for me (WIIFM) factors.

- **Anger** – After learning that this change is not going away, the next natural step is to go through the anger phase. At this point, people affected often can't see a way out of the situation, and often resort to anger and bitterness, or even hostility and rejection including blocking and disruptive behaviours. At this point the key as a change agent is to involve yourself in informal channels and use multiple communication forms. Give people time to understand the change, while keeping communication channels open.

- **Exploration** – By maintaining the commitment to working with individuals, and facilitating them through the change curve, it will eventually become clear that the change is here to stay. At this point, people will often try to compromise to find a favourable outcome to the change. Comments like, "What if we do this?", "What about this alternative?" or "Can we just do this instead?" are apparent. In this we need to be clear on timelines, and set boundaries in a firm but considered way that use rational and logic, in a language that the affected people understand. This requires absolute transparency and honesty.

- **Acceptance** – Congratulations! The individual has successfully come through the change curve. The need to change is understood, and now the person is learning to live with the change, getting involved in change and dealing directly with it. This is a time to capitalise and reinforce the positives, as well as reinforcing objectives and strategy; build buy-in and create good feedback mechanisms, including rewarding people and celebrating successes.

Implementing a change will ALWAYS consume more resources pre-, during and post-change to ensure sustained and stable steady state. A factor to be aware of is that most change initiatives where the resources requirement post-change are less than the previous organisational resource load, lead to a common mistake of ramping resources down too quickly and keeping them artificially low. This can quickly unravel into a downward spiral of lost control, which then needs an effective recovery programme that was/is costlier than doing it in a structured and balanced way the first time. This can be driven by optimism bias – "'We're there, let's reduce headcount and save money", or "The benefits case showed all the resources being offloaded the day the programme was declared complete, contrary to the reality of the situation", along with many other optimistic prospects.

So, in summary the prerequisites should include at least the resource, time and budget to achieve:

- A plan that connects each individual.
- Has a bottom-up aspect.
- Communication that is tailored not a generic one-size-fits-all.
- Active sponsorship.
- Clear vision.
- Enables feedback and listening (and responding) to those impacted.
- Transparency and honesty as a guiding principle.
- Supports people in being part of the solution to drive ownership
- Breaks things down into manageable phases or stages.
- Avoids the jargon (systems people speaking a foreign language to business people, especially where this has a different meaning to what people know and use in the organisation pre-change!).

Turning to behavioural interventions, these are slightly more nuanced and need real insight into the DNA, culture and people in the business. Therefore, this has to be a planned activity, best left to the behavioural specialists in major programmes.

I liken this phase to that of the hostage negotiator that cannot afford to disclose their agenda, ensuring they are actively listening and translating the emotional and behavioural layers of communication and status. This can be used not only at the beginning, but at critical points in the major change programme to detect underlying issues and subsequently design behavioural interventions to counter negative biases or activities that are likely to put the programme at risk.

Another very effective way of delivering interventions is through nudging, recognising that this must be done in an ethical way, without invoking unintended consequences or limitations in entitlements, etc. The essence of this is to encourage and promote supportive behaviour for the change and its intended outcomes.

The approaches through intervention were summarised in the UK House of Lords Select Committee for Science and Technology[6], which I have shown opposite.

While this is, in my opinion, a more formal representation of change interventions, it is however intended for wider public application. Therefore, is reasonable to suggest it can be used to derive what would be acceptable and possible at an organisational level.

Interventions, particularly nudges, if used at an organisational level in a considered manner will help "signpost" the direction for the organisation, as well as help to overcome known biases and/or heuristics that would be harmful for designing and implementing organisational change.

Simple examples might be targeted e-mails to groups that are yet to adopt a desired change, by referencing other groups that have adopted the change, with what positive impacts at a personal level these people have witnessed, measured or quantified.

This could be something as simple as declaring improved 3-way matching of invoices, enabling automated payments, lower queries, better job satisfaction for accounts payable staff, audit, etc. This could be seen as an initial intervention, and as a pre-measure prior to involving the need for costlier one-to-one engagement of stakeholders and affected parties. This can then be supplemented by measures to convert reticent departments to align with new ways of working organisationally that may have lower perceived benefits for a department.

---

6. House of Lords: Science and Technology Select Committee 2nd Report of Session 2010–12. *Behaviour Change Report*, published 19 July 2011: Published by the Authority of the House of Lords London: The Stationery Office Limited HL Paper 179 – page 10

Table of interventions

	Regulation of the individual		Fiscal measures directed at the individual		Non-regulatory and non-fiscal measures with relation to the individual					
							Guide and enable choice — Choice Architecture ("Nudges")			
Interventions category	Eliminate choice	Restrict choice	Fiscal disincentives	Fiscal incentives	Non-fiscal incentives and disincentives	Persuasion	Provision of information	Changes to physical environment	Changes to the default policy	Use of social norms and salience
Examples of policy interventions	Prohibiting goods or services e.g. banning certain drugs	Restricting the options available to individuals e.g. outlawing smoking in public places	Fiscal policies to make behaviours more costly e.g. taxation on cigarettes or congestion charging in towns and cities	Fiscal policies to make behaviours financially beneficial e.g. tax breaks on the purchase of bicycles or paying individuals to recycle	Policies which reward or penalise certain behaviours e.g. time off work to volunteer	Persuading individuals using argument e.g. GPs persuading people to drink less, counselling services or marketing campaigns	Providing information in e.g. leaflets showing the carbon usage of household appliances *Regulation to require businesses to use front of pack nutritional labelling, or restaurants to provide calorific information on menus	Altering the environment e.g. traffic calming measures or designing buildings with fewer lifts *Regulation to require businesses to remove confectionery from checkouts, or the restriction of advertising of unhealthy products	Changing the default option e.g. requiring people to opt out of rather than opt in to organ donation or providing salad as the default side dish	Providing information about what others are doing e.g. information about an individuals energy usage compared to the rest of the street *Regulation to require energy companies to provide information about average usage

Note: * Demonstrates how regulation of businesses might be used to guide the choice of individuals, thus distinguishing it from regulation which restricts or eliminates the choice of individual.

Table 15.5. Table of interventions – UK House of Lords Select Committee

15.3 Cognitive Hurdles

In many situations where you enter an organisation where there is significant underperformance, or a disconnect with the organisation, or a plain and simple turnaround, the hardest battle is simply getting people to agree on the causes of current problems and the need for change. A high proportion of CPOs try to make the case for change simply by pointing to the "numbers" (a quantum of savings, cost avoidance, working capital improvement as tangible illustrations that are easy to derive, report and justify), insisting that the organisation can achieve better results. But messages simply communicating the need for change through numbers seldom stick.

The very people the CPO needs to win over are often spread across the organisation, and oftentimes to them the need for change seems abstract and remote. It can be a simple case of not recognising or accepting the criticism that the problem is not theirs but the C-suite's, or conversely, they see the position as a threatening one that could expose weaknesses and derail their careers. For these reasons, breaking through those cognitive barriers organisation-wide poses a complex challenge.

In the first instance it is important that managers and team members experience the true reality of each and every situation, and experience the operational realities across the business. This needs to include all the aspects across a 24 hour spectrum if needed; the facilities as experienced on an everyday basis. This is vital in building relationships, and understanding exactly what the true realities of the situation are, not just a report that conveys a fraction of what can be observed, questioned, internalised, etc. This will also give insight into 'the art of the possible', what is realistic, what the people can offer at the point of operation, etc. This sensitivity to the reality is essential in being able later to engage, present real solutions and offer valuable insights into what is necessary, and with credibility bring the solution to life.

Sensitising people to the dynamics of an aspect of business that is sub-optimal, inefficient or uncompetitive if it were to continue, is essential and engenders a real motivation and ownership. This can then translate into the creative approaches, to highlight and share the experiences with key stakeholders to illustrate the issues and the need for change.

As an example, some years back (in the public sector) there was an urgent need to improve first call responses in a contact centre delivering the outsourced service provision to residents. However, this could only be achieved through a change to resources and by restructuring the service delivery model. This required a change to the contract to achieve this.

Having visited the location with the team, it was clear that the technology and prime time resourcing was wrong and needed to be changed. This despite the statistics which showed that the service had only dropped by a few percentage points; the real issue was customer call backs and ring outs, which meant that the service was deteriorating rapidly, staff morale at the outsourced provider was low and failing to deliver on staff recruitment and retention.

Simply by changing and investing in a new technology before the outsourced call centre contract end date, and avoiding sunk cost fallacy, we were able to not only resolve more calls first time, but volumes dropped off significantly (no second, third and fourth calls), and staff morale and satisfaction improved.

The simple need to invest mid-contract and turn the situation around meant the relationship was back on track, and over the duration of the contract costs were actually lower.

The internal communications strategy of any change initiative or programme also plays an important role in breaking through the cognitive hurdles. As I outlined earlier, the layering and personalisation and/or channels used for communication can't be treated as a one-size-fits-all. If not addressed, this again becomes another cognitive hurdle to enabling change. Furthermore, as I witnessed in one major programme, the communications emanating from the programme were often out of synchronisation with what the functions themselves were communicating – this became a further hurdle, self-imposed by the programme that simply needn't have occurred.

Once people in an organisation accept the need for change, and more or less agree on what needs to be done, leaders are often then faced with the stark reality of limited resources, in terms of both people and budget. Fighting for more resources from the Executive board and/or shareholders is a process that can take time and divert attention from the underlying problems. This is where CPOs need to re-prioritise resource to attain the maximum pay-offs, or simply change the resource mix to have fewer, better quality resources delivering more. This means also deciding where those resources are best-placed relative to the activity, spend, etc.

A careful examination of the facts can also reveal where changes in key policies can reduce the need for resources. This is a classic case of deciding where thresholds for when and where procurement and Contract Management expertise only can do the task, and at what point can you enable the organisation's resources to do tasks, with support or defined thresholds to operate within. The latter greatly removes Purchasing and Supply Chain Management as the blocker to become the enabler too. This is where data combined with organisational insight becomes powerful.

I have more than once heard CPOs claim that the very thing that stops them initiating a change are the policies and procedures that procurement puts in place in the first instance – again, a classic case of needing to make it light and frictionless to enable more through the organisation.

A database that is fit for purpose and not just a financial instrument is a significant hurdle to overcome, especially because finance is always established before procurement. Again, the opportunities to help reduce invoice volumes, invoice matching, reducing payment queries are all positive ways to frame the need for a different approach, and one that needs careful thought before embarking on a change.

If a new strategy and embracing change is to become a step change, then employees must not only recognise what needs to be done, they must also want to do it. Many CPOs recognise the importance of getting people motivated to make changes, but fall into the trap of reform through monetary incentives as the only way have limited success.

Solving the motivation hurdle is a question of identifying the key influencers/enablers – both inside and outside the organisation – with disproportionate power due to their connectivity or network. i.e. their ability to persuade or enable resources positively or negatively towards a change. Identifying these people or service providers/suppliers and understanding what energises them is key. Create a community from this cohort to signal that what they are representing and owning in regards to the change agenda in an empowered and trusted way produces a step change to overcome the hurdles encountered.

By making results and responsibilities clear to everyone, and demonstrably showcasing projects and/or programmes that supported the change agenda reinforces a culture of performance. As I have said throughout this book, people are the key denominator above all else, not groups or functions, as they will be enabled by the people within them.

Framing the size and scale of the change needed is one of the most subtle and sensitive tasks of the CPO; unless people believe that a/the plan can be realised, then a change programme is unlikely to succeed. Breaking down the tasks as a cascade at each and every level shows not only how the task can be achieved, but also how everyone has a role to play in pulling it off.

Finally, not understanding the political dynamics of the organisation (public, private, VC, etc.) is a dimension that has undone many change programmes. This requires the need to recognise all the "terrorists and assassins" with pronounced biases and vested interests. While there are no magic formulas to assuage this issue, having a senior sponsor and allies across different parts of the organisation is a way of monitoring and diffusing certain political activity at the source. Tackling status quo bias, which is often a prime mover against change, the not-invented-here brigade will almost always be present, so you should expect it and prepare for it and have your counter positions, data, etc. ready. Recognise though that this may be met by those displaying confirmation bias too, so be careful to avoid that trap.

We know that challenging change resistance with pure logic and rational won't work, so developing an approach that counters that hurdle, as I have outlined earlier at an individual level is a necessity. Recognise the challenger's motivatorions and ambitions, frame the change that positively nudges in a direction you need it to be. Recognise the difference in a staged approach versus a full plan, etc.

A balanced approach with flex from the change agent will probably be both realistic and achievable, meet expectations and inspire an appetite for more. Fight the good fight, but live to fight another day!

15.4 Anchoring, Framing, Status Quo Bias and Optimism Bias in Change Programmes

At the outset of any major change you need to establish some vital information points:

- What are your heuristics and biases, relative to the change programme and how will you keep them under control?
- What are the heuristics and biases of the team, stakeholders, sponsors, owners, relative to the change programme and how will you map them?
- How can you ensure you use an approach, language and frequency that resonates with that of the people to be collaborated with, influenced, etc?
- What does your behavioural architecture look like for improving or ensuring success?

Establishing these core attributes at the outset, through a structured and active listening approach are, without question, the imperative. All procurement and contract people consider that they are good negotiators.

However, you need to unlearn and relearn the guiding principles of a hostage negotiator. This nuanced approach will not be the same for a commercial negotiation as traditionally taught through many programmes.

In essence the 6 key topics are:

1. Active Listening
2. Time
3. De-escalate
4. Empathy and rapport
5. Influence
6. Control

Look at these in more detail, and consider the approaches that encompass and embrace these into a more open interview style. This should or could embrace all or most of the following, as you formulate your questions to gain insight and build trust:

- Appear as a reasonable problem-solver.
- Adopt the position of a companion and empathiser of the person's role.
- The 'help me understand' approach.
- A confident and almost accepting-directing approach to show that you want a way forward.
- Non-judgemental and helpful.
- Compassionate but competent.
- Reinforce the things you hear that will set you in the right direction.
- Reinforce positive behavioural signs.
- Be the "authentic chameleon" that has flexibility.
- Avoid confrontation.
- Be neutral as possible to the situation.
- Don't respond to anything on the spot as it may be construed that you are giving direction or casting judgement.
- Recognise and define the emotions you witness.
- Paraphrase in a careful and consider way to build trust and empathy.
- Adopt all the active listening skills I highlighted earlier in chapter 2.5.
- Don't rush the conversation.
- Accept silence and pauses as this will encourage others to talk more and tell you more of what you want to know.
- Avoid framing and inferences that could be construed negatively.
- Buy time to come back with responses.
- Remember your questions should be open-ended.
- Don't use any form of anchoring.
- Avoid deadlines or commitments to time or deliverables.
- Look for positive signs and bank them.

What you should (aim to) construct from the above is a unique set of approaches and considerations to suit the circumstances, the situation and the people involved. This is not a process, but a competency-based approach designed to answer and give insight to the introductory questions as a starting point.

Also note that admissions of deficiencies or failures is hard to do, so you need to make that as easy as possible and without judgement, even if that is bestowed on another party or someone whose failures are already known. Remember, everyone is connected and any attributions you make have consequences!

15.5 Change Leadership from a Behavioural Perspective

Understand and accept that your evidence is not persuasive enough on its own. With a quantum of charts, numbers, metrics, data, and statistics being only partially sufficient, you must strengthen the power of your approach with emotional argumentation and alternative forms of persuasion. Be aware though that on receipt of such rational and logical arguments, it is likely that you will be confronted with the Conservatism bias or the tendency to revise beliefs or positions insufficiently when presented with new evidence. This brings us full circle to the central premise that all change is associated with behaviours, in whatever dimension you wish to ascribe them.

Leader's actions and their ability to become role models remains central to change. Winning hearts and minds is every leader's job across the spectrum, it is not singular in its attribution.

Leaders who have been with the business or in the sector many years are not a good recipe for change, as they are as prone to bounded rationality just like everyone else. Having the courage to recognise and confront this is a sign of a strong leader.

Distinguishing between a complex change and other types of change is essential to derive the right approach. To illustrate what is meant by this, we can look at a spectrum of Operational (redundancies) and Tactical (re-engineering) to Strategic (new operating model or transformational re-design of the organisation). The classic trap of misunderstanding the implementation of an ERP system as central to facilitating workforce efficiency is perhaps one of the biggest failures of recent times. As a change agent you will get criticism, decide which of that criticism merits consideration and which is just 'noise'.

Ensure you have the time, resources and intervals to re-assess progress continually, as this will allow you to refine and re-calibrate approaches to reduce friction and increase embeddedness of the new arrangements. In major change, uncertainty is the new normal – be comfortable with this state as the behaviours needed for this are different to steady state.

Recognise that most behavioural scientists will want to carry out pilots, Randomised Control Trials (RCTs)[7] and ensure the solution is scalable. Sadly, in most organisations that is not possible, so look for parallel projects and

---

7. A Randomised Controlled Trial is a form of scientific experiment which aims to reduce bias when testing a new approach. The people participating in the trial are randomly allocated to either the group following the new customised way of working or system under investigation or to a group receiving standard way of working (or placebo) as the control, or previously tested approach or benchmark (a positive-control study). Randomisation minimises selection bias and the different comparison groups allow the researchers to determine any effects of the approach when compared with the standard approach (control) group, while other variables are kept constant.

programmes to guide your approach and be prepared to be agile and flexible along the way. Where possible, having a pilot phase to any change programme is best practice, so lean on that opportunity too.

The piloting phase, or RCT, can be used to further validate the approach, especially when there are still people to convince about the new ways of working, new supply arrangements, or outsourced activity, etc.

People do not adopt changes in supply or outsourced arrangements just because they are rational and deliver savings; there have to the emotional and behavioural attributes that they not only accept, but fundamentally trust and believe in.

"In the middle of difficulty lies opportunity"
– Albert Einstein (1879-1955)

CHAPTER 16 | THE SILENT PILLAR: SUPPLIER RELATIONSHIP MANAGEMENT (SRM)

16.1 The Traditional Pillars of Supplier Relationship Management

The concept of Supplier Relationship Management, despite having been introduced originally in the 1980s, is still a relatively new concept. It was introduced as an approach more formally into organisations in the 1980s, but it took until the late-1990s before companies really started to adopt Supplier Relationship Management principles. Consistently, Supplier Relationship Management programmes provide procurement process and performance improvements leading to significant savings and other benefits, such as reduced risk in the supply chain, improved quality, access to innovations as a first mover advantage, etc.

In addition to the above benefits, the typical value propositions from Supplier Relationship Management programmes include:

- Supply risk management and mitigation.
- Identification and elimination of non-value added work.
- Reduced internal costs.
- Better flow of the money supply.
- Provision of real partnership with clear accountabilities and incentives to deliver the increased value.
- Improved operational performance and value delivering capability of suppliers.
- Access to market intelligence.
- Innovation and Research & Development benefits flowing as a priority to those adopting a Supplier Relationship Management programme.
- Improved manufacturing slots.
- Resources from the supplier to work on value-adding initiatives.
- Potential to collaborate on new initiatives and products.
- Leveraged marketing.

There have be numerous iterations by various bodies, as you will see in table 16.1 overleaf, to set out the key pillars of Supplier Relationship Management.

STAGES	BODY/AUTHOR	Archstone (2006) Five key elements of Supplier Relationship Management	Park et al (2010) An integrative framework for Supplier Relationship Management - 5 steps	CIPS (2013) Supplier Relationship Management Knowledge paper	COFELY (2015) Supplier Relationship Management	PWC (2013) Supplier Relationship Management maturity model	State of Flux (2016) Six pillars of Supplier Relationship Management	Loseby (2018) Soft Skills for Hard Business
1		Supplier stratification	Establishment of purchasing strategies	Pre-contract phase	WHAT • Value • Innovation • Performance improvements • Effectiveness • Risk reduction	Strategy and governance	Value	Value
2		Governance and organisation	Selection of a supplier	Contract phase	WHO • Strategic • Preferred • Major • others	Process	Engagement	Governance
3		Supplier development	Collaboration	Supplier Management Phase	HOW • with immediate suppliers • entire supply base • full supply chain	People	Governance	*People Behaviours*
4		Service and performance management	Supplier assessment and development	Relationship Management		Technology	People	Engagement model
5		Supplier Relationship Management systems	Provision of CI			Performance management	Technology	Collaboration
6						Risk management	Collaboration	Technology, systems and processes
7								*Trust, PDI, and Cognitive diversity*

Table 16.1. The key pillars of Supplier Relationship Management, as compared between different

Some have referred to them in different terminology from a governance to a management perspective, but they amount to much the same when looking at the key steps and actions to implement Supplier Relationship Management.

Supplier Relationship Management has evolved from a relatively simple 3 or 4 pillar approache that was more process-focused to a more considered approach that recognises people skills more dominantly. This shift from process to people will, I believe, be the next generation of Supplier Relationship Management practice, that moves this discipline forward. The reason is that we have had and enjoyed the tools, processes and systems for some time, but the step change will be in recognising behaviours, which I will cover in the next section.

Supplier Relationship Management is an approach that should be reserved for only strategically important relationships for a business, given the resource required to execute this effectively and get a return on that investment. Accordingly, it is worth clarifying that Contract Administration and Contract Management are activities that preceded Supplier Relationship Management and require significantly less resource. For the sake of clarification:

Contract administration is:
Manage the supplier to the contract, and ensure that the supplier is delivering and operating within the terms agreed in the contract and to the agreed specifications.

Contract Management is:
An activity concerned with the process of managing contracts, deliverables, deadlines, and contract terms and conditions while ensuring customer satisfaction. Public agencies and private companies know that the purchasing process does not end when the contract is awarded.

Effective post-award Contract Management is essential to the seamless acceptance of supplies and services. Contract Management impacts many areas within an organisation and can significantly influence its budget, operations, customer service, and public image.

Earlier models have, as previously mentioned, tended to focus more on the steps and processes that underpin the approach, rather than the people. However, in my opinion it is the people involved that make the difference between success and something more akin to Contract Management, which is executed at a more defined deliverable level, rather than necessarily seeking innovation. Some of the steps and processes can focus on aspects such as the following:

- Supplier base segmentation.
- Purchase to pay processes.

- Contract aspects.
- Workflow.
- Selection by value.

While some of these aspects may be as a result of an agreement between the parties, it should be recognised that the centre and focus of Supplier Relationship Management is about people and the respective strategic objectives of their respective organisations. The selection process of who to partner with should be not be about financial value alone, but about all the factors that create true strategic value, such as:

- Assurance of supply.
- Quality that is fit for purpose or differentiated (if required).
- Service that allows the recognition of cost in the service delivery to be understand and consciously selected, not simply a default.
- Cost parameters for all aspects and how they can be continuously improved upon.
- Innovation, not just for the sake of it, but where it will create competitive advantage for both parties.
- Constantly aware of regulatory changes and how these can be turned into opportunities rather than a cost or a problem.

Real value is unlikely to be delivered merely by putting a system in place – it needs people to collaborate and develop trust to empower changes that drive competitive advantage. Equally, it is likely that the traditional approach will be driven by policies, hard metrics that don't change over time. A one-size-fits-all approach, which is not tailored to the organisation, will similarly flounder. Consider too that buyer-centric, purely procurement-led and owned, non-inclusive approaches will meet resistance. Finally, mechanisms that carry penalties for noncompliance will suffocate any potential innovation.

There will be a need to consider what changes in an existing relationship or contract are required. This is what I will explore in the following sections.

16.2 The Behavioural Pillars (People behaviours, Trust, Power Distance Index (PDI) and Cognitive Diversity)

In this section we will see how bringing together many of the aspects I have set out in previous chapters provide a more scientific and structured approach to the competences needed. This is a fundamental change to the concept and structure of Supplier Relationship Management and I believe the missing link needed to address the full spectrum of people skills. Combined with the ability to "make sense and translate" this into a language and approach that the whole business can assimilate, this will allow the process to be monetised more readily and hence enhance its true value.

Supplier Relationship Management is an area that will benefit significantly from an approach that embraces Behavioural Science, Social Science, Decision Sciences, collaboration, people (soft) skills combined with a natural business acumen that integrates itself as part of the business (on both sides). In a similar way to effective procurement it is a facilitated approach that is part of the business that can flex to empathise and maximise the uniqueness of each and every organisation in an intelligent way.

The full spectrum of Behavioural Science should be part and parcel of the competences in the development of an effective Supplier Relationship Management approach, as it is the people involved both directly and indirectly that will be the key determinant of success (or failure).

Firstly, the approach should very much start with a personal review of heuristics and biases, and how they will play into the role both positively and negatively. Also, how will manage any biases to ensure the best possible outcome? Secondly, recognise that this will need time and effort to not only build trust with all parties, but also map what heuristics and biases will be evident from others and what you may need to do to respond to them appropriately.

Thirdly, it is a change to the ways of working and as such should be recognised as such – a transformation not just in your own organisation, but in the supplier or service provider's organisation too. Fourthly, one's communication skills and effective listening skills will be tested fully, especially where new cultures (organisational and/or geographic) play a part. Remember that the cultural Power Distance Indexes are between not just HQ functions, but where the business is being operationalised too.

Fifthly, developing high levels of, or selecting people with above-average EQ will ensure the approach is empathetic, yet effective. Lastly, remove the hurdles to doing business and make it frictionless, ensuring things don't get "stuck" internally in any part of the respective organisations.

Not surprisingly, this is a complex task with many "human dimensions" across both organisations, and it thus needs significantly more effort than simply monitoring and responding to KPIs. It relies upon heavy doses of reciprocity and the flexibility that enables and binds activity together as needed. Results are not often instant, although they can occasionally be so, but generally require long-term commitment to realise the potential of significant benefits that are reported. In State of Flux's (SofF)[1] *Annual 2017 Survey Report*, the following example of cost savings was given:

"...Brammer, a distributor of maintenance, repair and overhaul products to industry, hit on a novel way to prevent customers "rogue stock-piling" products. It installs vending machines in customers' premises which allow their employees to "buy" products using a code. It means the customer consumes less, while inventory is more tightly controlled and demand more easy to foresee. Some customers have achieved a 45% cost saving with this approach".

Some of the key findings from the SofF 2017 report were as follows:

- 46% of leaders achieved post-contract signature financial benefits of more than 4%.
- 66% report improved collaboration as a direct result of their Supplier Relationship Management programme.
- 8 in 10 companies are actively seeking more supplier innovation.
- Only around a third of companies have defined their Supplier Relationship Management role.
- 21% have identified the requisite skill set.
- Just 11% have carried out a skills and competency assessment.

As you can see from the above, the skills needed and available are relatively low from the survey results. This in turn continues to support the theory that Behavioural Procurement and people skills have all too often been left in the "too difficult to do" box. Accordingly, a coherent structure and approach to set out and articulate what the skills are is an essential aspect of effective Supplier Relationship Management. Drawing on all the previous chapters, the matrix of these, not just one singular strand, is what makes it so challenging, but at the same time so rewarding.

State of Flux's survey sets out and ranks the people aspects as surveyed from their perspective, calling out communication as one of the major aspects. A more integrated and comprehensive approach, as illustrated in Table 16.2 opposite, shows many aspects already covered, but at the same time illustrates the opportunities:

1. Day, Alan and Shutes, Mel. (2017). *State of Flux Global Supplier Relationship Management Research Report. Entrepreneurial Supplier Relationship Management: Solving the Value Puzzle.*

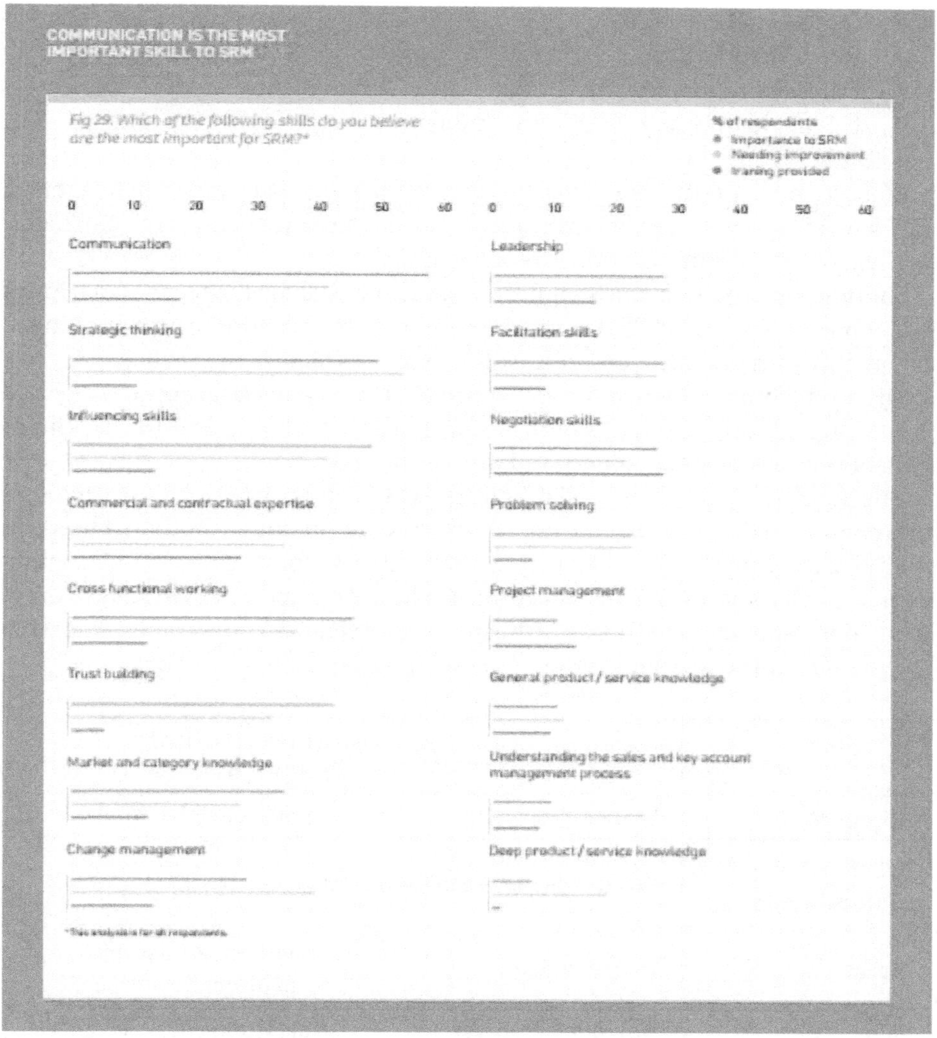

COMMUNICATION IS THE MOST IMPORTANT SKILL TO SRM

Fig 29. Which of the following skills do you believe are the most important for SRM?*

Table 16.2. People skills ranked in terms of importance to Supplier Relationship Management (State of Flux)

A more comprehensive and fuller suite of competences augment what we have already established at the leading edge of today's Supplier Relationship Management programmes, which need to include:

- Active listening skills.
- A deep understanding of heuristics and biases (self and others).
- Frictionless.
- Cultural practices (PDI) and Social Sciences.

- Decision Sciences.
- Reciprocity.
- Bounded rationality.
- Cognitive diversity (within the team(s)).

The richness of the competences and added perspectives, when applied, can address some of the key call-outs from the survey, such as Trust, Change Management, Communication (and Listening), etc.

Shifting the Procurement/Supplier Relationship Management functions into a wider business approach that is not the confine of the function, but something to be practiced on organisation-wide, will enhance its value as a practice.

The shift from a more traditional approach to a behavioural approach would see the agenda shift from less of the 'how', to the 'who has the requisite skills to collaborate across stakeholders and organisations?'

The next generation of collaborators will seek to be more creative and entrepreneurial. This will be especially true as business models, based on digital disruption, complexity in supply chains, and greater uncertainty economically and politically, shift immeasurably from what we know today. Consider some of the strands of business we see and know today, and what they will become in a new model as shown in Table 16.3 below:

	CURRENT PRACTICE	BEHAVIOURAL PRACTICE
Approach	Process-based	Competency-based
Relationship equilibrium	Biased to buyer organisation	Equality based
Incentivisation	Annual targets	Long-term growth and breakthrough
Value	Cost and KPI driven	Dual Competitive advantage
Dynamics	Reactive	Proactive
Primary biases	Confirmation, Self-serving, Bounded rationality, zero-sum risk	Loss aversion, GroupThink
Governance	Procurement/Supplier Relationship Management-led	Dual organisationally-aligned
Transformation	Year-on-year incremental	Disruptive step changes, driven by digital, AI and other entrants

Model	Standard	Customised and Agile
Primary drivers	Policies and procedures, plus annual KPIs	Trust, collaboration, mutual gain
Team	Functional	Cognitively diverse
Culture	Singular	Diverse PDI and compensated for through transparency and approach

Table 16.3. Comparison of traditional and new practices in Supplier Relationship Management

The behavioural architecture will drive the competitive advantage, through innovative and agile ways not a one-size-fits-all approach anchored to a fixed process. The unlearning and re-learning process will be key for organisations as they embrace a newer, more collaborative approach with cognitively diverse teams that negate much of the bounded rationality found in static, unidimensional teams.

A true peer-to-peer relationship on multiple levels will be needed. Complexity will increase as a consequence, which should be viewed as an opportunity and not a problem, satisfied through collaboration portals that are truly organisation-wide.

A clear recognition of attitudes and (self and team) behaviours over processing skills will become the differentiators in this space. The aim is to create a way of working that promotes transferable skills and broader appreciation of the organisational objectives in a language that everyone recognises, not just the function leading the activity.

16.3 Attitudes and Behaviours Matter

Entrepreneurial Supplier Relationship Management will embrace the all that Behavioural Science has to offer, and challenge the current slow adoption of Supplier Relationship Management, given that the principle is right and has been proven to add value to those who adopt and invest in it.

Creative and able leaders will realise that they will need to *make sense and translate* what Supplier Relationship Management is in a more behaviourally-centric approach and put this into a format, language and context that the business recognises and understands. We cannot and should not avoid the need to recognise cost savings and cost avoidance, but recognising the value of customer retention, up-selling, reduced inventory (lower working capital), product differentiation, product Unique Selling Points (Apple have done this successfully for years) can be monetised just the same.

As I referenced earlier, attitudes and behaviours should be the selection criteria over and above the skills needed to manage processes and be fully rational. That might suggest a totally irrational approach, which is probably true from where we look to source, educate, train and develop people from today, however, the importance of people skills will surpass the logic-based skills in the shift to a new paradigm. To paraphrase Benjamin Franklin, Albert Einstein, Voltaire and many others, "You know, doing the same thing repeatedly with expectation of differing results would be the definition of stupidity, not insanity".

Recognise that behaving badly in a negotiation, post-contract phase, or at any other time will only result in one outcome, you lose! We must recognise that the tactical levers of delayed payments, shorting suppliers of information on a timely and agreed basis (and still expecting an on time in full (OTIF) delivery), petulant and inflexible behaviour (diverting delayed shipments to warehouses by 24 hours, just because you can) are all short-term, self-inflicted injuries due to poor behaviour.

This short-termism is a mental safety blanket for people behaviours that no longer have a place in a more collaborative economy. This behaviour only serves to backfire too – as history has shown us, and something I have personally witnessed in my career – shortages through economic, political or natural events have abruptly ended supply chains for lengthy and sustained periods. Continuity of supply will then win over any form of short-term tactical/operational attitudes and behaviours.

Coming full circle, we look at the Working Relations Index (WRI) – used by Henke – and we can see how this has altered the fortunes of the American automotive industry as an example. The shift in WRI was mirrored by the fluctuations of the stock market prices as analysed and reported on by Henke.

The really interesting aspect comes when you look at the headings they have taken, versus the ones I showed earlier in Table 16.1. – I have shown the full detail in Table 16.4 opposite:

COMPONENTS	VARIABLES
Supplier – Company relationship	1. Supplier trust of company. 2. Supplier-company overall working relationship.
Company Communication	1. Company open and honest communication with suppliers. 2. Company communicates timely information. 3. Company communicates adequate amounts of information.
Company help	1. Help company gives to suppliers to reduce costs/hourly rates. 2. Help company gives to suppliers to improve product/services quality.
Company hinderance	1. Company late/excessive product/services design/specification changes (reverse measure). 2. Conflicting objectives across company functional areas (reverse measure). 3. Supplier given flexibility to meet established cost/quality objectives. 4. Supplier involvement in company product/services development.
Supplier profit opportunity	1. Company shares savings from supplier's cost reduction proposals. 2. Company rewards high performing suppliers with new/continued business. 3. Company covers sunk costs or cancelled or delayed programmes. 4. Company concern for supplier profit margins when asking for price reductions. 5. Suppliers opportunity to make acceptable return over long term.

Table 16.4 – PPIs WRI components and variables (calculated by combining a weighted average response to each variable of a specific component)

The effect of buyer behaviours has been scientifically-validated[2] to show a

2. Ellis, Scott, John W. Henke, Jr., and Thomas Kull. (2012). "The Effect of Buyer Behaviours on Preferred Customer Status and Access to Supplier Technological Innovation: An Empirical Study of Supplier Perceptions" in *Industrial Marketing Management*, 41:8 (November 2012): 1259-1269.

correlation between the two buyer behaviours – early supplier involvement and relational reliability positively affect preferred customer status, while a third behaviour – share of sales – has no effect. Looking at the financial implications as stated earlier, Henke[3] – after six years of research – found that 14% of revenue and 33% of profit was attributable to trusting supplier working relations. Secondly that up to 75% of the revenue of manufacturing organisations and up to 40% of service of organisations were being spent on purchased goods or services and therefore the impact of suppliers and service providers on economic success is significant. In later reports from PPI and Henke, they refer to trillions of dollars lost through poor working relationships. The chart below, available from PPI, shows the moving index in the American automotive industry over the last 14 years.

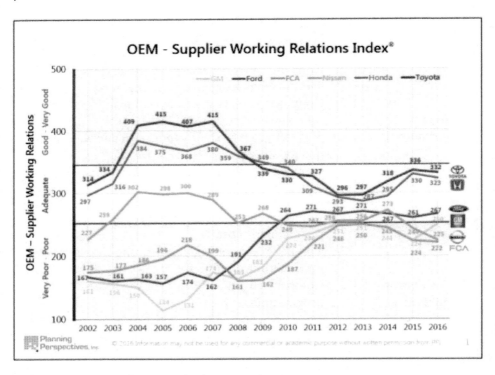

Chart 16.5. PPI index over the last 14 years

This link to behaviours (relationships) and competitive advantage and how value is delivered is partly where I started my journey of connecting the two elements of behaviour and competitive advantage, and takes the journey through heuristics, behaviours, EQ, reciprocity, frictionless, bounded rationality full circle.

---

3. Henke, John. (2009). *CPO Agenda, Spring 2009*: p16-17

Increasing supplier innovation – a direct product of effective relationships and behaviours – is something Peter Drucker[4] identified over 60 years ago as one of the basic ways an organisation can build and maintain competitive advantage in the marketplace. This suggests yet again that some of the fundamentals remain:

- Early engagement.
- Commercialisation of products.
- Timely and efficient information sharing
- Helping and supporting suppliers.
- Reciprocity.
- Collaborative approach.
- Unified platform to aid efficiency, remove duplication/errors.
- Technology enabled – open architecture.
- Risk sharing.
- Joint marketing
- Responsive.
- Avoidance of biases and bounded rationality.
- Cognitively diverse teams.
- TRUST.

In drawing this chapter to a close, the essence of great collaboration and true Supplier Relationship Management is where it is tailored to suit the organisations involved, and not just a generic process – and that's often the opening and deciding aspect to all this. This is followed of course by having the right people with right skills in the right place at the right time, irrespective of where they come from organisationally.

---

4. Drucker, Peter. (1954). *The Practice of Management*. Harper and Row: New York.

CHAPTER 17 | LEADERSHIP, INNOVATION AND MORE...

17.1 Leadership Styles and Impacts

The reality of modern leadership is that we cannot have certainty, but that complexity is guaranteed. Rigid models must give way to agility, with a pathway to competitive advantage through innovation and the diversity of people behaviours.

In looking at the Behavioural Sciences, I believe this can offer a comprehensive and indeed a new lens on critical business activities such as key decisions, change and team dynamics that will allow us to operate more coherently as a result. This will ultimately lead organisations who embrace this approach to a more sustainable pipeline of innovation and competitive advantage through an engaged employee base.

The Social, Decision and Behavioural Sciences will coalesce to provide a more colourful and expansive, yet clearer picture, leading towards an understanding your own behaviours and those of others can be more readily found. When managed effectively, they will undoubtedly rebalance what I call the fourth leg of the stool, people (systems, processes, and data being the other three).

Because the people leg is the most complex, it has often been neglected. Also, it should be remembered that foundational attributes such as trust, collaboration and cognitive diversity that are nascent need further encouragement, but not to the detriment of the other legs of the stool.

The transferability of these skills and competences will, I believe, not be bounded within Purchasing and Supply Chain Management and related fields, but equally applicable across the full business spectrum. Leadership therefore needs to understand that this is pivotal to success, and must be fully integrated with the wider business at all levels. While each leader will have their own style and approach, it is clear that certain attributes will be an expectation from successful organisations. This means that having sector knowledge, high IQ, desired qualifications, position and title will not be enough if they do not possess the behavioural skills and competences to engage and deliver high levels of engagement effectively.

I believe the behavioural skills will be a differentiator when you consider that technical skills, such as systems knowledge, process expertise and the ability to access data can more readily be delegated. People skills are the one competency that cannot. This will be the defining competency of a leader that will make or break teams, programmes and whole organisations.

17.2 Surveys and Interviews

During 2017 and early 2018 I carried out a series of surveys (circa 113) and interviews (27) to both validate the approach as well as test certain aspects of behaviours both in academia and in organisations (public and private) across an international audience. I was intentionally practicing what I am preaching by trying to de-bias my opinions and summaries of the last 16 chapters!

The results showed some interesting outcomes, some of which I had not fully predicted. In terms of those who took the survey, only 14% said that formal education and professional training provided the skills and competences needed in relation to Purchasing and Supply Chain Management. This contrasted sharply with 73% who said that they had received sufficient training in-house to provide the skills and competences necessary for Purchasing and Supply Chain Management. This gap of nearly 60% suggest that most professionals rely upon post-formal education training to equip themselves as leaders.

Of equal interest was the following – for the statement "All decision-making in organisations is entirely based upon facts and data to deliver a totally rational outcome", only 6% of people agreed. During the interview sessions it became clear that people in public sector roles in particular were more inclined to support this, given the legislation that supports public procurement. Moreover, some senior leaders indicated that forward-thinking in advance of a public procurement process was necessary to deliver innovation and competitive advantage, illustrating a different approach to that afforded in the private sector.

Turning to the views of Purchasing and Supply Chain Management leaders and CEOs, again there was a difference in terms of what CEOs expected and were looking for in their Purchasing and Supply Chain Management leaders, and what those leaders thought their CEOs expected of them. Using a 2015 survey of CEOs[1] you will see the differences between the two groups, with some clear omissions in attributes such as Curiosity, Creativity, Problem-solving, Agility and Adaptiveness (see table 17.1).

The gap between the two groups could be as large as 18% or more depending on the weighting from the CEOs, which was not available. This is more interesting when we look at the missing attributes as opposed to the scores themselves.

---

1. MacAskill, Andrew. (2015). *Behavioural traits boards are demanding from procurement leaders.* Accessed at https://www.procurious.com/procurement-news/behavioural-traits-boards-are-demanding-from-procurement-leaders, 15/12/2015

ATTRIBUTE	P&SCM percentage of votes	CEO VIEW	
CURIOSITY	6%		↓
EMOTIONALLY INTELLIGENT	16%	███████	↑
HIGH IQ AND TEAM PLAYER			
CREATIVE AND PROBLEM SOLVER	12%		↓
ROLE MODEL			
FUNCTIONAL EXPERT			
INNOVATOR			
INFLUENCER AND COMMUNICATOR	13%	███████	↑
RESULTS DRIVEN	6%	███████	↕
AGILE AND ADAPTIVE	5%	███████	↓
SELF AWARE-SELF MANAGED-REFLECTIVE			
RELATIONSHIP DRIVEN	6%	███████	↕
OBJECTIVE AND DATA RATIONAL			
PLANNER AND DISCIPLINED			
STRATEGIC FOCUS	12%	███████	↑

Table 17.1. Purchasing and Supply Chain Management leadership versus CEO view of attributes needed/expected

The survey sought to identify what skills and competences were most important for highly successful and effective teams, with nearly 80% listing the following as the top FIVE skills and/or competences, with a clear preference for collaborative skills:

1. Collaborative.
2. Focused and driven for results.
3. Effective communications and listeners.
4. Trusting and highly respectful.
5. Creative and Innovative.

In 2016 the World Economic Forum[2] listed SEVEN critical skills for jobs for the future as the following:

1. Critical thinking and problem-solving.
2. Collaboration across networks and leading by influence.
3. Agility and adaptability.
4. Initiative and entrepreneurship.
5. Effective oral and written communication.

2. World Economic Forum: *The Future of Jobs: Employment, Skills and Workforce Strategy for the Fourth Industrial Revolution*; January 2016.

6.   Assessing and analysing information.

7.   Curiosity and imagination

Interestingly this challenged some of the skills and competences listed in the CEO survey of 2015, in particular the critical thinking and problem-solving skills. The survey responses gathered told a very different story, perhaps showing that getting consensus or indeed what the Purchasing and Supply Chain Management leadership community view as important is bounded by their rationality?

Clearly further research will be needed to explore this disparity between what a profession sees as what they need to provide versus what organisations expect to be provided. In table 17.2 I have shown the results from the survey, cutting off all responses below 2%.

	Competency descriptive	Survey count	Percentage score
1	ADAPTABILITY	18	11.92%
2	INNOVATIVE	17	11.265
3	EMOTIONAL INTELLIGENCE	16	10.60%
4	PROBLEM SOLVING	13	8.61%
5	AGILITY	13	8.61%
6	LEADERSHIP	11	7.28%
7	CRITICAL THINKING	9	5.96%
8	STRATEGIC	9	5.96%
9	CURIOUS	6	3.97%
10	LEARNING	6	3.97%
11	TEAM PLAYER	5	3.31%
12	TRUSTING	5	3.31%
13	GOOD COMMUNICATOR	4	2.65%
14	TECHNOLOGY AWARENESS	4	2.65%

Table 17.2. Critical future skills as viewed by Purchasing and Supply Chain Management survey respondents

An area that has been the subject of research is that of *fairness,* and how this needs to be present to ensure there is acceptance of an outcome, even when this is unfavourable. I have commented upon this in chapter 4.3, but felt it was necessary to see how this would be viewed by a diverse survey base from public sector, private sector and academics in the field of Purchasing and Supply Chain Management. This can be summed up by the following SIX key words, drawing over 75% of the word count:

1. Transparency.
2. Equality, including "win-win" and mutuality.
3. Respect for the other party.
4. Equitable to both parties.
5. Trust and Integrity.
6. Honesty.

Turning to the whole ecosystem of competences and skills we need in the profession (and I suspect this is true of many other professions), it became abundantly clear during the interviews that people skills are the differentiator. The entry ticket, so to speak, is the knowledge of good processes (such as category management), systems (ERP, E-proc, etc.), and a respected educational background. This is further supported by the move to an ever more complex and faster-paced environment with greater economic uncertainty.

The resonance of certain terms or attributes, at the risk of my own confirmation bias kicking in, was part of what I was hoping to gain from the interviews. In no particular order, here they are:

- Self-awareness.
- Social skills (science of)
- Networker.
- Forming emotional connections.
- Trust.
- Collaboration – the "Bridge builders".
- Use of Decision Sciences.
- Outcomes versus process following.
- Bounded rationality (lack of awareness of).
- Data smart (not data scientist).
- Broader business skills (entrepreneurial, acumen, creative, critical thinker, influencer and a curious mindset).
- Storyteller.

In essence what I concluded from the interviews was more about the destructive effect of not having the behavioural skills, as opposed to wondering whether we should we have them, or need them. This was equally reinforced by the call to teach Social Sciences and Decision Sciences through the academic curriculum, correlating with the 86% of people surveyed who believed that this is either not or only partially provided for today.

This input and the science of the last 16 chapters supports the link between behavioural competences and the creation of competitive advantage and/or value for organisations. The thorny question of how we place a monetary value on this for the finance department and others remains, though, and perhaps begs the question of whether we should/could place value on science over art? Clearly, we can produce and deliver effective metrics, such as the Virgin Atlantic Airways fuel trial[3], but each scenario will be unique. Therefore, parallels and associations between different interventions and architectures from project to project and organisation to organisation will need to be constructed and applied.

The suggestion that there is irrational behaviour perhaps deserves better qualification as being an act or omission that is significantly distant to the populous of the group or team involved (large or small), and the gap between the two is not reconcilable.

This is the point at which we can't find a compromise to what we are trying to achieve or are presented with something diametrically opposed to our values. For me this is the outer area in the diagram I set forth in chapter 6, figure 6.2 and this is where it becomes material to the outcome. The fact, and it is a fact, is that we all have our own unique set of heuristics and biases, cultures, value sets and ethical/moral standards that form our unique behavioural DNA.

Therefore, we should accept that some situations and circumstances are irreconcilable, and therefore focus on what treatment and/or intervention would work and how we should go about designing and implementing this to ensure optimal outcomes aligned to our stated goals.

17.3 Innovation through Behavioural Practice in Purchasing and Supply Chain Management

Innovation is not an exclusive domain of Purchasing and Supply Chain Management. However, it can and should be one of the key areas of the business where this can be driven by Purchasing and Supply Chain Management, given the accessibility to a wide and diverse supply and service base that can represent between 40 and 80% of an organisation's turnover. Furthermore, during the interviews I carried out I explored the statement that Drucker made in 1954[4],

3. Metcalfe, Robert; Gosnell, Greer and List, John. (2016). "Virgin Atlantic Tested 3 Ways to Change Employee Behaviour" in *Harvard Business Review*; 1 August 2016.
Mooney, Chris. (2016). "Virgin Atlantic just used Behavioural Science to 'nudge' its pilots into using less fuel. It worked" in *Washington Post*; 22 June 2016.
4. Drucker, Peter. (195p4). *The Practice of Management*. Harper and Row: New York.

"Innovation creates differentiation between organisations, which in turn creates competitive advantage". The clear message I got back was unanimous agreement, and in most cases leaders felt that this was even more relevant than when first put forward by Drucker over 60 years ago!

Additional comments during the interviews sought to support the theory that most effective procurement functions had reached base cost on commodities and services, and therefore value could only be created through new ways of working (innovation). Furthermore, the pursuit of innovation in some cases was defined as "incremental innovation", versus a step change. Additionally, an approach towards pure cost savings alone was acting against the best interests of organisations.

In pursuit of innovation some sectors, such as pharmaceuticals, have taken to buying-out more agile and innovative smaller enterprises to drive the innovation pipeline. Creating an "active bridge" into the supply chain, as internal innovation often lacks resources and funding, is where some leading organisations are taking this and hence the salience of leadership through Purchasing and Supply Chain Management was seen as a good practice to adopt.

The big "however" resounded around the lack of creative skills, or "big dreamers" as some referred to it, in a profession steeped in process and methodology. Moreover, the resonance around a lack of cognitive diversity in teams remained an issue for those I interviewed. This was further supported by a criticism that all too often procurement is the blocker rather than the enabler in this space. Lamentably, this is the opposite to what it ought to be, given procurement's position across the organisation. Alarmingly, most survey respondents stated that they thought procurement generally only had a 10-15% positive impact at best!

Many interviewees referenced the "short-termism" of many organisations that prevented more substantive innovation being initiated, as often the timeline to benefit realisation was beyond the fiscal year. The pressure to deliver at every consecutive reporting interval, driven by investors, was often cited as a key reason for this. However, those that were able to balance short-term with long-term gains would clearly win in the end. As we read earlier, the impact of the "not invented here" and status quo bias are particularly hard at work, and will need skilled practitioners to navigate out and away from these obstacles.

Contrasting the more predictable world of 1954 with the faster changing and more complex world of today, innovation will in itself become harder to achieve as a significant game-changer. Therefore, as referenced earlier, the term incremental innovation may be a more appropriate goal or realistic expectation to enable.

Drawing on earlier references across the book, I would summarise the SIX behaviours that I believe that need to be in place, with all of them being evident, observed and recognised by other parties to the process of promulgating innovation:

1. Trust-enabling.
2. Collaborative and supportive across the total supply and value chain.
3. Results focused, but clear reward and recognition for everyone in a fair and equitable manner.
4. Agility and flexibility to be creative without bias.
5. Balance creativity with structure and pragmatism to move quickly to implementation.
6. Cognitive diversity.

It is equally recognised that this process involves taking higher levels of risk than normal, accepts failure, but learns from it as a positive outcome and does not become bounded by current culture and knowledge. As I have stated before, just changing a few critical behaviours can often bring about the majority of the change needed to realise the benefit. This will also be easier to enable as it does not represent wholesale change, which scientifically, is a lot more difficult to achieve, if not impossible.

Cognitively diverse teams generate healthier overall teams that are more capable of problem-solving and challenging established thoughts and practices, so this needs to be embraced. Being honest about what you are missing or lacking and bringing these skills and insights into the organisation is a must. It will stimulate and accelerate the process.

Just because an initiative is intended to be an innovation generator, a structured approach is still needed, if not more so. All great ideas need prioritisation too, as even the ones you have the greatest affinity with personally may not be the right ones, so avoid your personal biases as a leader. However, don't lose these ideas as they may become part of a future pipeline of ideas that have synergy and value as a collective. Getting to market first is critical too, so be ruthless. Above all, avoid the sunk cost fallacy of investing in an equivalent just because it's your best idea!

Reward is not always in the form of a monetary bonus, there are so many other ways, especially if you understand what motivates your team and the whole ecosystem involved. In my experience this can range from providing/ sponsoring training, a book, a certificate and the *experience* of the process will last long after the money has been spent! Ensure you don't miss anybody out, because as a leader it is your job to promote others and not yourself. If you have done your job well, then the team will promote you. The ownership and cross-recognition from this approach is witnessed beyond the functional or company boundaries. Eyal Winter[5] describes incentives as being, social, emotional and moral.

Innovation that simply becomes process optimisation or incremental improvement needs to be handed on to those that integrate this into business as usual. The pay-off for you and your team will come next time around when you need agile and flexible collaboration to make the next big idea work, fast. Continuous improvement is just as important to organisations in continuing to deliver value, growth and sustainability, and helps create the behaviours that you need to have a collaborative enterprise.

Innovation brings with it change, and this needs to be recognised both in terms of what the implications are for systems, process and more importantly people. If you believe that certain people – and there will always be some – can't or don't want to make the change, you need to recognise this and manage accordingly for all parties concerned, including those committed to change.

Creating innovative new ways of working, services and/or products is a stressful business and needs to recognise all the factors that prevail, even down to the organisational cultures you may be collaborating with. You will need to endure the duration of the journey, the challenges from those that display overt status quo bias (and who may be senior) and more. It is often said that in adversity, problems can sometimes, if approached in the right way, deliver an opportunity for change for the better. I believe this is to be true in so many ways, and breaking out of our bounded rationality can help us do this.

I don't intend to address the process or programme management aspects needed to deliver structured change, as these can be accessed in more focused articles or publications. However, the principles of having the following are still evident, in no particular order:

- Evaluation criteria for acceptance or rejection of new ideas.
- Risk management.
- Clear strategy.
- Functional specifications.
- Clarity of scope (in and out of).
- Market forces.
- Technology roadmaps.
- Benefits articulation.
- Communication plan.
- Programme management discipline.
- Underpinning data and analysis.
- Systems for collaboration.

---

5. Winter, Eyal. (2014). *Feeling Smart: Why our emotions are more rational than we think*. Public Affairs

- Legal structure for handling Intellectual Property, etc.
- Budget and spend management control.

Ultimately the leadership goal is to develop a deep sense of zen-like harmony of rationality and behaviours, to manage a critical imperative such as innovation. The business of being innovative and creative is a disciplined one that requires high levels of trust and collaboration, as well as the rigour and discipline of broad programme management and business acumen. The emphasis and focus of the many aspects of consideration will change and evolve for each and every team and idea, to mirror the complexity and speed of business disruption. Leaders can no longer be afforded the luxury of 'business as usual'.

Erik Maskin[6], in Mechanism Design Theory, presents a powerful coalition of Game Theory, Behavioural Economics and engineering to account for the differences in response that independent, intelligent people display. This is further supported by Winter who shows that, although our emotions are thought to be at odds with rationality, they're actually a key factor in rational decision-making.

Leadership needs to understand what motivates and drives teams and individuals, as well as what will have been decided and determined rationally inclusive of behavioural bias or emotion. The stark reality that the process, the systems and the data will be a constant, and only people will be the variable – in all likelihood the determining factor in making a breakthrough or not. This is at the heart of why the skills and competences involved in maximising the contribution from individuals and teams is the most difficult of all things to master.

17.4 A Summary and some concluding thoughts

As I look back over the book and reflect on the hundreds or thousands of academic and professional journals, papers and books I have read, a number of factors re-occur and resonate time and again, irrespective of whether in a Purchasing and Supply Chain Management context or not.

- To lead you need to be a behavioural performance coach.
- Consider the aspect of people over process.
- Complexity and speed become exponential in their rise and won't stop!
- Continuous Personal Development (not just professional) is an imperative.
- Invest time and understanding in your biases.

---

6. Maskin, Erik. (2016). Quoted in *McKinsey Quarterly*; October 2016

- Humility and openness are markers of experience, not weakness.
- You can't control everything – recognise this!

Purchasing and Supply Chain Management as a profession is at a crossroads I believe. Will there be a profession in the future, or is it procurement but not as we know it? Perhaps the answer lies in evolving to become Value Architects that span the business as integrators and aggregators across the commercial ecosystem, and practice the "make sense and translate" both internally and externally to enable the integration and aggregation needed. This is a collaborative role within the business, as the hunter/gatherers of salient data, new insights, early innovations, trust builders, creating emotional loyalty as we go.

Behavioural Science is actually in its infancy, despite a legacy that spans as far back as Adam Smith in the late 1740s. What I have set out is a start, not an end.

So, you may ask yourself, "What does this all mean?"

I have attempted to summarise this in a few bullet points:

- Knowing yourself and the impact you do or don't have on others is a key factor to start with, and an attribute that needs to be part of our conscious mind.
- The people skills relative to Social, Decision and Behavioural Sciences will enable us to understand and make sense of what is happening or needed, but each situation is unique and should be treated as such.
- Correctly framing problems from the outset is critical, either challenging testing or removing assumptions (the ask and clarify test) before we conclude how we have framed the problem.
- People are more consumed with loss than a gain, so it would always be wise to remember this.
- Be careful how you define irrationality, as this varies from person to person!
- Obsess about people and outcomes, not process.
- Relationships are between people; contracts are between companies.
- Be careful about building rational systems and procedures as they are for use by people with varying sets of rationality.
- We can't impose behaviours, but we can create a culture that others can align to.
- According to Gartner research, the skills needed to the capabilities in the talent pool shows a deficit of 30-40%.
- Bias neutral is utopia, deal with it!
- Recognise and avoid socially-constructed traits (labels or stereotypes).
- Concentrate on where an intervention or choice architecture will work.
- Ensure people see change as fair, even if they don't like it or it impacts them.

- Provide new experiences and references to challenge bounded rationality.
- Focus on providing an awareness of behaviours rather than simply saying "don't do that".
- Tackle the "Weinstein effect": recalibrate for everyone what acceptable behaviour looks like.
- Story telling is powerful, don't underestimate its value.
- For large and complex issues, consider deploying a decision support system.

One of the issues I have not researched or commented upon is an aspect that was cited by nearly half the of the people I interviewed – the question of behaviour in the C-suite: "I am therefore, I can", as I refer to it. There is a link between what has been described by others as the more extreme and counter-culture behaviours from the top and a reason why some left the organisation. This is a subject for further consideration, I am sure.

In writing this book, I realise I have only made a first foray into the complex and diverse subject of Behavioural Science. I have, through this process, accumulated a vast list of topics to research and write about in the future, such is its breadth and depth.

My final thoughts: we know business is hard, and requires some hard skills and attributes. But to counterbalance these to achieve maximum efficacy in leadership, process and people management we need soft (people) skills. The aim should be to become a Value Architect – I look forward to seeing the next generation of these people soon!

GLOSSARY and DEFINITIONS

Analytical Hierarchy Processing (AHP): a structured technique for organising and analysing complex decisions, based on mathematics and psychology.

Anchoring and adjustment (or focalism): is a cognitive bias that describes the common human tendency to rely too heavily on the first piece of information offered (the "anchor") when making decisions.

Antecedents: means 'to go before' in Latin. It gets its name from the idea that a pronoun refers to something previously mentioned in the sentence. Look at this example: When you see the professor, please tell him I'll be 10 minutes late this evening (in this example, the antecedent is professor. It is the word that the pronoun 'him' refers to).

Apophenia: is the tendency to attribute meaning to perceived connections or patterns between seemingly unrelated things. The phrase was coined by psychiatrist Klaus Conrad in his 1958 publication on the beginning stages of schizophrenia. He defined it as "unmotivated seeing of connections [accompanied by] a specific feeling of abnormal meaningfulness". He described the early stages of delusional thought as self-referential, over-interpretations of actual sensory perceptions, as opposed to hallucinations. More recently it has come to imply a universal human tendency to seek patterns in random information, such as gambling.

Attribution theory: is concerned with how and why ordinary people explain events as they do. Heider (1958) believed that people are naive psychologists trying to make sense of the social world. People tend to see cause and effect relationships, even where there are none! Heider didn't so much develop a theory himself as emphasize certain themes that others took up. There were two main ideas that he put forward that became influential.

1. Internal Attribution: The process of assigning the cause of behaviour to some internal characteristic, rather than to outside forces. When we explain the behaviour of others we look for enduring internal attributions, such as personality traits. For example, we attribute the behaviour of a person to their personality, motives or beliefs.

2. External Attribution: The process of assigning the cause of behaviour to some situation or event outside a person's control, rather than to some internal characteristic. When we try to explain our own behaviour, we tend to make external attributions, such as situational or environment features.

269

Availability heuristic: A mental shortcut that occurs when people make judgments about the probability of events by the ease with which examples come to mind.

Bandwagon effect: This reflects what researchers have long identified as the impact of social conformity in shaping how people think and act.

Behavioural Assessments: The process is designed to be part of and not a substitute for the evaluation and award criteria for a project bid. This can range in the overall criteria of award (out of 100%) of between 15 and 40% of the total. Behavioural assessments typically use the following approaches as part of the process:

- Behavioural profiles using psychometric tools to understand the motivation and preferred style of the bidding team.
- Behavioural CVs focused on specific values or questions that draw out real examples of behaviour.
- Behavioural interviews of all the key players to test leadership, management, communication and collaborative working.
- A behavioural assessment centre to reveal how your operational team will act under pressure.

Behavioural Insights Team (BIT): introduced by the UK Government and sometimes referred to as the "Nudge Unit", because of what they do in nudging we, the UK public, into better decisions

Behavioural Procurement: (definition) and the related field of Behavioural Economics study the effects of psychological, social, cognitive, and emotional factors on the commercial decisions of individuals and institutions and the consequences for competitive advantage, innovation and resource allocation. BP is primarily concerned with bounds of rationality of commercial agents and factors. BP models typically integrate insights from BE, psychology, Decision Sciences, Social Sciences, market theory, as well as implicitly nudging; in so doing these behavioural models cover a range of concepts methods and fields.

Behavioural psychology: (also known as behaviourism) is primarily concerned with the theory of learning based upon the idea that all behaviours are acquired through conditioning. Conditioning occurs through interaction with the environment. Behaviourists believe that our responses to environmental stimuli shape our actions. According to this school of thought, behaviour can be studied in a systematic and observable manner regardless of internal mental states.

Biases: These can be said to be the influencing factors or prejudices based on known limits of knowledge, experience, etc. Sometimes people often see this as a way of changing what some may see as a more logical, rational or expected outcome. Often the changes we experience in ourselves and that of others can be explained by such biases.

A Black Swan Event: must have extreme impact, and retrospective predictability and the following three attributes: 1. It is an outlier, beyond the realm of regular expectations, because experience can't point to its possibility. 2. It carries an extreme impact. 3. After the fact we produce explanations for its occurrence, making it explainable and predictable.

Bounded rationality: relates to the concept that when individuals make decisions, their rationality is limited by the tractability of the decision problem, the cognitive limitations of their minds, and the time available to make the decision. Decision-makers in this view act as satisficers, seeking a satisfactory solution rather than an optimal one. Herbert A. Simon proposed bounded rationality as an alternative basis for the mathematical modelling of decision-making, as used in economics, political science and related disciplines.

Charrette Procedure: is an intense period of design or planning activity. The word charrette is French for "cart" or "chariot." Its use in the sense of design and planning arose in the 19th century at the École des Beaux-Arts in Paris, where it was not unusual at the end of a term for teams of student architects to work right up until a deadline, when a charrette would be wheeled among them to collect up their scale models and other work for review.

Choice architecture: is the design of different ways in which choices can be presented to consumers, and the impact of that presentation on consumer decision-making. For example, the number of choices presented, the manner in which attributes are described, and the presence of a "default" can all influence consumer choice. As a result, advocates of Libertarian Paternalism and asymmetric paternalism have endorsed the deliberate design of choice architecture to nudge consumers toward personally and socially desirable behaviours like saving for retirement, choosing healthier foods, or registering as an organ donor.

Clustering illusion: This is a cognitive bias, which occurs as a consequence of seeing a pattern where none actually exists.

Cognitive-Experiential Self-Theory (CEST): an adaptive view of heuristic processing.

Cognitive psychology is primarily concerned with the science of how people think, learn, and remember.

Collaboration: Collaboration is where two or more people or organisations work together to realise or achieve something successfully, such as a new or innovative product or service. Collaboration is very similar to, but more closely aligned than, cooperation. Most collaboration requires leadership. Teams that work collaboratively can obtain greater resources, recognition and reward when facing competition in all manner of respects. Structured methods of collaboration encourage introspection of behaviour and communication. These methods specifically aim to increase the success of teams as they engage in collaborative problem-solving.

Collaboration platforms: At a very high level this is a platform, in the form of business software, that adds broad social networking capabilities to work processes. The goal is to foster innovation and effective working practices and approaches by incorporating knowledge management into business processes so employees can share information and solve business problems more efficiently. In short, they:

- Aid communication in all its forms.
- File sharing and development of content, etc.
- Reduce Task and Project difficulty in order to give space in functional workflows.
- Avoid abortive processes or quickly re-focus efforts back to the agreed outcomes.
- Remove bias.
- Remove scope creep.
- Consistency and alignment in relative or actual real time.

Corporate Social Responsibility (CSR): is a form of corporate self-regulation integrated into a business model. CSR policy functions as a self-regulatory mechanism whereby a business monitors and ensures its active compliance with the spirit of the law, ethical standards and national or international norms. With some models, an organisations implementation of CSR goes beyond compliance and statutory requirements, engaging in "actions that appear to further some social good, beyond the interests of that organisation and that which is required by law".

Critical thinking: is the purposeful and reflective judgement about what to believe or what to do in response to observations, experience, verbal or written expressions or arguments. Critical thinking involves determining the meaning and significance of what is observed or expressed or concerning a given inference or argument, determining whether there is adequate justification to accept the conclusion as true.

Cultural Dimensions Theory: a framework for cross-cultural communication, developed by Geert Hofstede. It describes the effects of a society's culture on the values of its members, and how these values relate to behaviour, using a structure derived from factor analysis. Hofstede developed his original model as a result of using factor analysis to examine the results of a worldwide survey of employee values by IBM between 1967 and 1973. It has been refined since. The original theory proposed four dimensions along which cultural values could be analysed: individualism-collectivism; uncertainty avoidance; power distance (strength of social hierarchy) and masculinity-femininity (task orientation versus person-orientation). Independent research in Hong Kong led Hofstede to add a fifth dimension, long-term orientation, to cover aspects of values not discussed in the original paradigm. In 2010, Hofstede added a sixth dimension, indulgence versus self-restraint.

The Cynefin Framework (pronounced: KUN-iv-in): This is a conceptual framework used to help managers, policy-makers and others reach decisions. Developed in the early 2000s within IBM, it has been described as a "sense-making device".

Decision trees: A decision tree is a flowchart-like structure in which each internal node represents a "test" on an attribute (e.g. whether a coin flip comes up heads or tails), each branch represents the outcome of the test, and each leaf node represents a class label (decision taken after computing all attributes). The paths from root to leaf represent classification rules. In decision analysis, a decision tree and the closely related influence diagram are used as a visual and analytical decision support tool, where the expected values (or expected utility) of competing alternatives are calculated.

A decision tree consists of three types of nodes:

- Decision nodes – typically represented by squares
- Chance nodes – typically represented by circles
- End nodes – typically represented by triangles

Decision trees are commonly used in operations research and operations management. If, in practice, decisions have to be taken online with no recall under incomplete knowledge, a decision tree should be paralleled by a probability model as a best choice model or online selection model algorithm. Another use of decision trees is as a descriptive means for calculating conditional probabilities.

Economic incentives: something, often money or a prize, offered to make someone behave in a particular way: e.g. the state has an economic incentive program that provides an additional incentive to companies that already are located and employ workers here and are considering expansion.

The Edelman Trust Barometer: is Edelman's annual trust and credibility survey, currently in its 17th year (2017). A global measurement of trust across the world, the Trust Barometer is produced by integrated research, analytics and measurement proprietary to Edelman.

Enneagram types: the nine types of Enneagram are: 1 THE REFORMER: The Rational, Idealistic Type: Principled, Purposeful, Self-Controlled, and Perfectionistic, 2 THE HELPER: The Caring, Interpersonal Type: Demonstrative, Generous, People-Pleasing, and Possessive, 3 THE ACHIEVER: The Success-Oriented, Pragmatic Type: Adaptive, Excelling, Driven, and Image-Conscious, 4 THE INDIVIDUALIST: The Sensitive, Withdrawn Type: Expressive, Dramatic, Self-Absorbed, and Temperamental, 5 THE INVESTIGATOR: The Intense, Cerebral Type: Perceptive, Innovative, Secretive, and Isolated, 6 THE LOYALIST: The Committed, Security-Oriented Type: Engaging, Responsible, Anxious, and Suspicious, 7 THE ENTHUSIAST: The Busy, Fun-Loving Type: Spontaneous, Versatile, Distractible, and Scattered, 8 THE CHALLENGER: The Powerful, Dominating Type: Self-Confident, Decisive, Wilful, and Confrontational, 9 THE PEACEMAKER: The Easy going, Self-Effacing Type: Receptive, Reassuring, Agreeable, and Complacent

Emotional Intelligence (EI or EQ): the capability of individuals to recognise their own and other people's emotions, discern between different feelings and label them appropriately, use emotional information to guide thinking and behaviour, and manage and/or adjust emotions to adapt to environments or achieve one's goal(s).

Framing effect: this is essentially the way in which an argument and/or proposal has been drafted to present choices to a recipient. Further, whether it has been couched as potential loss or as a potential gain.

Frictionless: the aim of frictionless is to make solutions in business, technology, enterprise wide activity, design, transactions, decision-making, governance and compliance as intuitive and easy as possible. This extends to removing barriers, simplifying choices, reducing the number of steps/stages to a decision, use of clearer/simpler language or any action that enables and simplifies anything pre-existing. Also, the ten commandments of frictionless (David L Loseby – April 2017)

Game Theory: is "the study of mathematical models of conflict and cooperation between intelligent rational decision-makers". Game Theory is mainly used in economics, political science, and psychology, as well as logic, computer science and biology. Originally, it addressed zero-sum games, in which one person's gains result in losses for the other participants. Today, Game Theory applies to a wide range of behavioural relations, and is now an umbrella term for the science of logical decision-making in humans, animals, and computers.

The Gestalt Theories or Principles: The school of Gestalt practiced a series of theoretical and methodological principles that attempted to redefine the approach to psychological research. This is in contrast to investigations developed at the beginning of the 20th century, based on traditional scientific methodology, which divided the object of study into a set of elements that could be analysed separately with the objective of reducing the complexity of this object.

The **GLOBE**: Global Leadership and Organisational Behaviour Effectiveness Research

Group Serving bias: the tendency to credit the group for its successes but to blame external factors for its failures.

Heuristic: Generally taken as being the "rule of thumb" or the procedure that helps find an adequate, though often imperfect, answer to difficult questions. A form of shortcut in some cases to help us quickly make judgements or decisions. This is often comprised of all the many "layers" of experience(s) we have had in our lives, even from childhood.

Human decision-making and Status quo bias: *Reversal tests* When a proposal to change a certain parameter is thought to have bad overall consequences, consider a change to the same parameter in the opposite direction. If this is also thought to have bad overall consequences, then the onus is on those who reach these conclusions to explain why our position cannot be improved through changes to this parameter. If they are unable to do so, then we have reason to suspect that they suffer from status quo bias. The rationale of the Reversal Test is if a continuous parameter admits a wide range of possible values, only a tiny subset of which can be local optima, then it is *prima facie* implausible that the actual value of that parameter should just happen to be at one of these rare local optima.

ISO 44001: published 1 March 2017 by the International Organisation for Standardisation. It is based on British Standards BS 11000, initially developed from 2006 as PAS 11000 (2006). ISO 44001 is now aligned to the high-level structure that covers all ISO management standards, and incorporates the eight stage life cycle model that was the basis for BS 11000 to help business partners maximise the value of collaborative working: Operational awareness, Knowledge, Internal assessment, Partner selection, Working together, Value creation, Staying together, Exit strategy implementation.

Intertemporal choice: the study of how people make choices about what and how much to do at various points in time, when choices at one time influence the possibilities available at other points in time. These choices are influenced by the relative value people assign to two or more payoffs at different points in time. Most choices require decision-makers to trade off costs and benefits at different points in time. These decisions may be about savings, work effort, education, etc.

Judgements: based on 2 systems: intuitive and simple decisions (System 1) and/ or more complex decisions considerations that require research or greater effort (System 2).

Keynesian Theory: The General Theory of Employment, Interest and Money was written by the English economist John Maynard Keynes. The book, generally considered to be his magnum opus, is largely credited with creating the terminology and shape of modern macroeconomics. Published in February 1936, it sought to bring about a revolution, commonly referred to as the "Keynesian Revolution", in the way some economists believe. Especially in relation to the proposition that a market economy tends naturally to restore itself to full employment after temporary shocks. Regarded widely as the cornerstone of Keynesian thought, the book challenged the established classical economics and introduced important concepts such as the consumption function, the multiplier, the marginal efficiency of capital, the principle of effective demand and liquidity preference.

Loss aversion (see also Endowment Effect in self-biases): This particular phenomenon might be translated into common parlance as: "You don't know what you've got until it's gone". In economics and decision theory, loss aversion refers to people's tendency to prefer avoiding losses to acquiring equivalent gains.

MINDSPACE: a simple mnemonic introduced by BIT, which can be used as a quick checklist when making policy:

1. Messenger: we are heavily influenced by who communicates information
2. Incentives: our responses to incentives are shaped by predictable mental shortcuts such as strongly avoiding losses
3. Norms: we are strongly influenced by what others do
4. Defaults: we "go with the flow of pre-set options,
5. Salience: our attention is drawn to what is novel and seems relevant to us
6. Priming: our acts are often influenced by sub-conscious cues
7. Affect: our emotional associations can powerfully shape our actions
8. Commitments: we seek to be consistent with our public promises, and reciprocate acts
9.Ego: we act in ways that make us feel better about ourselves.

Modern Day Slavery Act (MDSA): is an Act of the Parliament of the United Kingdom. It is designed to tackle slavery in the UK and consolidates previous offences relating to trafficking and slavery.

Molotov Cocktail: The name "Molotov cocktail" was coined by the Finns during the Winter War. The name was an insulting reference to Soviet foreign minister Vyacheslav Molotov, who was one of the architects of the Molotov–Ribbentrop Pact signed in late August 1939. It is a generic name used for a variety of bottle-based, improvised incendiary weapons. Due to the relative ease of production, Molotov cocktails have been used by street criminals, protesters, rioters, gangsters, urban guerrillas, terrorists, irregular soldiers, or even regular soldiers short on equivalent military-issue weapons. They are primarily intended to set targets ablaze rather than obliterate them.

Negativity bias: also known as also known as the negativity effect and refers to the concept that, even when of equal intensity, things of a more negative nature (e.g. unpleasant thoughts, emotions, conversations, acts, etc.); they will have a greater effect on a person's psychological state and processes than do neutral or positive things.

Negativity effect: the more negative/offensive the comment/remark the bigger the impact it has in our minds and our concept of 'self'. Hence the saying, "Bad news sells better than good news every time".

Nemawashi: The Japanese business practice of speaking to every stakeholder prior to the meeting.

Neuroscience: is the scientific study of the nervous system. It is a multidisciplinary branch of biology, that deals with the anatomy, biochemistry, molecular biology, and physiology of neurons and neural circuits. It also draws upon other fields, with the most obvious being pharmacology, psychology, and medicine.

OECD: The mission of the Organisation for Economic Co-operation and Development (OECD) is to promote policies that will improve the economic and social well-being of people around the world.

The OECD provides a forum in which governments can work together to share experiences and seek solutions to common problems. We work with governments to understand what drives economic, social and environmental change. We measure productivity and global flows of trade and investment. We analyse and compare data to predict future trends. We set international standards on a wide range of things, from agriculture and tax to the safety of chemicals.

OECD also looks at issues that directly affect everyone's daily life, like how much people pay in taxes and social security, and how much leisure time they can take. We compare how different countries' school systems are readying their young people for modern life, and how different countries' pension systems will look after their citizens in old age.

Drawing on facts and real-life experience, we recommend policies designed to improve the quality of people's lives. We work with business, through the Business and Industry Advisory Committee to the OECD (BIAC), and with labour, through the Trade Union Advisory Committee (TUAC). The common thread of our work is a shared commitment to market economies backed by democratic institutions and focused on the wellbeing of all citizens. Along the way, we also set out to make life harder for the terrorists, tax dodgers, crooked businessmen and others whose actions undermine a fair and open society.

Parkinson's Law (of trinity): is the adage that "work expands so as to fill the time available for its completion". It is also sometimes applied to the growth of the bureaucratic apparatus in an organisation.

Partisan nudge bias: Presenting participants of varying political persuasions with short descriptions of various behavioural policy nudges (e.g. designating enrolment in a programme as a default). To explain how such policy tools could be applied, we illustrated them using either an example of a liberal policy priority (e.g. encouraging low-income individuals to enrol in food stamps programmes for which they were legally eligible) or a conservative policy priority (e.g. encouraging the wealthy to take advantage of capital gains tax breaks they were legally eligible for). The participants were then asked to rate how ethical, manipulative and coercive they found the nudge to be, as a general policy approach. In almost every case, respondents on the left of the political spectrum supported nudges when they were illustrated with a liberal agenda but opposed them when they were illustrated with a conservative one; meanwhile, respondents on the political right exhibited the opposite pattern.

Personality psychology is primarily concerned with the branch of psychology that focuses on the study of the thought patterns, feelings, and behaviours that make each individual unique. Classic theories of personality include Freud's psychoanalytic theory of personality and Erikson's theory of psychosocial development.

Power Distance Index (PDI): is defined as "the extent to which the less powerful members of organisations and institutions (like the family) accept and expect that power is distributed unequally." In this dimension, inequality and power is perceived from the followers, or the lower level.

Pre-mortems: is a managerial strategy in which a project team imagines that a project or organization has failed, and then works backward to determine what potentially could lead to the failure of the project or organisation. The technique breaks possible group think too, by facilitating a positive discussion on threats, increasing the likelihood the main threats are identified. Management can then analyse the magnitude and likelihood of each threat, and take preventative actions to protect the project or organization from suffering an untimely "death". According to a Harvard Business Review article from 2007, "unlike a typical critiquing session, in which project team members are asked what might go wrong, the premortem operates on the assumption that the 'patient' has died, and so asks what did go wrong."

Present bias: refers to the tendency of people to give stronger weight to payoffs that are closer to the present time when considering trade-offs between two future moments (O'Donoghue, and, Rabin, 1999).

Pro-innovation bias: this is the belief that an innovation should be adopted by the whole of society without the need for any alteration.

Prospect Theory: The whole concept of Prospect Theory (*Prospect Theory: An analysis of decision under risk*) came from a paper written by Daniel Kahneman and Amos Tversky in 1979, which was further revised in 1992. The principal concept was to describe the way people choose between probabilistic alternatives that involve risk, where the probabilities of outcomes are known. Further Prospect Theory terms are embodied in Chapter 11.

Randomised Controlled Trial (RCT): is a form of scientific experiment which aims to reduce bias when testing a new approach. The people participating in the trial are randomly allocated to either the group following the new customised way of working or system under investigation or to a group receiving standard way of working (or placebo) as the control, or a previously tested approach or benchmark (a positive-control study). Randomisation minimises selection bias and the different comparison groups allow the researchers to determine any effects of the approach when compared with the standard approach (control) group, while other variables are kept constant.

Regressive bias: The regression (or regressive) fallacy is an informal fallacy. It assumes that something has returned to normal because of corrective actions taken while it was abnormal. This fails to account for natural fluctuations.

Regret Avoidance: is a situation where an investor would not accept the bad investment decision made to avoid the unpleasant feelings. In general emotions have a negative effect on investment decisions. There may be times when the markets are at the peak and an investor might invest money without any rationale just by sentimental value, if the market goes down from there then the investor would have made a bad decision riding on emotions. People usually throw good money after bad in these situations.

Representativeness heuristic: A mental shortcut used when making judgments about the probability of an event under uncertainty. Or judging a situation based on how similar the prospects are to the prototypes the person holds in his or her mind.

Social psychology: is primarily concerned with the study of topics such as group behaviour, social perception, nonverbal behaviour, conformity, aggression, and prejudice.

Stakeholder Management: A structured approach which leads to the identification, analysis, planning and implementation of actions designed to engage with individuals (stakeholders) at all levels who have an interest in a project or activity.

Sub-addivity effect: is the tendency to judge probability of the whole to be less than the probabilities of the parts. A form of underplaying or watering down of what is factually correct.

Sunk Cost Fallacy: This relates to the principle that the prospect of losses has become a more powerful motivator on your behaviour than the promise of gains. Whenever possible, you try to avoid losses of any kind, and when comparing losses to gains you don't treat them equally.

Superfund sites: These are polluted locations requiring a long-term response to clean up hazardous material contaminations. CERCLA authorised the United States Environmental Protection Agency (EPA) to create a list of such locations, which are placed on the National Priorities List (NPL).

Supplier Relationship Management (SRM): is the systematic, enterprise-wide assessment of suppliers' assets and capabilities with respect to overall business strategy, determination of what activities to engage in with different suppliers, and planning and execution of all interactions with suppliers, in a coordinated fashion across the relationship life cycle, to maximise the value realised through those interactions. The focus of Supplier Relationship Management is to develop two-way, mutually beneficial relationships with strategic supply partners to deliver greater levels of innovation and competitive advantage than could be achieved by operating independently or through a traditional, transactional purchasing arrangements.

Supply Chain Management (SCM): Is concerned with the management of the flow of goods and services, of an enterprise. This involves the movement and storage of raw materials, of work-in-process inventory, and of finished goods from point of origin to point of consumption. Interconnected or interlinked networks, channels and node businesses combine in the provision of products and services required by end customers in a supply chain. Supply Chain Management has been defined as the "design, planning, execution, control, and monitoring of supply chain activities with the objective of creating net value, building a competitive infrastructure, leveraging worldwide logistics, synchronising supply with demand and measuring performance globally."

Trust, Ability, Integrity and Benevolence: Ability refers to an assessment of the other's knowledge, skill, or competency. This dimension recognizes that trust requires some sense that the other is able to perform in a manner that meets our expectations. Integrity is the degree to which the trustee adheres to principles that are acceptable to the trustor. This dimension leads to trust based on consistency of past actions, credibility of communication, commitment to standards of fairness, and the congruence of the other's word and deed. Benevolence is our assessment that the trusted individual is concerned enough about our welfare to either advance our interests, or at least not impede them. The other's perceived intentions or motives of the trustee are most central. Honest and open communication, delegating decisions, and sharing control indicate evidence of one's benevolence.

Zero-risk bias: a tendency to prefer the complete elimination of a risk, even when alternative options produce a greater reduction in risk (overall).

RECOMMENDED READING LIST

Agnoli, F. (1991). Development of judgmental heuristics and logical reasoning: Training counteracts the representativeness heuristic. *Cognitive Development*, 6, 195–217.

Anderson, N. H. (1996). *A functional theory of cognition*. Hillsdale, NJ: Erlbaum.

Ariely, D., and Loewenstein, G. (2000). When does duration matter in judgment and decision-making? *Journal of Experimental Psychology: General*, 129, 524–529.

Bernoulli, D. (1954). Exposition of a new theory on the measurement of risk. *Econometrica*, 22, 23–36. (Original work published 1738)

Buehler, R. (2007). The Planning Fallacy. In R. Baumeister and K. Vohs (Eds.), *Encyclopedia of Social Psychology*. Sage.

Buehler, R., Griffin, D., and MacDonald, H. (1997). The role of motivated reasoning in optimistic time predictions. *Personality and Social Psychology Bulletin*, 23, 238-247.

Buehler, R., Griffin, D., and Ross, M. (1994). Exploring the "Planning Fallacy": Why people underestimate their task completion times. *Journal of Personality and Social Psychology*, 67, 366-381.

Buehler, R., Griffin, D., and Ross, M. (2002). Inside the Planning Fallacy: The causes and consequences of optimistic time predictions. In T. D. Gilovich, D. W. Griffin, and D. Kahneman (Eds.), *Heuristics and biases: The psychology of intuitive judgment* (pp. 250-270). New York: Cambridge University Press.

D. Griffin, and D. Kahneman (Eds.). *Heuristics and biases* (pp. 489–509). New York: Cambridge University Press.

Chapman, G. B., and Johnson, E. J. (2002). Incorporating the irrelevant: Anchors in judgments of belief and value. In T. Gilovich, D. Griffin, and D. Kahneman (Eds.), *Heuristics and biases* (pp. 120–138). New York: Cambridge University Press.

Epley, N., and Gilovich, T. (2002). Putting adjustment back in the anchoring and adjustment heuristic. In T. Gilovich, D. Griffin, and D. Kahneman (Eds.), *Heuristics and biases* (pp. 139–149). New York: Cambridge University Press.

Finucane, M. L., Alhakami, A., Slovic, P., and Johnson, S. M. (2000). The affect heuristic in judgments of risks and benefits. *Journal of Behavioural Decision-making*, 13, 1–17.

Gilbert, D. T. (1991). How mental systems believe. *American Psychologist*, 46, 107–119.

D. Kahneman (Eds.). (2002). *Heuristics and biases* (pp. 167–184). New York: Cambridge University Press.

Gilovich, T., Griffin, D., and Kahneman, D. (Eds.). (2002). *Heuristics and biases.* New York: Cambridge University Press.

Hammond, K. R. (2000). *Judgment under stress.* New York: Oxford University Press.

Hsee, C. K. (1998). Less is better: When low-value options are valued more highly than high-value options. *Journal of Behavioural Decision-making*, 11, 107–121.

Isen, A. M., Nygren, T. E., and Ashby, F. G. (1988). Influence of positive affect on the subjective utility of gains and losses: It is just not worth the risk. *Journal of Personality and Social Psychology*, 55, 710–717.

Kahneman, D. (1994). New challenges to the rationality assumption. *Journal of Institutional and Theoretical Economics*, 150, 18–36.

Kahneman and A. Tversky (Eds.), *Choices, values, and frames* (pp. 693–708). New York: Cambridge University Press.

Kahneman, D., Knetsch, J. L., and Thaler, R. H. (1986). Fairness as a constraint on profit seeking: Entitlements in the market. *American Economic Review*, 76, 728–741.

Kahneman, D., Knetsch, J. L., and Thaler, R. H. (1991). The endowment effect, loss aversion, and status quo bias. *Journal of Economic Perspectives*, 718 September 2003.

Kahneman, D., and Lovallo, D. (1993). Timid choices and bold forecasts: A cognitive perspective on risk taking. *Management Science*, 39, 17–31.

Kahneman, D., and Miller, D. T. (1986). Norm theory: Comparing reality to its alternatives. *Psychological Review*, 93, 136–153.

Kahneman, D., Slovic, P., and Tversky, A. (Eds.). (1982). *Judgment under uncertainty: Heuristics and biases.* New York: Cambridge University Press.

Kahneman, D., and Tversky, A. (1979). Prospect Theory: An analysis of decisions under risk. *Econometrica*, 47, 263–291.

Kahneman, D., and Tversky, A. (Eds.). (2000). *Choices, values, and frames.* New York: Cambridge University Press.

Kahneman, D., and Lovallo, D. (1993). Timid choices and bold forecasts: A cognitive perspective on risk taking. *Management Science*, 39, 17-31.

Kahneman, D., and Tversky, A. (1979). Intuitive predictions: Biases and corrective procedures. *TIMS Studies in Management Sciences*, 12, 313-327.

Klein, G. (2003). *Intuition at work: Why developing your gut instincts will make you better at what you do.* New York: Doubleday.

Kopp, R. (1992). Why existence value should be used in cost-benefit analysis. *Journal of Policy Analysis and Management*, 11, 123–130.

Lovallo, D., and Kahneman, D. (July 2003). Delusions of success: How optimism undermines executives' decisions. *Harvard Business Review*, 56-63.

Mellers, B., Hertwig, R., and Kahneman, D. (2001). Do frequency representations eliminate conjunction effects? An exercise in adversarial collaboration. *Psychological Science*, 12, 269–275.

Samuelson, W., and Zeckhauser, R. (1988). Status quo bias in decision-making. *Journal of Risk and Uncertainty*, 1, 7–59.

Shafir, E. (1993). Choosing versus rejecting: Why some options are both better and worse than others. *Memory and Cognition,* 21, 546–556.

Simon, H. A. (1955). A behavioural model of rational choice. *Quarterly Journal of Economics*, 69, 99–118.

Simon, H. A. (1979). Rational decision-making in business organizations. American Economic Review, 69, 493–513.

Sloman, S. A. (1996). The empirical case for two systems of reasoning. *Psychological Bulletin*, 119, 3–22.

Slovic, P., Finucane, M., Peters, E., and MacGregor, D. G. (2002). The affect heuristic. In T. Gilovich, D. Griffin, and D. Kahneman (Eds.), *Heuristics and biases* (pp. 397–420). New York: Cambridge University Press.

Stanovich, K. E., and West, R. F. (1999). Discrepancies between normative and descriptive models of decision-making and the understanding/acceptance principle. *Cognitive Psychology*, 38, 349–385.

Stanovich, K. E., and West, R. F. (2000). Individual differences in reasoning: Implications for the rationality debate. *Behavioural and Brain Sciences*, 23, 645–665.

Staats, B. R., Milkman, K. L., and Fox, C. R. (2012). The team scaling fallacy: Underestimating the declining efficiency of larger teams. *Organizational Behaviour and Human Decision Processes*, 118, 132-142. doi: 10.1016/j.obhdp.2012.03.002

Thaler, R. H. (1999). Mental accounting matters. *Journal of Behavioural Decision-making*, 12, 241–268.

Tversky, A., and Kahneman, D. (1971). Belief in the law of small numbers. *Psychological Bulletin*, 76, 105–110.

Tversky, A., and Kahneman, D. (1973). Availability: A heuristic for judging frequency and probability. *Cognitive Psychology*, 5, 207–232.

Tversky, A., and Kahneman, D. (1974, September 27). Judgment under uncertainty: Heuristics and biases. *Science*, 185, 1124–1131.

Tversky, A., and Kahneman, D. (1981, January 30). The framing of decisions and the psychology of choice. *Science*, 211, 453–458.

Tversky, A., and Kahneman, D. (1986). Rational choice and the framing of decisions. *Journal of Business,* 59, S251–S278.

Tversky, A., and Kahneman, D. (1992). Advances in Prospect Theory: Cumulative representation of uncertainty, *Journal of Risk and Uncertainty*, 5, 297–323.

Tversky, A., and Redelmeier, D. A. (1992). On the framing of multiple prospects. *Psychological Science*, 3, 191–193.

Wilson, T. D. (2000). *Strangers to ourselves: Discovering the adaptive unconscious.* Cambridge, MA: Harvard University Press.

Wilson, T. D., Centerbar, D. B., and Brekke, N. (2002). Mental contamination and the debiasing problem. In T. Gilovich, D. Griffin, and D. Kahneman (Eds.), *Heuristics and biases* (pp. 185–200). New York: Cambridge University Press.

Zajonc, R. B. (1980). Feeling and thinking: Preferences need no inferences. *American Psychologist*, 35, 151–175.

Zajonc, R. B. (1998). Emotions. In D.T. Gilbert, S.T. Fiske, and G. Lindzey (Eds.), *Handbook of Social Psychology* (4th ed., Vol. 1, pp. 591–632). New York: Oxford University Press.

CASE STUDY 1 | BEHAVIOURAL ASSESSMENTS

This case study has been written with the cooperation and collaboration with the A14 Integrated Delivery Team Supply Chain Team (Andrew Spencer - Procurement and Supply Chain Director; Ben Cross – Supply Chain Collaboration Lead; Cameron Bell – Assistant Supply Chain Manager).

The use of behavioural assessments is largely intended for use within the construction, infrastructure and outsourced contracting domains, due to its intended use for long-term, complex and high-value projects. This is largely to do with the upfront investment in costs and resources to deliver such a relational contract in the first instance. The approach considers, therefore, technical, financial and people factors, not just simply the cost, quality, service triangle that has not always ensured the best outcomes.

I will begin by setting out a brief, intended application description and overview of the approach. The process is designed to be part of and not a substitute for the evaluation and award criteria for a project bid. This can range in the overall criteria of award (out of 100%) of between 15% and 40% of the total. Behavioural assessments typically use the following key steps as part of the process:

- Evaluating behavioural profiles, by trained professionals, using psychometric tools to understand the motivation and preferred style of the bidding team.
- Review of behavioural CVs (in a standardised format for consistency of measurement) focused on specific values or questions that draw out real examples of behaviour.
- Structured behavioural interviews, by trained professionals, of all the key players to test leadership, management, communication and collaborative working.
- Finally, a behavioural assessment centre to reveal how the operational team(s) will act under pressure.

Looking at each component in turn:

- Behavioural profiles for each senior and key member of the team complete an online questionnaire to create their individual profile. The profiles provide the insight and information that will be needed by the selected evaluation team throughout the entirety of the process and all its stages.
- The key players (primary teams) from each party to the project are subject to

287

a behavioural review. An analysis of the people in the teams, which identifies and defines the culture and behaviour of them as a collective and then recommends how the team profile can be improved.

- Behavioural training and coaching of the proposed delivery team is an essential part of bringing newly-formed teams together as a more cohesive and collaborate unit. Defining team dynamics, collaborative strengths and weaknesses will be drawn out as part of the awareness and understanding of the teams' effectiveness and overall cohesion as a collective. This includes skill levels, maturity, experience, cognitive diversity and general background. This is particularly key as the team may be in a consortium and therefore drawn from different companies, as was the case on the A14 Cambridge to Huntingdon improvement project. The individuals forming the new team may even benefit from some pre-assessment coaching too, as part of the process. However, this can be agreed on a case-by-case basis.
- Behavioural CVs and interviews usually take the form of a predefined CV template format for each person. This is complemented by one-to-one interviews, by trained professionals, to identify and define behaviours stated and those displayed.
- Assessment centres are used to expose the proposed team to a pressurised and challenging experience. This is intended to test levels of restraint, composure, comportment, active listening, communication and responding skills. This will also try to expose any default to type behaviours that manifest themselves under pressure that may be detrimental to the new team dynamic.

The aspects of active listening, communication, collaboration and trust enabling attributes have been covered earlier in the book.

Introduction to the Case Study (content provided by A14 IDT Supply Chain Team):

United Kingdom: Highways project

The A14 Integrated Delivery Team (A14 IDT) is an organisation currently working on behalf of Highways England, delivering a £1.5-billion major highways infrastructure project on the A14 between Cambridge and Huntingdon.

TheA14 IDT comprises the project client Highways England, several delivery partners including main contractors Costain, Skanska, Balfour Beatty, with designers CH2M and Atkins. At the heart of the A14 IDT organisation is an innovative and pioneering integrated delivery model. This was designed with Highways England through the realisation of the overwhelming potential for synergy, quality and timeline benefits. The integrated delivery model involves representatives from the key partners working together as one team to achieve common project goals. This has fostered a highly collaborative organisational culture which has been driven through behaviours, cross-functional interaction and shared core values. An essential component is this integrated way of working was extended to our supply chain partners. It is imperative for the success of the project that the supply chain partners selected share the same philosophy and align with the desired culture and values.

Principal aims and objectives of the project were stated as follows:

The successful procurement and Supply Chain Management (SCM) of the pivotal traffic management sub-contractor was highlighted as critical to ensuring a successful delivery of the project. This was reflected by several important factors including the high safety risk of the work activities, the public-facing nature of the package and the inherent reputational risk, the high level of effective collaboration required from the supplier; and the commercial impact as a significant £12.5-million element of spend.

To achieve industry-leading standards and performance outcomes, selecting a supply chain partner who demonstrated alignment to our values and behaviour needs was a crucial success factor. The A14 IDT set about developing a strategy to maximise the cross-functional collaborative working methods within the procurement and subsequent supplier management activities.

The collaborative approach to this concept is demonstrated in the model below, and has completely raised the bar for procurement approaches within the highways industry. The collaborative approach to involvement with various functional stakeholders in a new behavioural approach has created best practice within the highways industry and learning for the wider procurement community.

A set of common aims applied to all teams involved in the behavioural procurement and SCM project driven by the A14 IDT's 'three exemplar pillars' and our client's 'three imperatives' outlined below.

- Health Safety and Wellbeing (H, S and W).
- Economics.
- Stakeholder and Legacy.
- Safety.
- Customer Service.
- Delivering the Road.

The specific aims of the traffic management cross-functional project were to select a supply chain partner, on this occasion for traffic management, which had the following aspects embedded within their organisation:

- Leading behaviours to H, S and W both in working practices and culture.
- Value adding commercial offering to the A14 IDT.
- World class attitude of continuous improvement to create legacy benefits for future projects.
- Collaborative behaviours for true integration with all A14 IDT functional team.
- A clear set of objectives were outlined to allow us to achieve the above aims:
- To develop a world class procurement and supply chain strategy.
- The procurement process included a 15% scored behavioural element.
- Cross-functional involvement in all planning, scoring and delivery of this project.
- Deep dive supplier audit and KPI process to further confirm above embedded project aims.

The assessment centre day consisted of the following tasks for the team to accomplish:

Task 1 - Any Question
Opportunity for team work and collaborative behaviours to shine through in their own teams. Opportunity for active listening, constructive challenging and developing the ideas of others.

Task 2 - Lemons and Oranges
A fantastic game that really tests people's competitive nature, but can they understand the bigger picture and collaborative with the competition so everyone wins?

Task 3 - Pieces
This task will test the patience of the calmest people in the world. This requires a huge amount of encouragement and influencing to ensure a system is in place so all can work together to achieve the shared goal. If not, chaos is on the cards.

Task 4 - Toward power
You need leaders in this task who have a clear strategy that the team have developed together and effective communication to ensure the plan is delivered. Too many leaders and limited team work will soon have disappointment and frustration knocking on the door.

Task 5 - Viking Attack
An absolutely mind-boggling riddle that seems impossible to solve. The individual teams need to grasp the bigger picture quickly to ensure they

don't travel round the houses. There may be others who hold the key to their success. Your ability to motivation of others is really tested to the full in this game.

Task 6 - Collaboration Briefing

A great end to the day, the opportunity to work on all of the collaboration lessons that have been learned throughout the day, and the opportunity is given so the two teams can come together again for one last time to agree a common understanding. Remember it has been a long day and people are tired, so this task can demonstrate some new behaviours.

The A14 team, facilitated through an external resource, executed these stages with the following cross-functional ways of working:

- Collaborative planning session to agree package acquisition strategy.
- Invitation to tender involved all teams to identify and scope the desired behaviours.
- Cross-functional assessor panel in the supplier behavioural assessment.
- Subject matter experts from a cross-section of teams adjudicated all tender returns.
- An extensive supplier audit, with representatives from across the project teams, looked into the supplier's organisation ensuring alignment to our behaviours.
- Use of 360 KPIs as a platform to bring together cross-functional stakeholders.
- A formal behavioural maturity framework (BMF) was used, which included online and a face-to-face workshop bringing together the A14 IDT and the supplier's teams.

Following the above stages and after proving alignment to our behaviours and an offering in line with our specific aims, H.W. Martin were selected as the traffic management supplier for the A14.

Organisational Benefits Achieved

Our world-class approach to procurement and SCM has created extensive value across three key areas for the project.

Health, Safety and Wellbeing (HSW) Benefits

- The initial supplier assessment, which helped form the tender list, included a check of accident frequency rate, pre-qualification and accreditations.

This raised the bar, ensuring the suppliers were leading in health, safety and wellbeing.

- The use of behavioural assessment within the tender allowed the A14 IDT to ensure positive HSW behaviours were evident within the supplier organisation. Due to the significant HSW risk to the project of these activities this approach has been extremely beneficial.
- The behavioural validation audits conducted collaboratively with A14 IDT team have made the H.W. Martin workplace a healthier, happier and safer place to work. Long term this has helped set the A14 IDT standards by the implementation of a corrective action plan and follow-up by the supplier. The behaviours resulting from the audit have clearly improved their HSW management system, workplace safety and safety delivery.

Economic Benefits

- The cross-department approach added significant value by selecting a partner with aligned behaviours which also proved very commercially advantageous. The budget for the package was £12,496,670, and using our collaborative approach resulted in a saving of £622,815.
- The alignment of selecting a supplier based on behaviours results in a much more collaborative partner. This supports commercial management going forward, where both parties work together to resolve any contractual issues.
- The robust approach to SCM through KPIs demonstrates we are 'spending money wisely' by ensuring our partner is performing to our standards. It ensures we embed positive behaviours. Validation supplier auditing has driven opportunities to identify efficiencies which all lead to cost savings for both parties.

Stakeholder and Legacy Benefits

- The use of the scored behavioural assessment highlights the importance of the A14 IDT values and culture, and is not just a commercial submission. Our project really has raised the bar regarding client expectations of suitable supply chain partners.
- Our supplier, H.W. Martin has embraced the Behavioural Maturity Framework (BMF)[1] as well as the Collaborative Performance Framework (CPF)[2], advocated by Highways England. The BMF and CPF has helped improve the wider industry understanding of behaviours which has driven improvements in the desirability and inclusivity of our industry.

---

1. O'Neill, David: Supply Chain Development Director (Highways England): presentation June 2016: http://www.highwaysdelivery.com/programme/david-o-neil-presentation.pdf
2. Atkins et al. (2017). *Highways England Supply Chain Capability Review: Office of Road and Rail*; June 2017, page 23. Accessed at http://orr.gov.uk/__data/assets/pdf_file/0005/25169/atkins-highways-england-supply-chain-capability-review-2017-06-30.pdf

- Our selection of H.W. Martin has seen the creation of 16 trainee jobs, further supporting the A14 IDT's ambition of leaving a legacy for unemployed people.

Further commentary

There are a number of reports and approaches that have begun to take place in this space[3] which is encouraging and have largely been driven by government initiatives, but also private hedge funds looking to produce certainty of outcomes and better performance. Of particular note is the systems approach advocated by the Royal Academy of Engineering and Highways England. The Royal Academy of Engineering report, *Creating systems that work*[4/5], identifies six principles for an integrated system:

1. Debate, define, revise and pursue the purpose.
2. Think holistically.
3. Follow a disciplined procedure.
4. Be creative.
5. Take account of the people.
6. Manage the project and the relationships.

They argue that the key strengths of a systems approach are that it takes a holistic view of the project and identifies the interactions and interdependencies of individual elements of the project. This allows the identification of critical interfaces – whether physical interfaces like regional boundaries in a rail system or supplier interfaces between two ICT systems – and assists in identifying early the ways that they could fail. It is clear that this approach if using behavioural assessments helps in the key areas of:

1. Risk mitigation.
2. Innovation.
3. Long-term sustainability.
4. Ability to manage change more effectively and efficiently for clients.
5. Provide a reflective platform for all parties to self-assess behaviours and understand the impacts of them on the wider team.
6. Self-development.

3. *Highways England: Supply Chain Strategy 2015*. Publications code PR72/15. https://www.gov.uk/government/uploads/system/uploads/attachment_data/file/471743/N150251_Supply_Chain_Strategy_2015_V11.pdf
4. *Creating systems that work: principles of engineering systems for the 21st century*. The Royal Academy of Engineering; June 2007. www.raeng.org.uk/education/vps/pdf/rae_systems_report.pdf
5. *Public projects and procurement in the UK sharing experience and changing practice*. The Royal academy of Engineering; February 2014. https://www.raeng.org.uk/publications/reports/publicprojects-and-procurement-in-the-uk-sharing

This is but to name a few, including the very raw comments of "it was a reality check to us all", and brought out some very nervous and anxious behaviours going into new areas for most of the people on the teams.

Commercially developed platforms to engender and sustain collaboration are an effective way of helping diverse or consortium teams. Furthermore, these platforms can be used to aid cross-geography teams too, externally and internally.

Some of the collaborative approaches set out in the Supply Chain Strategy 2015 by Highways England provides some of the more succinct and visual attributes for those considering this approach.

It specifically references the development of more mature relationships, and creation of value versus the use of penalties, most of which can be recognised in the diagram below:

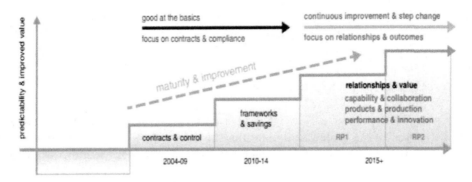

Diagram 1. Maturity and Improvement model: Highways England

According to Highways England the routes to implementation are structured on three dimensions. This can be seen in Diagram 2:

1. Delivering exceptional performance by developing and deploying Value Chain Plans.
2. Building best practice capability by developing leadership, skills and intelligence.
3. Developing relationships that underpin delivering performance and capability.

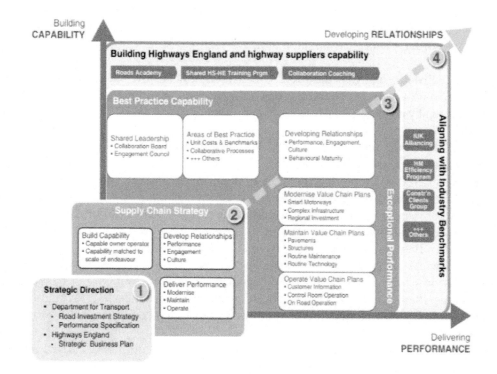

Diagram 2. Highways England 3 dimensions

In public procurement, where most of the work has been done, there are of course legal considerations to be taken into account, and this should be done as part of the upfront planning work prior to market engagement. I have provided a summary here, but of course the final direction on how you decide to proceed for each project should be validated with a legal expert, reflecting on current legislation.

Key principles – The Regulations are intended to provide a "level playing field" where all bidders are given equal treatment. Their guiding principles are transparency, objectivity and consistency. Where evaluation of bids includes an assessment of behaviours and matters of culture and approach – all of which give rise to subjective interpretation – it is particularly important that these are observed and recorded in a consistent way.

Stage 1 Procurement: Selection – An assessment of bidders' capability and resource to perform the contract in question, based on experience, resource and track record, typically is a basis for shortlisting.

Stage 2 Procurement: Evaluation – Consideration of how particular bidders will deliver and execute the intended contract, in order to determine the "most economically advantageous tender" for contract award.

The distinction between "selection" and "award" criteria is important, because legal challenges have been brought on the grounds that a contracting authority has considered selection criteria at the evaluation (or award stage) of the public procurement process. Simply mixing criteria from one to the other is not allowed.

General issues of attitude and/or culture can be relevant to an organisation's suitability for a particular project, but if these issues are addressed in a shortlisting stage then they should not be reassessed at evaluation stage.

Conversely, if the shortlisted bidders' behaviours are to be assessed by way of simulation exercises, interviews and questionnaires, or a combination of these methods, then in the later stages of a procurement issues of corporate "culture" and attributes of individual personnel should not be re-examined at the award stage.

Generally, the behavioural assessment process is most commonly carried out at evaluation stage. Where these are broken down into sub-criteria, these must also be disclosed to the bidders.

Evaluation criteria must in turn be clearly linked to contract terms and outcomes, i.e. salient to the bid. Tender documentation must be explicit as to the specific behaviours and how they align to outcomes/contract delivery.

Both the behavioural criteria being tested and the relative weight given to those scores must be linked and proportionate to their likely impact on contract performance. So, for example, a low weighting of 5-10% associated with behavioural criteria is unlikely to be appropriate if there are low levels of definition, high risks and unknown factors requiring high levels of collaboration by the parties.

By example some practical considerations of:

- Communication methodology.
- Collaboration platform to be used.
- Cultures of client body and the market.
- Physical constraints.
- Language/translation needed.
- Can the methodology be replicated?
- Is the methodology a recognised and scientifically validated?

- Ethical considerations – personal and organisational.
- Cascade through the supply chain of the bidder.
- Corporate culture and alignment to core values, e.g. commitment to Modern Day Slavery goals – passive, active, leading, etc.
- Ensure this will be the delivery team and not a sales team!
- Will the team be committed for the duration and risk of loss of named individuals? Tie-in agreements, etc.
- Ensure there is recognition positively and negatively for replacement of personnel during the assessment phase. Also, will you allow this or not?
- Ensure the breakdown of assessment elements is clear, concise and connected to each attribute.
- Ensure the approach is tested before use!
- Independence of the assessors and a means for declaring any conflicts of interest.
- Training or briefing for assessors is key to consistency. The assessors need a common understanding of what scores indicate and what "good" looks like. The scoring matrix must be clear and ideally transparent to bidders.
- All scores are moderated objectively to make sure that any extremes are understood.

This is by no means an exhaustive list, but sets out what a comprehensive and detailed programme and methodology needs to consider in outline. Equally, it should be thoroughly planned with sufficient time and resource to complete adequately.

CASE STUDY 2 | POTENTIAL BEHAVIOURAL BIASES IN A PROJECT OR PROGRAMME

This is an area of consideration that is of interest to all practitioners and leaders who have a vested interest in maintaining and delivering outcomes when engaging with multiple stakeholders.

Some of the insights that inform this case study are informed by the work of BIT in the body of work[1] they have produced over the last few years in collaboration with various public bodies. There are a number of recurring themes that affect both how the project or programme is structured, as well as how the team interacts and collaborates. These also affect aspects that are reliant on a change to policies, procedures and codes and which needed to enable implementation, and thus realisation of value of benefits to be made.

Before going any further, it should be said that in the vast majority, if not all cases, nobody sets out to do a bad job in the first instance. Hence, the context in which these should be viewed is that there are a large number of *socially constructed* factors as to how these occur. That is to say that due to shared assumptions,what we think the reality is versus the imagined state are different. This is usually derived as a consequence of dialogue/discourse even before we have begun the project in question. In the course of a typical project, it is most common to encounter the following biases and/or attributes of behaviour:

- Confirmation bias.
- GroupThink.
- Planning Fallacy.
- Sunk cost fallacy.
- Optimism bias.
- Bounded rationality.

Many of these biases depend upon the dynamics of culture, short-termism (as evidenced particular in shareholder-held businesses that want continuous and/ or constant returns) and a range of other salient influences. These behaviours or attributes will manifest themselves from the very top of the organisation, such as a sponsor or board member, to the team you are working with. Equally as I

---

1. The Behavioural Insights Team (BIT). (2017). *An exploration of the potential biases in project delivery in the Department for Transport*, July 2017. The Behavioural Insights Team (BIT). (2017) *Using data science in Policy*; released in 2017 undated.

have evidenced before, the self-awareness of your own behaviours and impact is just as much a factor in the matrix of people involved. At the end of this section I will suggest some ways in which these biases and/or attributes can be recognised as well as mitigated to a greater or lesser extent. Further, in some cases they can be managed to a point where they have no material impact on the project. This should be a reflection back on the diagram 6.2 in chapter 6.

In approaching a project, you will need to consider what usable and/or useful data sources you can draw upon to begin to understand the environment within which you are operating. This often becomes a harder task for those that have worked in an organisation for many years, as their ability to separate pertinent information from bounded rationality becomes harder. Therefore, the objectivity (Critical Thinking Methodology)[2] you use is of the utmost importance.

At the root of a good outcome is the balance between the use of technology (and the data and insights that go with this) and motivating people to be creative, engaging and committed to delivery of the outcomes. In real world situations time will be of the essence and the ability to trial and test will not be to the same level or scale as an academic setting, so this will necessitate the need for effective and timely decision-making.

However, most decisions are more likely to be supported where there is evidence to back them up, whether that is quantitative or qualitative, in a form that comes be readily assimilated. Remember, of course, for the most part presenting data visually with senior decision-makers tends to be more effective, however this will still need to be backed up by the tables and data sheets that identify with this format too.

Remember too all the aspects we have covered in the book in terms of framing, anchoring and saliency bias as a component part of the approach when you are defining the choice architecture. This needs to be done at the very outset and not something that is considered part way down the track. However, this doesn't mean that you shouldn't be flexible and agile in the way you respond to situational dynamics.

While a pragmatic approach to project delivery is necessary, it is still worth considering and contemplating where and how a behavioural assessment mindset will identify the area to focus on. This should recognise, of course, that this should not result in a formal or intentional pursuit of this route, but act more as a prompt to consider what should be prioritised in the mix of all the stakeholders, sponsors and team in general. Appended opposite in Table 1 you will see the ISO Octagon.

---

2. Critical thinking is the purposeful and reflective judgement about what to believe or what to do in response to observations, experience, verbal or written expressions or arguments. Critical thinking involves determining the meaning and significance of what is observed or expressed or concerning a given inference or argument, determining whether there is adequate justification to accept the conclusion as true.

Table 1. ISO Octagon[3]

Turning to some of the ways in which we can begin to look at improving project and/or programme success, there are a number of ways in which we can approach this, all of which are consistent with the previous chapters. In essence, in no particular order, they are as follows:

1. Pre-mortems.
2. Data collection and enhancement.
3. Lessons learnt from prior initiatives or projects.
4. Decision trees.
5. Collaboration platforms.

---

3. John Doyle, March 2017; *ISO 10667 A professional standard for delivering behavioural assessments – lessons for the procurement teams.* www.b2bppm.co,/blog/iso-10667- a-professional-standard-for-delivering-behavioural-assessments-lessons-for-procurement-teams-1110

6. Effective sponsorship and governance.
7. Behavioural mapping (pragmatically constructed along the lines of ISO10667).

Dealing with each item above in turn, but recognising that the order, selection and/or use and applicability will be dependant on each and every single project's needs.

Pre-mortems are a managerial strategy in which a project team imagines that a project or organisation has failed, and then works backward to determine what potentially could lead to the failure of the project or organisation. The technique breaks possible GroupThink too by facilitating a positive discussion on threats, increasing the likelihood that the main threats are identified. Management can then analyse the magnitude and likelihood of each threat, and take preventative actions to protect the project or organisation from suffering an untimely "death".

According to a *Harvard Business Review* article from 2007[4], "Unlike a typical critiquing session, in which project team members are asked what might go wrong, the pre-mortem operates on the assumption that the 'patient' has died, and so asks what did go wrong." The pre-mortem analysis seeks to identify threats and weaknesses via the hypothetical presumption of near-future failure. But if that presumption is incorrect, then the analysis may be identifying threats/weaknesses that are not in fact real.

Data collection and enhancement – Enhancing the data collection can begin with defining what attributes and data you need to collect and why, as well as if there are gaps, how these are proposed to be closed. This needs to be a shared and collaborative effort across the whole team and its extended members at the outset. This may also include an acknowledgement of what data has never been collected, but would be advantageous to collect in the future. Also, where will benchmark data come from and how will it be validated?

Constructing templates, and where possible pre-populating the sheets with what data you can assemble, often helps other functions and areas of the business collaborate with you to assemble to full picture. Recognise of course that the more factual markers you have, the lower the tendency for biases to creep into the decision-making process!

Additive data sets are usually a good way to start too. Sharing the data collected also helps allay fears that things are being hidden or for other purposes that are not transparent and evident.

---

4. Klein, G. (2007). "Performing a Project Premortem". *Harvard Business Review*. 85 (9): 18–19.

Lessons learned from prior initiatives or projects – this may be stating the obvious, however, the additional benefit of engaging with the organisation shows that you are intent on getting the outcome right, and not repeating issues from the past. Furthermore, thinking objectively about what areas and how you will construct questions or surveys should be approached with skill and care in the same way that qualitative methodology[5] might be applied to a research thesis.

Decision trees – A decision tree is a flowchart-like structure in which each internal node represents a "test" on an attribute (e.g. whether a coin flip comes up heads or tails), each branch represents the outcome of the test, and each leaf node represents a class label (decision taken after computing all attributes). The paths from root to leaf represent classification rules. In decision analysis, a decision tree and the closely-related influence diagram are used as a visual and analytical decision support tool, where the expected values (or expected utility) of competing alternatives are calculated. A decision tree consists of three types of nodes:

- Decision nodes – typically represented by squares
- Chance nodes – typically represented by circles
- End nodes – typically represented by triangles

Decision trees are commonly used in operations research and operations management. If, in practice, decisions have to be taken online with no recall under incomplete knowledge, a decision tree should be paralleled by a probability model as a best choice model or online selection model algorithm. Another use of decision trees is as a descriptive means for calculating conditional probabilities.

Collaboration platforms – At a very high level this is a platform, in the form of business software, that adds broad social networking capabilities to work processes. The goal is to foster innovation and effective working practices and approaches by incorporating knowledge management into business processes, so employees can share information and solve business problems more efficiently. In short, they:

- Aid communication in all its forms.
- File sharing and development of content, etc.
- Reduce Tasks and Projects difficulty in order to give space in functional workflows.

---

5. Yin, Robert K. (2016). *Qualitative research from start to finish*. Second edition published by The Guilford Press, New York.

- Avoid abortive practice or quickly re-focus efforts back to the agreed outcomes.
- Remove bias.
- Remove scope creep.
- Consistency and alignment in relative or actual real time.

Effective sponsorship and governance – Whenever a project is about change to the ways of working or a new commercial arrangement, these two requirements are key. Requesting a sponsor that is active and engaged is the start, as well as ensuring that the project is something that he/she recognises and identifies with the investment and resources needed. Sounds obvious and choose wisely!

Governance needs to follow the principles of frictionless and be as "light" as possible. Keeping it in as simple a form of language as possible is also critical. Recognise always that governance is not an instrument to delay or obstruct projects, but to keep them honest and true.

Behavioural mapping (pragmatically constructed along the lines of ISO10667) – For large projects in the Construction, Infrastructure or Outsourcing space where long term contracts are intended this is a good practice to adopt. If formally used, it will need to be resourced effectively with external support, along with the associated costs. However, as a consideration for how large and complex procurement and commercial activities can be improved, the approach can be considered as an effective decision support tool or approach. This will inform where, when, who and how biases and other attributes might positively and/or negatively impact a project/programme.

Going forward there will be a need to research, collaborate and share experiences as to where and how to effectively provide interventions that aid outcomes as a result of the Behavioural and Social Sciences.

CASE STUDY 3 | TAKING PARALLELS FROM OTHER BEHAVIOURAL INTERVENTIONS

Having done a lot of what I refer to as "make sense and translate" – that is taking something written for another audience, application, sector and/or opportunity and representing the opportunity to another group in a different way and context – this has become the norm for me. This was true of the trial carried out in Virgin Atlantic Airways (VAA) and the design of an approach to reduce CO_2 emissions and save cost from air fuel usage[1].

In essence, the approach was to understand the trial and utilise the learnings from this to apply into a live organisational context without trials (RCTs), with the aim of delivering a reduction in electricity consumption. The common call from organisations is to take an approach that is aimed at taking action, without necessarily factoring in pilots or trials to pull forward positive impacts. This is far more synonymous with the short-termism demanded in many sectors – retail being one of them.

Appended below is an overview of the trial's objectives, scope and methodology:

Understanding how the behaviour of employees – in this case, airline captains – influences fuel efficiency, and how low-cost company interventions can influence their behaviour for positive impact. This prompted VAA to partner with Chicago University (CU) and the London School of Economics (LSE) to carry out a study to test the effectiveness of an intervention to change behaviours.

The study involved analysing 335 captains across 40,000 flights while informing captains that their fuel performance was being monitored. Giving the pilots personalised performance targets dramatically increased their fuel efficiency. Changes in their behaviour led to the saving of 6,828 metric tons of fuel, worth £3.3-million; that also prevented the emission of 21,507 tons of CO_2 to the atmosphere, according to VAA, over the eight-month study period (February-October 2014).

At the end of 2013, the CU/LSE team randomly allocated the captains to three treatment groups and one control group. In January 2014, all captains

1. Lambert, Dr Emma Harvey; Kistruck, David; Gosnell, Greer; List, Professor John and Metcalf, Dr Robert. (2016). *The effects of giving Captains feedback and targets on SOP fuel and carbon efficiency information: Results of the Virgin Atlantic, University of Chicago and London School of Economics Captains' Study*; 20thJune 2016.

were told that their flight and fuel behaviour would be monitored for the next eight months. The vast majority of this impact came simply from the captains in the control group knowing that Virgin Atlantic was studying their behaviour, but the actual experimental interventions pushed the savings up still further. Captains were randomly allocated to one of four groups:

- Group 1 – Control: this group carried on with business-as-usual (BAU), with access only to information provided through VAA's SOPs documentation, which includes information on fuel efficiency procedures;
- Group 2 – Information: this group received monthly tailored feedback on their performance on the SOP behaviours described below;
- Group 3 – Targets (information + targets): this group received the same information as above, alongside information about their attainment of expected targets for that month;
- Group 4 – Charity (information + targets + charitable incentives): this group received the above information and targets plus a charitable donation incentive for each target met every month.

In conclusion the University research team found that notifying Captains that fuel efficiency was being studied, as well as providing them with tailored information, targets and feedback, was a highly cost-effective method for changing behaviours and achieving change. This represented a win for the triple bottom line: people, profit, and the environment.

Armed with this information, I was asked to consider how we might change behaviours within a retail business to deliver a reduction in electricity consumption, with a view to cost reduction as the primary focus. However, for me this represented an opportunity to deliver something more through the triple bottom line approach. On the plus side I had an executive sponsor. However, I also had to contend with challenges, including:

- Status quo bias – keep things as they are and don't accept any additional workload.
- Not invented here (IKEA affect) – It was not my idea therefore, why should I adopt it?
- Present bias – The tendency of people to give stronger weight to payoffs that are closer to the present time. This month's sales bonus versus an annual pay-off.

In addition to this the above sentiment, when Gillingham and Palmer[2]

2. Gillingham, K and Palmer, K. (2013). *Bridging the Energy Efficiency Gap - Policy Insights from Economic Theory and Empirical Evidence.* January 2013; revised October 2013. RFF DP 13-02-REV. 1616 P St. NW Washington, DC 20036 202-328-5000. www.rff.org

referenced consumers they could equally have been referring to corporate behaviour. Their research referred to the issue (definition) of self-control problems as a behavioural failure. Self-control problems are situations in which consumers (corporate employees) appear to have time-inconsistent preferences. That is, consumers appear to take a long-term view of decisions about outcomes that will occur in the distant future (an investment to save), but as the future approaches, the discount rate used to evaluate decisions increases.

These decisions may concern unfulfilled plans or commitments to make "good" investments such as exercising more, stopping smoking, eating healthier, or, as suggested by Svetlanov and Sigerson[3], investing in more energy efficient products.

Accordingly, the approach needed careful consideration given all the factors that negatively weighed against success. The design of the approach considered the following:

- Make execution easy and engaging ("frictionless").
- Offer a selection of alternatives and empower leaders and teams to choose (geographically spread on multiple continents).
- Reporting easy; photograph meters + initial base information (site address, meter number, etc.).
- Make tracking easy and engaging.
- Competition.
- Awards.
- Photo each month.
- Informs future approach to allow a tender

Even given this approach flexibility and adaptability, there was a need to recognise that there was not a common language. In some cases, this meant accepting that we would retrospectively receive an information feed from the accounts function in an Excel spreadsheet to allow for translation.

We also provided a menu approach to investment decisions to allow local teams to choose how they wanted to control and take ownership for what they did. Appended overleaf in Table 1 you can see how this was presented as a way of taking action early in the fiscal year to aid success of the challenge.

---

3. Tsvetanov, Tsvetan, and Segerson, Kathleen. (2013). "Re-Evaluating the Role of Energy Efficiency Standards: A Behavioural Economics Approach". *Journal of Environmental Economics and Management*.

	Opportunity	Typical payback in years
1	Upgrade pipework insulation on heating distribution	0.7
2	Reconfigure showroom/office heating controls	0.1
3	Put timers on car park lights	0.01
4	Timers on office equipment	0.4
5	Computer power down software	0.1
6	Install timers on beverage machines	0.05
7	Compressed air system maintenance/leaks	0.6
8	Reduce hot water temperature	0.4
9	Heating –replace warm air with gas radiant heating	0.8

Table CS 3.1. Investment options for energy reduction (based on industry validated standards)[4]

The challenge was presented with a multiple level of factors:

1. Consumption reduction of 9%, which would lead to estimated value reduction based on current tariffs.
2. CO_2 reduction based on industry standard figures per region (group effort).
3. Gifting to charities for most successful operations, sanctioned by Regional CEO.

This was a combination of approaches from a collection of interventions and designs to bring about the desired change. The programme was successful, aggregating around a 13% saving in energy and CO_2 for all those countries that participated. However, there was only a 70%+ adoption rate over the course of the 9 months I tracked the project.

As we entered the second half of the year, a few factors I observed made quantifiable differences in engagement and delivery:

- Publication of the results in months 4 and 7 following the data collection, and putting this in the hands of the senior stakeholders accountable for

---

4. *Society of Motor Manufacturers and Traders Report.* Accessed at http://www.smmt.co.uk/wp-content/uploads/sites/2/Dealer-Energy-Efficiency-Guide.pdf

the business. This was a move to ownership and a transparency of the data and performance – a way of working recognised and used by the business.

- Market movements in energy prices, especially in Asia, brought a very immediate focus – much closer to that of the present day.
- Translation of the cost impact into a sales relative context – a more common and understood lexicon across the business.

Individual locations clearly bought into the environmental impact value and celebrated this, despite this not being a value-owned at a senior level within the business. The project had a number of lessons for me, which I have summarised as follows:

- Provide sufficient, but not too many attributes for the teams to relate to in order to enable the programme.
- Communication and exposure of the results is key, whether good, bad or indifferent.
- Be flexible in your approach and show reasonable leniency in adoption.
- Be supportive.
- Understand the circumstance and situations for genuine opt-out and mitigating circumstances.
- Try and provide positive framing to encourage: more carrot and less stick to the approach.

Finally, I don't believe that there is a one-size-fits-all approach to the way the choice architecture is applied, as each and every organisation will have its own unique attributes that need to be accounted for. Hence the competences and understanding of what culture, behaviours, trust, collaboration need to be understood and reflected in the approach.

INDEX

6 Es framework 78
  see also MINDSPACE
8-Stage process for leading change
  see also Kotter, John; Change management 229

Active Listening Skills **40**, 41, 73, 210, 239, 240, 288, 290
Affinity bias
  see also Self Biases 88, 91
Algorithm of cognition
  see also Cognitive Framing 103
Analytical Hierarchy Processing (AHP) 39, 40, 269
Anchoring
  see also Focalism 4, 5, 80, 136, 137, 138, 139, 239, 269
  and adjustment
  see Heuristics 80, 137, 269
apophenia
  see Clustering illusion; Societal biases 121
Arica School
  see also Enneagram; Ichazo, Oscar 53
Ariely, Dan
  see also Behavioural Economics 17, 24, 138, 141, 282
Aristotle 11, 13, 49
Availability heuristic
  see Heuristics 80, 270
average speed cameras
  see Nudging 179

Baader-Meinhof phenomenon
  see also Frequency illusion 92
Bains, Gurnek
  see also Cultural differences 206, 209
Bandwagon effect
  see also Societal biases 122, 270
Bay of Pigs 194
Behavioural assessments
  key steps 287
  see also Case Study 1 287
Behavioural biases
  in a project/programme; *see* Case Study 2 299

Behavioural deviation to the norm 96
Behavioural Economics 3, 4, 5, 11, 13, 15, 17, 19, 36, 20, 23, 24, 25, 37, 93, 126,
    177, 266, 270, 307
Behavioural Insights Team (BIT)
  see also Nudge Unit 77, 94, 186, 200, 270, 299
  and nudging 187
Behavioural mapping 302, 304
Behavioural Procurement (BP) 7, 11, 12, 19, 20, 21, 22, 24, 25, 45, 248, 270
  definition 12, 24
  origins 20
Behavioural psychology 59
Behavioural Science 4, 5, 7, 11, 18, 23, 50, 57, 58, 69, 70, 71, 73, 171, 188, 190,
    193, 247, 251, 252, 262, 267, 268
  application in Purchasing and Supply Chain Management 73
Bias blind spot
  see also Self Biases 88, 90
Biases
  and Purchasing and Supply Chain Management 75
  dealing with Self biases 98
  defeating 75
  Group biases 75, 107
  Group serving 130
  Institutional biases 4, 3, 5, 73, 75, 98, 119, 130, **133,** 137, 270, 284
  see also Behavioural Science
  Self-biases 75, 87
  Self **87**
  Societal biases 75, **119**
  Societal examples 119–120
Bias Management considerations
  see also Biases 107
Black Swan Events 61
Bounded Rationality 14, 15, 19, 20, 23, 36, 62, 79, 184, 193, **226,** 241, 251, 254,
    255, 265, 268, 271, 300
Brain, functions and systems 67
  amygdala 68, 69
  hippocampus 68, 69
  hypothalamus 68, 69
  limbic 68
Bühler, Karl
  see Organon Model 42

Cacioppo, Dr John T. 120
CAPRICI (acronym) 27
Carbon Dioxide pollution reduction experiment
  see also Nudging 171, 179, 203, 305, 308
Castonguay, Mariah
  see also Social Impact Theory 123
Change Leadership Team
  see Global Leadership and Organisational Behaviour Effectiveness Research (GLOBE) 223
Change management 191, **225**
  behavioural interventions 230–232, 233–235, 234–236
  change curve 230, 232
  framing size and scale 238
  internal communications strategy 237
  key attributes and approaches 240
  key failure attributes 225–226
  Kubler-Ross Curve 230
  leadership from a behavioural perspective 241–242
  negotiation skills 239
  overcoming motivation hurdles 238
  prerequisites 230, 233
  process and phases 225
  process to create change 265
  understanding political dynamics 238
Changing As Three Steps (CATS)
  as foundation for subsequent works 228
  see also Change management; Lewin, Kurt 227
Charette Procedure
  see also Cynefin Framework 198
Chartered Institute of Purchasing and Supply (CIPS) 2, 19, 244
Cheerleader effect
  see also Group biases 97, 109
Choice architects 35, 171, 177, 178, 180, 181, 182, 183, 184, 185, 187, 267, 271, 300, 309
Classical conditioning
  see also Psychology 59
Classification of attitudes
  Ego-defensive 48
  Knowledge 48
  Utilitarian 48
  Value-expressive 48

Clustering illusion
  see also Societal biases 121, 271
coalitional game
  see Game Theory 152
Cognitive Bias Codex 85
Cognitive-Experiential Self-Theory (CEST) 79, 271
Cognitive framing **100**
  Evolution of skills 102
  Unidimensional, Hierarchical and Paradoxical frames 102
Cognitive hurdles
  in Change management 236
  internal communications strategy 237
Cognitive psychology 59, 271
collaboration
  importance of 50
Collaborative Performance Framework (CPF)
  see also Case Study 1 292
commercial society
  see also Smith, Adam 13
communication
  and Watzlawick, Paul 42
  effective vs ineffective 29
complete knowledge
  see Game Theory 155
conditioning
  see behavioural psychology 59
Confirmation bias
  see also Self Biases 88, 90, 97, 121, 299
Conservatism bias 241
Contract administration
  definition 245
  see also Supplier Relationship Management (SRM)
Contract Management
  definition 245
  see also Supplier Relationship Management (SRM) 1, 7, 20, 25, 46, 49, 52, 237,
    245
Cooperative Game Theory
  see also Game Theory 152
Corporate Social Responsibility (CSR) 35, 110, 272
CRAFT
  see Institute for Collaborative Working (ICW) 51

Creeping determinism
  see Hindsight bias 92
Critical Thinking Methodology
  see also Case Study 2 300
Cuban Missile Crisis 194
Cultural Layers and Models 214–216
Cultural Practices **205**
Cynefin Framework 195, 196, 197, 198, 199, 273
  5 domains 196

Data lakes 75
Debove, Stéphane 63, 64
decision problem
  see Game Theory 15, 39, 152, 271
Decision trees
  see also Case Study 2 273, 301, 303
de Courten-Myers, Gabrielle M. 67
Delaney clause 139
  see also Zero-risk bias 139
Descartes, René 11
digitalisation techniques
  see also Frictionless 204
Disadvantageous inequity aversion
  see also Fairness 64
Disposition effect
  see also Risk aversion; Prospect Theory 170
Distributive justice
  see also Fairness; Debove, S. and Rabin, M. 64
dominance equilibrium
  see also Equilibrium; Game Theory 156
dominance iteration
  see also Game Theory; equilibrium 156, 157
dominance solvable
  see also Game Theory; equilibrium 157, 158
Drucker, Peter
  see also Supplier Relationship Management (SRM) 255, 262, 263
Dynamic Social Impact Theory (DSIT)
  see also Latane, Bibb; Social Impact Theory; Societal biases 123

Edelman Trust Barometer 55
editing

see Prospect Theory 165
Emotional Intelligence (EI) 3, 3, 22, 30, 43, 44, 73, 209, 274
  definition 30
Emotional motivators
  see also Cultural differences 212
Emotional Quotient (EQ) 30, 31, 32, 209, 218, 247, 254, 274
Endowment effect 92, 126, 127, 128, 143, 283
  see also Self Biases 88, 92
Enneagram
  see also Ichazo, Oscar 53, 53
Enterprise Resource Planning (ERP) 225
equilibrium
  see Game Theory 155
Erikson, Erik 60, 278
Escalation of commitment
  see Heuristics 80
evaluation phase
  see Prospect Theory 165

Fairness
  and skills for good leadership 260
  evolution of human fairness
    see also Debove, S. 63
  primary inner brain areas diagrammatic 65
  see also Psychology 3, 47, 49, 50, 57, 63, 64, 283
Familiarity heuristic
  see Heuristics 80
Fearne, Professor Andrew
  see also Cognitive framing 100, 101
Fehr, Ernst
  see also Fairness 57, 64, 66
Focalism
  see also Anchoring 4, 136, 269
Fourfold pattern of risk
  see also Risk aversion; Prospect Theory 170
Four motives orientating against violence
  see also Pinker, Steven 131
Four-sides model/Communications square/Four ears model
  see also von Thun, Friedemann Schulz 41, 42
Four states of collaboration model 36
Framing Effect **124**

Frequency illusion
  see also Self Biases 88, 92
Freud, Sigmund 60, 278
Frictionless 5, **193**, 194, 195, 199, 200, 201, 237, 247, 254, 274, 304, 307
  definition 193
  ten commandments 201

Gambler's Fallacy
  see also apophenia; Societal biases; Clusting illusion 121
Game Theory
  and negotiation 21
  key terminology 149, 150–151
    backward induction 150
    common knowledge 150
    dominating strategy 150
    extensive game 150
    game 150
    mixed strategy 150
    Nash equilibrium
      see also Nash, John 150, 151, 159, 160, 163
    payoff 151
    perfect information 151
    player 151
    rationality 151
    strategic form 151
    strategy 151
    zero-sum game 151
  strategies for negotiation 154
  sub-disciplines
    classical 154
    combinatorial 154
    dynamic 154
    evolutionary 154
General Date Protection Regulations (GDPR) 172
Gestalt Theories 16, 275
  biotic experiment 16
  phenomenon experimental analysis 16
  Principle of Psychophysical Isomorphism 16
  Principle of Totality 16
Global Leadership and Organisational Behaviour Effectiveness Research
    (GLOBE) 222, 223, 275

Goffman, Erving
see also Cognitive framing 100
Goleman, Daniel
see Emotional Quotient (EQ) 30, 31, 43, 44
Griffin, Christopher
see also Sub-disciplines of Game Theory 153, 154, 282, 283, 284, 285
Group attribution error
see also group biases 4, 108
Group behavioural patterning 124
GroupThink 4, 94, 112, 114, 115, 194, 198, 250, 299
  avoiding pitfalls 116
  pitfalls 115
  see also group biases 112

Hammer, Dana Perkurson 46
Harsanyi, John
see Game Theory 150
Henke, Professor John W. Jnr. 5, 22, 252, 253, 254
Heuristics
see also Behavioural Science 4, 5, 73, **78**, 79, 97, 137, 282, 283, 284, 285
Hindsight bias
see also Self Biases 88, 92
Hofstede, Geert
see also Power Distance Index 206, 208, 215, 222, 272, 273
hot hand fallacy
see also Clustering illusion; Societal biases 122
House of Lords Select Committee for Science and Technology
see also Change management 234
Hume, David
see also Smith, Adam 13
hyperbolic discounting
see also Self biases 88, 93, 97

Ichazo, Oscar 53
IKEA effect
see also group biases; 'Not Invented Here' effect 109
illusory truth effect
see also Self Biases 88, 94
incentives 51, 77, 87, 113, 123, 162, 177, 179, 180, 182, 213, 238, 243, 265, 273, 276, 306
Individualism vs. collectivism (IDV)

see also Cultural differences 207
Indulgence vs. restraint (IND)
  see also Cultural differences 208
Ingroup bias
  see also Group biases 110
innovation
  and Change management 265
  incremental innovation 263
  in Purchasing and Supply Chain Management 262
  Six behaviours of 264
Institute for Collaborative Working (ICW) 51
Institute of Business Ethics (IBE) 56
internal communications strategy
  in Change management 237
International Standard ISO44001 50
  see also Collaboration 50
Intertemporal choices
  see Hyperbolic discounting 93
interviews
  in relation to Leadership 258
ISO Octagon
  see Case Study 2 300

Janis, Irving
  see GroupThink; eight symptoms of GroupThink 114, 115
Just In Time (JIT) 62

Kahneman, Daniel
  see also Behavioural Economics 17, 24, 61, 75, 79, 82, 89, 101, 112, 124, 125,
    126, 137, 138, 140, 143, 165, 166, 168, 170, 279, 282, 283, 284, 285
Katona, George 15, 16
  see also Behavioural Economics 15
Katz, Daniel 48
Kennedy, John F. 194
Keynesian Theory 15, 276
Keynes, John Maynard 15, 276
Klein, Gary
  see illusory truth effect 94, 284, 302
Kőszegi, Botond
  see Risk aversion 126
Kotter, John

see also Change management 225, 228, 229
Kübler-Ross Curve
  acceptance 232
  anger 232
  denial 232
  exploration 232
  see also Change management 230
Kübler-Ross, Elisabeth
  see also Change management; Kübler-Ross Curve 230, 232

Latané, Bibb
  see also Social Impact Theory 123
Leadership
  and innovation 263
  difference markers CEO vs CPO 259
  styles and impacts 257
Lewicki, Roy J. 55, 56
Lewin, Kurt
  and Change management processes 226
  see also Gestalt Theories 16, 226, 227, 228
Libertarian Paternalism 170
  in Procurement 170
Lilly, John
  see also Arica School; Ichazo, Oscar 53
Lin, Daniel
  see Bias blind spot 90, 91
Long-term orientation vs. short-term orientation (LTO)
  see also Cultural differences 207
Loss aversion **126**, 127, 140, 141, 143, 145, 167, 172, 173, 174, 175, 176, 226,
    276, 283
  see also Endowment effect 4, 126, 143, 250, 276
Lovallo, Dan
  see Planning fallacy 89, 283, 284

Managing diverse teams
  as applied to Purchasing and Supply Chain Management 217
Masculinity vs. femininity (MAS)
  see also Cultural differences 207
Maskin, Erik
  see Leadership innovation 266
Mayer, John D.

see also Emotional Quotient (EQ) 30, 43, 44
Mechanism Design Theory
  see also Maskin, Erik 266
Meyer, Erin
  see also Leadership dimensions; Cultural differences 30, 210
MINDSPACE
  see also Behavioural Insights Team (BIT) 77, 78, 276
mixed-motives games
  see also Game Theory; equilibrium 157
Modern Day Slavery Act (MDSA) 35, 277
Molotov Cocktail
  see Cultural practices 205
Morgenstern, Oskar 16, 17, 149

naïve diversification
  see Heuristics 80
Naranjo, Claudio
  see also Arica School; Ichazo, Oscar 53
Nash Bargaining Solution 163
Nash Equilibrium 150, 151, 159, 160, 163
Nash Existence Theorem 160
Nash, John
  see also Game Theory 149, 150, 151, 152, 159, 160, 161, 163
Negativity effect 126, **130**, 277
  four elements 130
  see also Societal biases 4, 120, 277
Neuroscience
  and behaviour 69
  see also Brain 3, 18, 69, 70, 277
Nietzsche, Friedrich 11
nine cultural competences
  see also Global Leadership and Organisational Behaviour Effectiveness
      Research (GLOBE) 222–223
Non-cooperative Game Theory
  see also Game Theory 152
'Not invented here' mindset
  see also Group biases 117
Nudging 4, 5, 12, **177**, 180, 181, 182
  9 step approach 189
  and Change management 234
  as applied to decision-making 180–181

as applied to Policy-making 186–187
ethics and governance 181–182
ethics of, 182
in procurement and contracting 188, 188–190, 188–189

operant conditioning
see also Psychology 60
Organisation for Economic Co-operation and Development (OECD) 45, 187,
277
Organon Model
see Bühler, Karl 42
Oskar Morgenstern
The Theory of Games and Economic Behaviour 16, 149
overconfidence
see also Self biases 98

Parkinson, Cyril Northcote
see also Parkinson's Law (of trinity) 135, 136, 278
see also Institutional biases 135, 278
Peltzman Effect (Risk Compensation) 116
personality psychology 59
P for Political, E for Economic, S for Social, T for Technological, L for Legal and
E for Environmental (PESTLE) 5, 96, 172, 218
see also Prospect Theory 172
Pinker, Steven 131
Planning fallacy 112
see also Self Biases 88, 89, 299
Plato 11
Pólya, George
see also Heuristics 78
Power Distance Index (PDI)
see also Cultural differences 206, 208, 246, 247
PPI index
see also Supplier Relationship Management (SRM) 254
predictably irrational
see also Ariely, Dan 24, 141
predictions and forecasts **95**
pitfalls of modern world 95
Pre-mortems 278, 301, 302
Prescription medication regulatory changes
see also Nudging 178

Preuss, Lutz Professor
  see also Cognitive framing 100, 101
Prisoner's Dilemma
  see Game Theory 157, 158, 159
Professional Attitudes and Behaviours: As and Bs of Professionalism
  see also Hammer, Dana Perkurson 46
professionalism
  attitudes and behaviours 45
  OECD definition 45
  attitudinal attributes (Hammer) 46
  structural attributes (Hammer) 46
Pro-innovation bias
  see also Group biases; Institutional biases 109, 133, 279
Pronin, Emily
  see Bias blind spot 90, 91
Prospect theory 5, 101, 126, 143, **165**, 167, 168, 170, 172, 173, 279, 285
  editing 165
  evaluation phase 165
  losses and gains table 167
  probability weighting to convert a sale 168
Psychology
  overview 59
public procurement
  legal aspects of 295
Purchasing and Supply Chain Management
  Contract Management 1, 7, 20, 25, 29, 46, 49, 52, 237, 245
  Supplier Relationship Management (SRM) 5, 6, 1, 7, 20, 35, 52, 162, 243, 244,
    245, 246, 247, 248, 249, 250, 251, 255, 244, 280
  Supply Chain Management (SCM) 3, 5, 6, 1, 7, 17, 20, 21, 22, 24, 25, 45, 71,
    73, 74, 75, 76, 80, 87, 100, 101, 120, 142, 149, 171, 185, 193, 197, 211, 214,
    237, 258, 259, 260, 262, 263, 266, 280, 289, 291, 292

Rabin, Matthew 63, 64, 126, 184, 279
Randomised Control Trials (RCT)
  see also Change management 241, 305
Reciprocity 4, 54, 57, 88, 90, 105, 250, 255
  main 54, 105
  see also Self biases 4, 54, 57, 88, 90, 105, 250, 255
Regional EQ skills summary 209
Regressive bias 134, 279
Relationship Lifecycle Management **51**

Representativeness heuristic 80, 280
reversal test
  see also Status quo bias 143
Risk Compensation
  see also Peltzman Effect 116
Ross, Lee
  see Bias blind spot 90, 91, 230, 232, 282
Rousseau, Denise M. 55
Royal Academy of Engineering
  see also Case Study 1 293
Royzman, Edward
  see also Negativity bias/effect 130
Rozin, Paul
  see also Negativity bias/effect 130

Sako, Mari
  see also Four contractual mechanisms 37
Salacuse, J.W. 216
Salovey, Peter
  see also Emotional Quotient (EQ) 30, 43, 44
sceptical generalist
  see also Frictionless; critical decision-making 194
Schmidt, Klaus M.
  see also Fairness 64, 66
Self-serving bias 88, 89
Selten, Reinhard
  see also Game Theory 150
Semmelweis, Ignaz
  see also Group biases 109
  Semmelweis reflex
Silva, Rohan
  see also Nudging 186
Simon, Herbert A.
  see also Theory of Corporate Decision-making 13, 14, 15, 62, 79, 271, 284
skills
  of effective teams 259
  World Economic Forum Seven Critical Skills 259
Smith, Adam 11, 12, 13, 17, 18, 61, 133, 173, 267
Snowden, David J.
  see Cynefin Framework 195, 196, 199
social cue

see Cognitive framing 101
Social Impact Theory
  see also Bandwagon effect; Societal biases 123
Social Psychology 59
Social Sciences
  as applied to Purchasing and Supply Chain Management 211–213
soft skills
  see also Behavioural Competences 45, 98
Software as a Service (SaaS) 172
Stakeholder management 3, 22, **32**
stakeholder management matrix 33
Status Quo bias 4, 97, 142, 143, 238, 239, 275, 284, 306
stepladder technique 198
Stock-Sanford corollary
  see also Parkinson's Law (of trinity) 136
strategic equilibrium
  see also Nash equilibrium; Game Theory 150
Strategic Negotiation Process Workshops 139
Strategic Relationship Context Model
  see also Sako, Mari 37, 38
Strengths, Weaknesses, Opportunities and Threats (SWOT) Analysis 96
sub-addivity effect
  see also Institutional biases 135, 280
Sunk cost fallacy 141, 142, 195, 237, 264
  see also Institutional biases 140, 280
Sunstein, Cass R.
  commentary on ethics of Nudging 181, 182
  see also Behavioural Economics; Libertarian Paternalism 17, 24, 170, 177,
    181, 183, 185
Superfund sites
  see also Delaney clause; Zero-risk bias 139, 280
Supplier Relationship Management (SRM) 5, 6, 7, 20, 35, 52, 162, 243, 244,
    245, 246, 247, 248, 249, 250, 251, 252, 255, 280
  and Behavioural Science 247–248
  behavioural pillars 246–248
  benefits 243
  entrepreneurial 251
  factors for strategic value 246
  new vs old practices 250–251
  skills required matrix 248
  traditional pillars 243

Supply Chain Strategy Dynamics (SCSD) 34, 35
  matrix 34
surveys 6, 258
  in relation to Leadership 258
System 1 judgements 82, 83, 185, 200
  intuitive and simple 82, 83, 200, 201, 219, 276
System 2 judgements 82
  research or greater effort 4, 82, 83, 200, 226, 276

Taleb, Nassim Nicholas
  see also Behavioural Economics 17, 61, 62
Thaler, Richard H.
  see also Behavioural Economics; Libertarian Paternalism 17, 24, 143, 170,
      177, 181, 183, 177, 283
The Better Angels of Our Nature: Why Violence Has Declined
  see also Pinker, Steven; Four motives orientating against violence 131
The General Theory of Employment, Interest and Money
  see also Keynes, John Maynard 15, 276
The "invisible hand"
  see also Smith, Adam 18
The Knowledge 69
The Organisation for Economic Co-operation and Development (OECD) 45,
      187, 277, 278
Theory of Administration
  see also Simon, Herbert A. 13
Theory of Corporate Decision-making
  see also Simon, Herbert A., Adminstrative Behaviour 13
Theory of Games and Economic Behaviour 16, 149
Theory of Moral Sentiments
  see also Smith, Adam 11, 12, 13, 61
The Wealth of Nations
  see also Smith, Adam 12, 61
Tomlinson, Edward C. 56
Tormala, Dr Zakary
  see PESTLE; Prospect Theory 173
trust 21, 49, 50, **54**, 55, 56, 107, 119, 244, 246, 250, 251, 261, 264, 274, 281
  Ability, Integrity and Benevolence 21, 56, 281
Tversky, Amos
  see also Behavioural Economics 17, 79, 89, 101, 112, 124, 125, 126, 135, 137,
      138, 140, 165, 166, 168, 170, 279, 283, 284, 285
Uncertainty Avoidance Index (UAI) 207

Unidimensional frames 103
United Kingdom: Highways project
  see Case Study 1 288
United Nations Global Compact (UNGP) 80
United Nations (UN) 80, 137, 187
  see also Nudging 80, 187
Utopian Principle
  see also Smith, Adam 17

Value Architects 267, 268
Virgin Atlantic Airlines (VAA)
  see also Carbon Dioxide pollution reduction experiment; Case Study 3;
      Nudging 179, 262, 305, 306
von Neumann, John 16, 17, 149
von Thun, Friedemann Schulz 41, 42

Watson, John B.
  see also Psychology 59
Watzlawick, Paul 42
Welsh, Jack 48, 195
Wertheimer, Max
  see also Gestalt Theories 16
Whole Life Cycle (WLC) 171
Willingness to Accept or Pay (WTAP) 92
  see also Endowment effect; Loss aversion 128
Winter, Eyal
  see also Incentives 46, 205, 265, 266, 277
Working Relations Index (WRI)
  buyer behaviours 253
  and Supplier Relationship Management (SRM) 252, 253
  see also Henke, Professor John W. Jnr 252

Zero-risk bias 139, 281
Zero-sum heuristic 111

Printed in Great Britain
by Amazon

39639431R00185